Convergence as Adaptivity

Convergence as Adaptivity

Understanding Policymaking in an Era of Globalization

ZHIYUAN WANG

SUNY PRESS

Published by State University of New York Press

For information, contact State University of New York Press, Albany, NY
www.sunypress.edu

Library of Congress Cataloging-in-Publication Data

Name: Wang, Zhiyuan, 1981– author.
Title: Convergence as adaptivity : understanding policymaking in an era of
    globalization / Zhiyuan Wang.
Description: Albany : State University of New York Press, 2023. | Includes
    bibliographical references and index.
Identifiers: LCCN 2022046499 | ISBN 9781438493794 (hardcover : alk. paper) |
    ISBN 9781438493800 (ebook) | ISBN 9781438493787 (pbk. : alk. paper)
Subjects: LCSH: Globalization—Political aspects. | Globalization—Economic
    aspects. | International cooperation. | Transnationalism. | Policy sciences.
Classification: LCC JZ1318 .W363 2023 | DDC 303.48/2—dc23/eng/20221202
LC record available at https://lccn.loc.gov/2022046499

10 9 8 7 6 5 4 3 2 1

Contents

Illustrations

Figures

Tables

Acknowledgments

For me, writing these acknowledgments is not merely a routine to complete a book for the purpose of publication. This project would have been impossible, or the book would at least have been in a very different shape, without the generous help, wise advice, careful guidance, and constructive suggestions from the colleagues I am so fortunate to have and whom I am about to list. Therefore, it is only right to document what I owe intellectually and beyond. First, I am indebted to David Cingranelli and Ekrem Karakoç. Without their guidance and encouragement in every step of my academic journey, I would not be in the position I am now, let alone writing a book. Their help to me is far beyond academics. I hope this book can at least show the worthiness of their efforts.

Colleagues in my department deserve hearty applause. Dan Smith, as the department chair, provided the most generous support that allowed me to concentrate on this project. Dan also played a major role in clearing hurdles on the path, one after another. I owe tremendous thanks to him. I draw incredible inspiration and motivation from countless interactions with Badredine Arfi, Michael Bernhard, Sebastian Elischer, Aida Hozic, Conor O'Dwyer, Dan O'Neill, Michael MacDonald, Michael Martinez, Bryon Moraski, Ido Oren, Beth Rosenson, Zach Selden, Laura Sjoberg, and Ben Smith. More importantly, they serve as great examples of the accomplishments that I try to achieve in my own intellectual pursuit. In many conversations with Hannah Alarian, Paul Gutierrez, Andrew Janusz, Nick Kerr, Steven Klein, Cristian Pérez Muñoz, Juliana Restrepo Sanín, and Andrew Rosenberg, I always find warm support and limitless energy to move forward.

I am greatly thankful to Susan Aarronson, Glen Biglaiser, Lily Che, Alice Evans, Wei Jiao, Amy Pond, Xiaoyu Pu, Alexander Thompson,

Jun Xiang, Lei Zhou, and Qiankun Zhou for their direct or indirect help, without which this book could not possibly have been completed as it is now. I am also grateful to the two anonymous reviewers. Without their constructive and insightful suggestions this book could not live to its full potential. My editor, Michael Rinella at State University of New York Press, provided timely feedback, clear instructions, and constant encouragement throughout the process. I feel really lucky to have had him in this important role.

I also thank Oxford University Press and Sage for generously granting me permissions to adapt two journal articles. Chapter 3 was originally published in *International Studies Quarterly* in 2020 in the second issue of volume 64 by Oxford University Press as "Thinking Outside the Box: Globalization, Labor Rights, and the Making of Preferential Trade Agreements." Chapter 4 was initially published in 2021 in *Political Research Quarterly* in the third issue of volume 74 by Sage as "Choosing a Lesser Evil: Partisanship, Labor, and Corporate Taxation under Globalization." Minimum alterations have been applied to the articles to facilitate their adaption into the book.

Last but absolutely not least, without the unwavering support and warm companionship of my wife, son, and daughter, without all the love and laughter they unconditionally give me, the book would have remained nothing but a faint idea. My parents and in-laws exhibited boundless patience with me all along the way, for which this book is merely a simple token of my gratitude.

I cannot mention all the people I have benefited from in the academic endeavor that has led to this book. I therefore dedicate this book to those who give me the love, care, and support that make the impossible possible. I take full responsibility for errors in the book but no sole credit for completing it.

Introduction

A Globalized World, yet Nationalized Policies

> The speed of light does not merely transform the world. It becomes the world. Globalization is the speed of light.
>
> —Paul Virilio

> It has been said that arguing against globalization is like arguing against the laws of gravity.
>
> —Kofi Annan

According to the World Bank (2021), the world ratio of trade to gross domestic product more than doubled over the past fifty years, expanding from approximately 25 percent in 1970 to 56 percent in 2019. World exports of goods and services multiplied from 383.55 billion dollars (dollar amounts in current US dollars) in 1970 to 24.78 trillion dollars in 2019. Accompanying the trade expansion, global foreign direct investment inflows soared from 12.36 billion dollars in 1970 to 1.51 trillion dollars in 2019. World portfolio equity inflows exploded from 1.36 billion dollars in 1970 to 376.96 billion dollars in 2019. These numbers indicate nothing but that national economies are more integrated into a global system of production and consumption now than they were half a century ago. In other words, the economic interconnectedness among states has incredibly intensified since the 1970s. The triumph of globalization is proclaimed.

Intensified economic interconnection changes the way that we perceive and interact with the world, as it has now been compressed into a tiny place (Friedman, 2005).[1] Is national politics then also globalized as a consequence? Put differently, when national borders are porous to impactful international economic flows, to what extent can governments continue to maintain their policy autonomy (if this is indeed possible at all)? This is the core question that this book seeks to answer. My brief answer is that states still manage to preserve policy autonomy but not in a conventionally understood manner. I will show that states adapt to an increasingly constrained environment imposed by globalization through policy convergence too.

Globalization implies integration and homogenization.[2] Economically, as previously noted, states are more intimately connected with one another (Bordo et al., 1999; Garrett, 2000; Goldstein et al., 2007; UNCTAD, 2016; WTO, 2014). On the ideational and institutional levels, states are becoming increasingly alike (Garrett, 2000; Held et al., 1999; Kriesi et al., 2006; López-Córdova & Meissner, 2011; Pinto, 2013; Smith et al., 1999). States also pursue similar or even identical policies, a phenomenon that is known as policy convergence. It seems that there is no place for diversity or differentiation in this process. In this sense, the prognostication that globalization will end the nation-state is not an exaggeration (Beeson, 2003; Ohmae, 1996), let alone the fact that it undermines democracy (Bloom, 2016; Rodrik, 2011; Wu, 2017). Since no states can escape from globalization (Garrett, 2000), no states can fight it. Globalization is the "golden straitjacket" on sovereign nations (Friedman, 1999).

However, this pessimism ignores the capacity of the state to adapt to this new policy environment and also overlooks the diverse forms and results of exercising policy autonomy (e.g., Clark, 2009; Jordana et al., 2018; Nooruddin & Rudra, 2014; Shin, 2017; Swank, 2002; Wang, 2017a). Accordingly, it overstates the threats of globalization as a constraining force. In this book, I hold that globalization indeed changes the policy environment in which states operate, but this does not mean that states had never existed in a constraining environment before. This new policy environment is new not in terms of its nature but in the degree and modality of the constraints (Krasner, 1999a; Zurn & Deitelhoff, 2015). Despite this constraining environment, states have exhibited extraordinary adaptivity (Stein, 2016), and they do so through both divergence and convergence.

Furthermore, the study conducted in this book suggests that globalization has not constrained states to the extent that the Westphalian system, which has structured inter-state interaction and intra-state governance for the past three hundred years, will soon dissolve and therefore require a replacement. Globalization changes the way in which sovereign states fulfill their functions but does not alter how they are organized to sustain their legitimacy (Thomson, 1995; Weiss, 1998; Zurn & Deitelhoff, 2015). In other words, the core of sovereignty is not endangered (i.e., the highest authority that an independent state can exercise remains intact; Thomson, 1995). Admittedly, what sovereigns can do is now more than ever subject to powerful structural constraints (Held et al., 1999; Sassen, 1995). However, there is currently no feasible polity model to replace the nation-state (Rodrik, 2011).[3] Later, I will critically review extant literature on globalization and national policymaking.

The Convergence Thesis: The Market Dominates the State

According to Kerr (1983), convergence is "the tendency of societies to grow more alike, to develop similarities in structures, processes, and performances" (p. 3).[4] Therefore, policy convergence refers to the tendency toward policy similarities across jurisdictions. Under globalization, it is held that national policies converge on neoliberal economic dictates (Davies & Vadlamannati, 2013; Jensen, 2013; Simmons & Elkins, 2004; Smith et al., 1999). Many globalization scholars believe that the fact that states compete for capital and markets at the global level is responsible for the observed policy convergence (Cao & Prakash, 2010; Davies & Vadlamannati, 2013; Elkins et al., 2006a; Garrett, 1995; Wang, 2018). In addition, this policy convergence is largely detrimental to public interests (i.e., a race to the bottom in regulations; Olney, 2013; Razin & Sadka, 2018). Consequently, as globalization accelerates, states are pressured into gradually conceding their decision-making power in vital policy areas to markets at the peril of social welfare (Hellwig, 2008). This is why scholars have predicted that globalization will eventually end the nation-state (Albrow, 1996; Ohmae, 1996).

There are two elements to this convergence argument. The first element is the belief that pursuing economic competitiveness must be achieved through policies that favor efficiency over welfare (Polanyi, 2001 [1944]; Wu, 2017). For example, it has been proposed that lowering the tax rate on capital guarantees a higher return and that doing so will help nations to increase capital flows (Cao, 2010; Hays, 2003). Furthermore, it has been claimed that loose environmental regulations attract investment and can help a nation to maintain a competitive advantage for its products on overseas markets (Cao & Prakash, 2012). The second element is the belief that such policies have strong and clear negative externalities (Franzese & Hays, 2008),[5] that is, policies that a state enacts increase the costs of refusing to adopt similar ones for its competing peers (also see Simmons & Elkins, 2004).

Indeed, there is evidence to support policy convergence in several issue areas, such as central bank independence (Bodea & Hicks, 2015a), corporate tax rates (Cao, 2010), economic liberalization (Simmons & Elkins, 2004), the environment (Cao & Prakash, 2010; Holzinger et al., 2008; Lee & Strang, 2006), investment protection (Elkins et al., 2006a), and social welfare spending (Brooks, 2005). It seems that a policy that a state adopts increasingly becomes a function of the policy choices of said state's economic competitors in the same issue areas.[6]

The aforementioned scholars have rightly pointed to the nature of the constraints that globalization imposes on states. It is true that globalization alters the policy space for states and that globalized economic competition strongly motivates cross-national policy convergence (Neumayer & Plümper, 2012; Simmons et al., 2006). Without globalization, convergence would be much narrower in scope or even less likely altogether. However, it is an overstatement to say that globalization is the only cause of convergence. Convergence can occur through learning, emulation, and/or coercion (Dobbin et al., 2007; Holzinger & Knill, 2005; Solingen, 2012). More importantly, convergence can happen as a result of states' strategic choices (Holzinger & Knill, 2005), such as substitution.

The Divergence Thesis: The State Still Matters

Counter to the convergence thesis, many studies have discovered that states can resist the pressure to converge in various issue areas. Because of this resistance, policy outcomes have successfully kept their diversity. Extant scholarship often ascribes this policy differentiation to variation in political institutions and organizations. For example, the proportional representation system more likely maintains higher tax rates (Hays, 2003) and more substantial social welfare spending (Swank, 2002) than the majoritarian system does. Political organizations also exert an influence. Kurtz (2002) has demonstrated that political parties, the organization of the poor, and the alliance patterns between the two account for the differences between Mexico and Chile in social policy, notwithstanding the fact that both countries embarked on a neoliberal economic reform, as dictated by globalization. Brooks (2002) finds that the party system is a robust causal factor in explaining the degree of pension privatization. Political legacies also shape the response to external pressure for policy changes. Brooks and Kurtz (2012) discover that import substitution industrialization influences the subsequent capital account reforms when faced with peer pressure to do so. Political regime is another significant factor that is conducive to variation in responses to international pressure to enforce deregulation. In two studies, Wang (2017a, 2017b) obtains evidence that when they are pressured to repress labor rights, more inclusive regimes are able to maintain better protection of such rights in practice.

A New Direction: Strategic Convergence

As demonstrated earlier, a race to the bottom does not invariably materialize in states across all issue areas. Policy autonomy may be eroded but not entirely lost, and there is still room for states to maneuver when globalization accelerates (Datz, 2019; Gritsch, 2005; Mosley, 2005; Naoi, 2020). However, resistance-generated divergence is not the only sign of policy autonomy. Convergence also results from states' policy adaptivity. Little current research specifically examines convergence from the perspective of strategic substitution, but several studies indeed help to lay the foundation for investigations into this topic. First, Hays (2003) describes a unique type of convergence. He has demonstrated that globalization does not simply set out to lower or increase corporate tax rates but that different electoral rules shape varying policy responses to other nations' corporate tax policy changes. Globalization makes the corporate tax rates of majoritarian nations fall rapidly while increasing those in places with consensus democracy, which makes corporate tax rates in these two types of nations converge in the middle. In other words, this convergence is a result of states' strategic choices that are based on their respective interests and policy priors within domestic institutional frameworks.

Second, with a focus on developing nations, Rickard (2012) finds that trade reduces social welfare spending, just as the convergence thesis predicts. However, these states offset such costs by increasing subsidies for the beneficiaries of social welfare programs. Taken together, these findings suggest that convergence should not be considered in isolation and that it may reveal states' policy ingenuity if it is carefully investigated in conjunction with other related policy changes.

Another study that merits our attention is Genovese et al.'s (2017) article, in which they illustrate that states can substitute internationally diffused policies with more politically advantageous alternatives. To the best of my knowledge, this study is among the first to deal with policy substitution in the context of globalization. Although Genovese et al. (2017) do not theorize their contribution to the framework of convergence, they do highlight policy substitution as a valid mechanism to exhibit states' policy adaptivity, which consequently leads to convergence in terms of policy instruments that differ from the diffused ones. Similarly, although not situated in a substitution-induced convergence theory, Shin's (2017) work verifies the practical possibility of such causal mechanisms. This work also reveals that leftist governments in some developed countries employ opaque tax policies to minimize tax burdens on firms and thus to alleviate concerns about these governments' retaining high nominal corporate tax rates.

In this book, I argue that states adapt to a constraining policy environment not only through plain resistance but also convergence, and that policy substitution leads to the latter. More importantly, this convergence can occur either within or across issue areas and either at the same analytical level or across analytical levels. In the following section, I present an overview of the book's theoretical framework.

An Overview of the Theoretical Framework

The globalization-convergence thesis has resulted from a misunderstanding of the type and the sources of convergence. Globalization mainly causes convergence in terms of policy input but not necessarily in terms of policy outcome or real-world impact. Differentiation in policy outcome has been revealed in a number of issue areas under globalization. Similarly, globalization constrains national policy autonomy through economic competition and international regimes that may or may not lead to convergence. Convergence can also occur by means of other mechanisms, such as transnational communication, hegemonic imposition, or substitution. Moreover, policy convergence is not unvaryingly harmful, and proximity in policy enactments across issue areas proves beneficial to societies. These policies' changes improve public welfare at the global level. Therefore, there is no inexorable causal link between globalization and perverted policy convergence.

States can adapt to changing policy environments in various ways, including by employing different and even opposing policy tools. Therefore, alternating policy instruments are not indicative of the shrinking of state capacity; rather, they constitute the embodiment of states' policy power. In other words, we should not attach absolute political significance to specific policy tools and equate them to state capacity itself. Which policy tool to deploy to maximize their interests is entirely at the discretion of states.

Globalization alters the policy environment in which states pursue prosperity and does so by channeling negative policy externalities through heightened cross-border economic competition and by creating webs of international rules and obligations that ensnare states. Undoubtedly, globalization reshapes national policy space. However, this fact does not suggest that such input change will categorically give rise to convergence in a way that was conventionally predicted. It is often costly to implement the policies that globalization demands; however, there are feasible alternatives at both domestic and international levels and either within or across issue areas, which allow states to substitute for the costly policies and are thus also conducive to convergence.

Overall, I contend that when faced with intensified globalization, states choose policies that minimize the costs of enforcing the dictates of globalization but remain compatible with its existence and deepening. Consequently, such behavior results in strategic, substitution-induced convergence, which embodies the policy adaptivity mastered by states. In the next section, I summarize evidence that supports this conjecture, evidence that has been obtained through the examination of selected policy areas.

Evidence from the Policy Areas Examined

To demonstrate the explanatory power and empirical validity of the proposed theoretical framework, I examine policy changes in four areas: bilateral investment treaties (BITs), preferential trade agreements (PTAs), corporate taxation, and central bank independence (CBI). These four policies are crucial to the evolution of globalization, as they intensively respond to and shape the principal elements of economic globalization, that is, trade and capital flows (FDI and portfolio investment). Owing to the lack of an effective global regime that governs cross-border direct investment, BITs are one of the most important and most widely used tools to protect overseas assets, particularly in developing countries (Elkins et al., 2006a; Jandhyala et al., 2011). Made in accord with the requirements of the General Agreement on Tariffs and Trade and the World Trade Organization, PTAs can further liberalize trade among members, which have grown exponentially since the end of the Cold War. PTAs also serve many other important functions, such as reinforcing the bargaining position in multilateral trade talks (Mansfield & Reinhardt, 2003) and promoting domestic reform (Baccini & Urpelainen, 2014). Corporate taxation is at the heart of the concern over the deregulatory power that globalization wields (Cao, 2010), as it is used to attract FDI and thus grow the economy but to the detriment of social welfare. CBI has diffused globally over the past 50 years (Bodea & Hicks, 2015a). An independent central bank is not only key to preserving monetary autonomy in an age characterized by enormous and fast capital flows but also to maintaining macroeconomic stability by taming inflation and shaping stable expectations.

Using rigorous statistical analysis and detailed case studies, I demonstrate that strategic substitution strongly drives policy convergence in these areas. First, BITs are used to substitute for difficult domestic judicial reforms. When states conclude more such treaties, the institutional benefits that these international instruments provide allow them to halt or even reverse judicial reforms that serve similar functions as these investment treaties do, causing deterioration in judicial independence. Causal inferential investigation and the case of Egypt illustrate this strategic consideration.

Second, making PTAs makes it possible for states to maintain a greater legal protection of labor rights. Concluding trade agreements does not incur substantial political costs in the way that reducing labor protection does, but it presents similar economic advantages. Analyzing dyadic treaty making and the formation of the China–New Zealand Free Trade Agreement (2008) lends support to this conjecture.

Third, by the same logic, leftist governments cut corporate tax rates in return for not diminishing laws concerning labor rights. In other words, lessening the tax burden on firms enables the leftist governments to retain policies that are important to their core constituencies. Quantitative evidence from examining corporate tax rate data substantiates this expectation.

Fourth, to secure their control of capital flows, states grant more independence to their central banks. Having more politically independent central banks sends a credible signal to investors that the value of their foreign assets will not be subject to inflationary fiscal expansion. Therefore, when neighboring states loosen capital control to attract investment, a state at issue tends to use CBI to achieve the same purpose while maintaining control of its own financial market. Multiple statistical analyses corroborate this theoretical postulate. A case study of the Philippine central bank reform offers complementary empirical support.

Contributions to the Literature

This study contributes to the literature on national policymaking under globalization on several fronts. First, unlike the majority of the literature that adheres to the notion of convergence as the sole evidence of globalization's constraining power (Bodea & Hicks, 2015a; Cao & Prakash, 2010; Elkins et al., 2006a; Garretson & Peeters, 2006; Notermans, 1993; Wang, 2018), I demonstrate that convergence can be a result of states' substituting feasible polices for costly ones. Therefore, under certain circumstances, convergence is also indicative of states' policy autonomy.

Second, focusing on convergence to locate states' policy adaptivity distinguishes this book from existing studies that mainly focus on policy differentiation to detect the policy independence of states when faced with intensified globalization (Bremer, 2018; Garrett, 1995; Garrett & Lange, 1991, 1995; Grieco et al., 2009; Hwang & Lee, 2014; Milner & Judkins, 2004; Mukherjee et al., 2009; Pinto & Pinto, 2008). Both policy divergence and convergence belie states' policy creativity, depending on the issue areas that are under investigation.

Third, extant scholarship on policymaking under globalization often confines itself to single issue areas (Bearce & Hallerberg, 2011; Brooks & Kurtz, 2012; Lütz, 2004; Milner & Kubota, 2005; Morrison, 2011; Ward et al., 2011). This book demonstrates that convergence can occur either within issue areas or across issue areas. Moreover, considering the policy instruments (domestic or international) that are deployed to implement substitution, convergence can be sought either at the same analytical level or across analytical levels.

Finally, the empirical exercises in this book also carry normative implications. When states enact policies such as signing BITs and PTAs, lowering corporate taxation, and granting independence to central banks, in practice, these policy enactments should be able to mitigate some of the pressure on states to deregulate labor market and other areas that are of economic significance and direct distributive consequences. In this sense, this book provides extra support to works that have shown globalization is not invariably harmful (Greenhill et al., 2009; Malesky & Mosley, 2018).

Plan of the Book

In the next chapter, I present the theoretical framework of this book. Unlike the literature holding that states' efforts to maintain policy autonomy necessarily foster policy divergence despite the pressure that globalization exerts to succumb to convergence, I theorize that convergence can also be emblematic of policy adaptivity. Substitution is the main mechanism through which such convergence occurs as a strategic response to globalized pressure for policy conformity. Building on issue areas and the level of analysis, I recognize four types of convergence based on how substitution operates. Chapters 2 to 5 examine three of these substitution mechanisms.

In chapter 2, focusing on convergence through within–issue area substitution across analytical levels, I highlight that developing capital-importing states' convergence in terms of BITs does not constitute an involuntary capitulation to the pressure from capital-exporting states. Rather, capital-importing states strategically use BITs to substitute risky and unstable domestic judicial reforms while maintaining their attractiveness to investors. In chapter 3, to illustrate convergence through across–issue area substitution across analytical levels, I explore how pressure from economic peers to deregulate labor markets can make it more likely for states to conclude PTAs. Chapters 4 and 5 are dedicated to exploring convergence through across–issue area substitution at the same analytical level. In chapter 4, I demonstrate that leftist governments' convergence on lower corporate tax rates is not so much a submission to the global tide of reduction in capital taxation as an active policy adjustment to avoid labor market deregulation. In chapter 5, I show that the diffusion of CBI can be accounted for by a strategic consideration: pursuing CBI is a better policy alternative to forfeiting the control of capital flows when states face high capital openness from their neighbors, which is economically costly to imitate.

In the conclusion, I summarize the theoretical arguments and findings of the book with an emphasis on the book's ability to enrich our understanding of policymaking under globalization. I further explore the book's relationship with a number of strands of literature. I then discuss the implications for policymakers. Finally, I present the prospective research directions that this book might open up.

1

Measured Adaptivity

Policy Convergence through Substitution under Globalization

Globalization and Policy Convergence

One of the gravest concerns about globalization is the fact that states are losing policy autonomy because of it.[1] States are forced to relinquish the control of their own policymaking to enact similar or identical policies that enhance competitiveness in a well-integrated world economy (Drezner, 2005; Rodrik, 1997; Wang, 2018). In other words, globalization compels policy convergence among states. It is in this sense that Ohmae (1995) proclaims that "states are no longer meaningful units in which to think about economic activity" (p. 120).

Its logic goes as follows. As globalization deepens, trade and foreign investment become increasingly important to a state's economy (Alfaro et al., 2010; Azman-Saini et al., 2010; Grossman & Helpman, 2015; Liu et al., 2002). To sustain a strong economy, states have to promote both economic flows through favorable policies (Blanton & Blanton, 2007; Kambourov, 2009; McKenzie & Lee, 1991; Zhang, 2001). Pursuing these policies means states have to prioritize economic efficiency over other policy considerations in order to gain larger shares of markets (domestic and international) and attract more foreign capital. Refusing to do so would be considerably costly. Economically competing states set in motion and reinforce this pressure to enact similar policies favoring markets. As a consequence, they can only passively react to the increasingly constrained environment by reluctantly following the dictates of globalization (Cao, 2010; Cao & Prakash, 2012; Davies & Vadlamannati, 2013; Olney, 2013; Rodrik, 2011; Wang, 2018). What results is a race to the bottom across policy areas, a race that produces significant economic implications that come at the expense of societal welfare at large (Cao & Prakash, 2010; Garretson & Peeters, 2006; Notermans, 1993; Wang, 2018).

Accelerating globalization will irrevocably intensify policy convergence (Rodrik, 2011; Strange, 1997), permanently eroding policy autonomy and eventually dissolving the nation-state (Albrow, 1996; Beeson, 2003; Ohmae, 1995). Such worries expose the latent assumption that convergence is taken to solely denote the denationalization of economic regulation. Through convergence, globalization detaches states from their territories and national constituencies. Nevertheless, globalization does not unavoidably lead to convergence, nor does convergence patently indicate the surrender of policy autonomy. In the following discussion, I will lay out problems with the convergence thesis in detail.

Problematizing the Globalization-Convergence Thesis

There are at least four problems with the policy convergence thesis held by globalization scholars. First, scholars often conflate different types of convergence. Hay (2001; also see Strunz et al., 2017) identifies four: input, policy, output, and process.[2] Input convergence refers to "convergence in the pressures and constraints placed upon a particular political economy." Policy convergence denotes "convergence in the policies pursued by (or the paradigms informing) particular states." Output convergence concerns "convergence in the consequences, effects and outcomes of particular policies." Finally, process convergence represents "convergence in the processes sustaining the developmental trajectories of particular states" (Hay, 2001, p. 514).

These four types of convergence are distinct from one another, and they do not vary in the same manner. A constraining environment contributes significantly to the first one—input convergence—but not to the remaining three. There is no guarantee that input convergence will invariably lead to policy, output, and process convergences at the same time. For instance, retaining investment does not require all states to pursue identical policies expected to benefit investors, work with the same effectiveness, and/or embark on similar developmental trajectories (cf., Bloom, 2016; Wu, 2017). Empirical research has borne out this conceptual difference. In their study of 15 advanced industrial democracies during the period 1960–1987, Garrett and Lange (1991) find that trade openness only produces small impacts on a limited range of macroeconomic policies toward factors such as the real interest rate and the money supply. Higher trade exposure incentivizes states to pursue less expansive macroeconomic policies. This exposure, however, does not affect other important partisan policies. Corporatist states are more likely to maintain a balanced budget than weak labor and incoherent states. In addition, this disparity is strongly pronounced in government interventions such as total spending, consumption spending, and total taxation.

The second problem with the policy convergence thesis is the fact that convergence can occur through diverse mechanisms (Hoberg, 2001). Economic competition, with which globalization scholars are primarily concerned, is merely one of them. For example, Holzinger and Knill (2005)—whose research builds on pioneering works by scholars such as Bennett (1991) and Drezner (2001)—have identified five major mechanisms for convergence: imposition, international harmonization, regulatory competition, transnational communication (lesson-drawing, transnational problem-solving emulation, and international policy promotion), and independent problem-solving (p. 780). In a similar way, Dobbin et al. (2007) have named the following causes of convergence: social construction, coercion, competition, and learning. It is important to note that these mechanisms do not necessarily work independently and exclusively from one another. They can operate in concert to bring forth convergence in a given policy area. It has been shown that some liberal economic policies—such as capital account openness, current account openness, and exchange rate unification—diffuse on the global level due to a mixture of economic competition and the emulation of successful examples or culturally similar peers (Simmons & Elkins, 2004). In other words, the logic that globalization compels convergence merely through economic competition is flawed.

In some issue areas, hegemons play a larger role in promoting policy convergence through intergovernmental negotiations, which produces harmonization (Bach, 2010; Drezner, 2005). In issue areas where hegemons lack the will to lead policy coordination, the level of policy convergence is driven by competition (Drezner, 2005), implying a greater influence of market power. Ultimately, the variety of mechanisms for convergence suggests that globalization does not dominate other mechanisms in shaping national policies. If a few national policies do converge, this cannot be attributed only to globalization.

The third problem with the policy convergence thesis is the fact that, contrary to conventional scholarly assumptions, convergence actually benefits states in many circumstances, even if it is induced by economic competition. Goldstein et al. (2007) demonstrate that from 1946 to 2004, the GATT and the WTO substantially increased bilateral trade between members, member-nonmember participants, and nonparticipants. They also find that such effects were reinforced by additional trade-facilitating institutions such as colonial ties and reciprocal preferential trade agreements. Bilateral investment treaties (BITs) attract investment from both protected and unprotected investors after the endogeneity issue is addressed. Such effect can be attributed to the high ex ante and ex post costs imposed by BITs' negotiation processes and legal stipulations (Kerner, 2009). Likewise, by providing "tax relief to foreign investors from double taxation" and "mitigating the uncertainty an investor faces when dealing with foreign fiscal systems and lessening the administrative effort," double taxation treaties substantially increase investment in member states (Barthel et al., 2009, p. 2). Vogel (2000) shows how regulations on car emissions in California diffuse to car-exporting states; this phenomenon is famously designated "the California effect," and it represents a climb to the top (also see Holzinger & Sommerer, 2011). Trading with states that have higher labor standards has been demonstrated to produce positive impacts on labor rights laws in the exporting states (Greenhill et al., 2009). Baccini and Koenig-Archibugi (2014) demonstrate that both competition and socialization facilitate the diffusion of labor rights treaties among states, which helps to mitigate possible social dumping. Bodea and Hicks (2015a) reveal that globalization promotes the proliferation of central bank independence and that policy diffusion helps capital-stricken states receive higher investment flows and borrow at lower rates. The benign convergence on display here, which results from states actively pursuing liberal economic policies that are conceived to improve societal welfare (Garrett, 2000; Yergin & Stanislaw, 1997), echoes the observation that globalization is a social construct created by states.

The fourth problem with the policy convergence thesis is that, despite a restrictive international environment, states often find ways to maintain their policies' distinctiveness. A plethora of studies has concluded that states do exhibit policy differentiation that can be attributed to variations in their respective political and economic landscapes. For example, the negative externalities of financial globalization fail to coerce states into a perfect convergence in the field of banking regulation (Lütz, 2004). Although states do seem to agree on some kind of broad institutional framework, any so-called convergence is limited, and both the timing and processes of reforms differ as a result of domestic institutional veto players. This limited convergence can hardly be traced back to globalization itself. Instead, it must be ascribed to "the international harmonization" that "was driven by domestic regulators pursuing national interests" (Lütz, 2004, p. 187). To that end, Clark (2009) shows that, despite the policy constraints imposed by globalization, politicians do not lose control over the economy. Instead, they manufacture policy flexibility by employing policies that are compatible with the macroeconomic goals under various political conditions.

To summarize, the globalization-convergence thesis is both theoretically and empirically problematic because it amalgamates distinct types of convergence into one category, assumes that all convergence occurs due to globalization, posits that globalization is irredeemably detrimental to societal welfare, and overlooks the ability of states to fend off the pressure to converge. There are, however, two pitfalls that we must avoid when criticizing the globalization-convergence thesis. First, because the thesis is problematic, we must reject the proposition that globalization is constraining. Globalization does reshape the environment in which states operate. The pressure to converge does exist, and it keeps growing (Wang, 2018). To use Hay's term, globalization supplies a new and uniform input for national policymaking. The existence of heterogeneous policies among states indeed indicates their strengths and therefore their autonomy, but it does not represent a lack of external pressure to follow the dictates of globalization.

There is, furthermore, a second pitfall that we must avoid. The fact that states have retained distinct policies should not lead us to identify the absence of convergence as the lone indicator of states' policy autonomy. States possess a wide range of tools to deal with external policy pressure. Outright resistance is merely one of them; convergence can be another. Therefore, convergence in one issue area is not equivalent to the abandonment of that area's policy autonomy. In other words, convergence can be strategic and desirable, just as Bennett (1991) has argued. I will explore this point in greater detail in a later section. Before I do so, I will outline how states manage policy adaptation. This discussion is important to understanding why convergence functions as a way to adapt through mechanisms such as competition, learning, and emulation, or any combination of the three.

Policy Adaptivity and State Capacity

State capacity implies making policy adjustments whenever it is necessary to do so. Policy adaptivity therefore embodies state capacity rather than its absence. As Ikenberry (1986) has adeptly put it, "It is the ability to transform the techniques of state influence or control that lies at the base of state capacity, and this ability may involve the devolution of formal, direct state responsibility as well as its recrudescence" (p. 136). Thus, to change policy instruments reflects not the weakening of state capacity, but rather its strengthening (Clark, 2009). We should not confuse the alteration in policy tools with the loss of the state's capacity to make policy adjustments. "The use and efficacy of particular instruments will vary over time, depending on the phase of development and its associated tasks; but it does not follow that state capacity must thereby ebb and flow" (Weiss, 1998, p. 32). States always adjust "both formally and informally, to changes in their environment in order to be able to continue to perform successfully their designated functions" (Peters & Savoie, 2000, pp. 43–44). As a policy environment changes—for instance, as a result of accelerating globalization—states need to adapt.

Policy adaptivity is practically feasible. Public policy literature has long demonstrated that there is often more than one solution to a given policy issue. At the extreme end of this literature is the garbage can theory (Cohen et al., 1972). This theory argues that there is no such thing as rational design in a policy decision process. Solutions, problems, and policy participants can be completely independent from one another. Indeed, solutions can even actively search for problems (Cohen Michael et al., 2012). In this study, I do not go as far as to argue for the disconnection between solutions and problems that policymakers face in a specific policy environment, nor do I believe that the policymaking processes in the issue areas that I investigate are random. I also do not probe how policymakers ascribe meaning to specific policy instruments or to the policy processes (Linder & Peters, 1989). Rather, departing from the basic fact that a multiplicity of policy instruments exists in any given issue area, I focus on policymakers' calculations—for example, how they maximize political benefits by providing the least costly policies to their constituencies.

States implement policy adjustments in different ways. Policy changes reflect the changes in the environment that states face (Weiss, 1998, p. 21). In the context of economic management, policy adjustment can manifest in the process of switching from action to inaction, or vice versa, without compromising the authority of the state.

> If a government intervenes in the economy to protect an existing industry, either by tariff or through subsidized loans, is its action an indication of state strength? If a government withholds action and allows a noncompetitive industry to decline, does it thereby indicate weakness? The problem for a priori judgment is that state capacities result in both action and inaction, intervention and nonintervention. The meaning of state capacity does not lie in the simple degree of state intervention in the economy and society. (Ikenberry, 1986, p. 135)

This inaction is akin to the delegation of power by the state to private actors, which may practically contribute to enhancing state capacity. "The increasing use of non-profit and for profit organizations to implement policy need not mean that government is abdicating responsibility but only that it has uncovered lower-cost and higher-efficiency means of achieving its collective ends. Given that these organizations may have greater legitimacy with public service clients than more 'bureaucratic' public sector organizations, the governance capacity may actually be increased rather than decreased" (Peters & Savoie, 2000, p. 44). Such delegation of power may even lead to "a system of central coordination based on the cooperation of government and industry" (Weiss, 1998, p. 39). This would create the appearance that the state is losing its policy capacity.

Therefore, when states delegate power, this delegation does not diminish their total capacity. The total capacity of a state does not dwindle. For a state, its policy space embraces its policy capacity across all issue areas. The state may delegate or concede power in some areas while enhancing or strengthening power in others. When states retreat in the field of economic decision-making, they may simultaneously introduce policies that intrude into areas that used to be beyond their purview—for example, social welfare (Mann, 1984). Embedded liberalism precisely reflects such a process of policy trade-off (Avelino et al., 2005; Hays et al., 2005; Lim & Burgoon, 2018; Ruggie, 1982). Kim and Pelc (2021) observe that, in the United States, workers who suffer job losses due to import competition are less likely to call for protectionist policies such as anti-dumping when they successfully secure compensation from the government. This tendency demonstrates that trading one policy—such as controlling trade—for another—such as providing social welfare—reflects not the diminishment of state power, but the state's shrewd use of the power that it possesses.

Scholars often mistake the alteration of policy instruments for the renunciation of state autonomy. This is because they believe that "the relevant instruments are somehow predetermined and fixed in character" (Weiss, 1998, p. 197). Therefore, "any diminution in the importance of a particular policy tool is taken as evidence of a loss of state power" (Weiss, 1998, p. 197). For example, evolving from mercantilism to liberalism does not eclipse states' capacity to control and manage their trade relations. States can still use non-tariff barriers to manipulate trade (Kono, 2008). Rickard (2012) finds that trade openness leads to retrenchment in social welfare spending in some developing nations, just as convergence thesis predicts. Nevertheless, states strive to mitigate such costs through higher subsidies.

To summarize, states that face a restraining environment can find various ways to adjust their policies and ensure they do not incur considerable losses in a given issue area merely because the policy environment is tightening. As I will demonstrate later, policy adjustment can lead to either divergence or convergence. Before moving to an in-depth exploration of how policy adjustment induces convergence, I will first examine globalization's constraining power, which contextualizes the mechanisms of policy convergence through substitution.

Globalization's Addition to a Constraining Policy Environment

Although globalists are incorrect to allege that globalization irrevocably chips away at state autonomy that culminates in expansive policy convergence, they are correct to contend that globalization's power vis-à-vis the state is growing. Intensifying globalization establishes specific parameters for national policymaking. In other words, it changes the input for national policymaking. Globalization does this through at least two channels. The first consists of globalized economic competition, which induces and amplifies the externalities of national policies. The second consists of diffusing the institutional structures that both support, facilitate, and promote globalization and those that remedy the issues that accompany it. I will explain each of these channels in turn.

First, globalization elevates the power of the market to an unseen altitude. Trade now accounts for 30–70 percent of the wealthiest states' national economies (World Bank, 2016). The economic significance of trade even holds true in relation to hegemons. Although the US is not as reliant on trade as other states, the share of trade in its economy has climbed for the past fifty years and ultimately reached almost 30 percent of the country's GDP (World Bank, 2016). Trade has become increasingly important for the developing world as well. Without trade, it would be hard to imagine the Four Asian Tigers (Haggard, 1990) or China's economic miracle (Naughton, 2007). Moreover, the contemporary features of trade make it more economically impactful. Trade in services, production for trade, and intra-industry trade all have grown to an unprecedentedly high level compared to 100 years ago (Bordo et al., 1999). In doing so, these kinds of trade have deeply reshaped national economic structures.

At the same time, foreign capital has evolved into an integral part of most states' economies (World Bank, 2016). It is true that, 30 years ago, the majority of foreign direct investment (FDI) was made in OECD countries. Now, however, a significant portion of FDI targets emerging economies such as China, South Korea, India, Singapore, Mexico, and Brazil (UNCTAD, 2016). In the current world, moreover, the sectors in which foreign capital is invested are much more diverse; this investment therefore produces a remarkably broader impact on states' economies than it did at earlier times in history (Bordo et al., 1999; Kobrin, 2017).

Unsurprisingly, states that are left out of this process fare very poorly. Examples include Latin American states that have pursued policies of import-substitution industrialization and African states that are unable to attract FDI to produce advanced industrial goods for trade. Both trade and investment operate according to their own logical processes. States whose policies follow these processes will earn rewards; those whose policies resist these processes will be punished (see Andrews, 1994).

Therefore, to achieve success in globalized economic competition, states must pursue undifferentiated policies that stimulate both investment and trade. The incentive to do so is particularly strong if a state's competitors have already taken this step; after all, economic peer states that refuse to adapt can suffer from negative externalities (Franzese & Hays, 2008; Neumayer & Plümper, 2012). Globalization fundamentally changes the calculus of costs and benefits in states' policymaking. It is in this sense that we can say that states are constrained by globalization (Thomson, 1995, p. 225).

To turn now to the second channel in which globalization affects state policymaking, it must be said that even if today's globalization is not unprecedented (Hirst & Thompson, 1995; Krasner, 1999a), globalization still tightens the constraints on national policymaking. It is undeniable that "the clearest relationship between globalization and state activity is that they have increased hand in hand" (also see Gritsch, 2005; Krasner, 1999a, p. 40). Nevertheless, "globalization has strengthened the importance of international legal sovereignty because one way in which states have dealt with challenges to their control has been to enter into international agreements that facilitate international regulation when unilateral policy is ineffective" (Krasner, 1999a, p. 36). This is particularly true that in light of "the new web of obligations and rights that states need to take into account under the rule of law in the making of policy" (Sassen, 1995, p. 32), "globalization has reconfigured the intersection of territoriality and sovereignty" (p. 31).[3] For example, a broad range of international institutions currently define and redefine how states behave in their domestic and external affairs. The collective security mechanism of the United Nations makes war illegal as an instrument to settle disputes, and it obliges members to fight common enemies. The WTO coordinates tariffs and other trade-related polices among its members.

Political scientists' call for intrusive global governance puts more constraints on states because sovereignty, the defining feature of the nation-state, is considered to be the barrier to harnessing globalization for public welfare (Goldin, 2013; Hameiri & Jones, 2016; Slaughter, 2004). Global governance emerges to better deal with the problems that arise in a globalized world. Even so, global governance is plagued by the same kind of ineffectiveness that characterizes international cooperation across many issue areas (Downs et al., 1996; Drezner, 2000). Sovereignty is blamed for this ineffectiveness. Efforts to disintegrate the state therefore become necessary to promote global governance (Goldin, 2013; Slaughter, 2004). The emergence and expansion of global governance as a form of state transformation attests to the intensity of such efforts (Hameiri & Jones, 2016). As expected, transitional governance will add more constraints to states' policy spaces. Overall, states are at present "more deeply enmeshed in global networks of interaction; crucially, they have seen their own expansion in size and absolute power diminished by the relatively greater increases in the direct power, exit options, and collective structural power available to foreign actors and global networks" (Goldblatt et al., 1997, p. 283). Undoubtedly, although "sovereign states must effectively patrol territory . . . the meaning of effectiveness, as well as the means of achieving it, changes as the global environment changes" (Thomson, 1995, p. 225).

It should be noted that even before globalization began to accelerate, states had never made policies in an environment free of restrictions on their decision-making power. The policy environment is always constraining. Sovereignty itself establishes the first constraint. While sovereignty as a concept empowers a political entity by legitimating it as a member of international society, it constrains that entity as well (Werner & De Wilde, 2001). Sovereignty establishes the external boundary of power for each sovereign state as a territorial authority. Under most circumstances, each state can only attend to its own business; it cannot interfere with the affairs of others. The mutual exclusiveness of sovereignty implies that sovereign states must operate in a constraining environment. They always do so, even if this environment is fundamentally characterized by anarchy. In the meantime, the constraints embedded in sovereignty also constitute the domestic confines within which any particular state exerts its control. Due to these constraints, states cannot make policies without worrying about the adverse consequences of bad behavior such as the abuse of human rights (Glanville, 2013). Power relationships are another factor that shapes how states behave (Mearsheimer, 2001; Waltz, 1979). The struggle among great powers not only costs themselves dearly but also forcefully involves weaker states. Put differently, states seek survival and prosperity in an imperfect political market.

It is because states lack absolute autonomy that Krasner (1999b) famously refers to the Westphalian sovereignty as an "organized hypocrisy." The idea of organized hypocrisy correctly emphasizes the constraints that sovereign states face when they exercise their power. States are invariably constrained. The only thing that varies with time and across territories is what constrains them and to what extent they are constrained.

Globalization profoundly changes the set of choices that states' policies can follow and establishes new standards for how states should govern and rule. In this sense, we can say that globalization constitutes a new type of constraint on the policy autonomy of states. Therefore, regardless of how globalization occurs (Garrett, 2000), it remains an important influence on national policymaking in the contemporary world (Chaudoin et al., 2015; Lake, 2009). No state can afford to ignore it.

As globalization imposes more constraints on the policy autonomy of states, some scholars anticipate that the traditional nation-state will eventually lose its appeal as an authoritative way to organize the basic political units of international society (Albrow, 1996; Ohmae, 1996). Nevertheless, the way in which today's states exercise their control does not mean that sovereignty will lose its significance as a mode of legitimation. The more constrained environment that globalization seems to produce may change the policy instruments of states, but this environment is not set to upend the nation-state itself, nor will it overturn the core of sovereignty: authority (Mann, 1997; Rodrik, 2011; Thomson, 1995; Zurn & Deitelhoff, 2015). Sovereign states have coped with restricted policymaking power since their very birth. Globalization does not create a unique venue in which states face constraints (Agnew, 2017; Krasner, 1999a). The Westphalian sovereignty as a whole has proven to be resilient across time and circumstances; therefore, it will remain so in the foreseeable future (Rodrik, 2011; Zurn & Deitelhoff, 2015).

Globalization may "weaken the efficacy of specific *policy instruments*" (Weiss, 1998, p. 197), but it cannot demand that states follow its policy dictates (Stein, 2016). To gain a better position in globalized economic competition means certain policies are more favored than others. A state can, however, either exploit such pressure to avoid more costly policy changes or deflect pressure by reverting to more politically feasible alternatives. These substitutive policies encompass both domestic and international instruments. Convergence can arise from policy changes that are made through the adoption of either type of instrument. Hence, contrary to the conventional belief that convergence indicates nothing but the capitulation of states to globalization, convergence can—depending on issue areas—also attest to policy adaptivity. I will make this argument in the following section and demonstrate its empirical validity in subsequent chapters.

Policy Substitution-Induced Convergence

As discussed earlier, globalization imposes growing constraints on states' power, but states do not automatically surrender their policy autonomy. Rather, they strive to find various ways to adapt to this new policy environment. This adaptivity manifests in not only divergence but also convergence. Variation in domestic institutions and political organizations drives divergence, while policy substitution sustains convergence.[4] I argue that states can substitute costly policy changes dictated by globalization with less costly ones that also advance it within or across issue areas.[5] This process leads to policy identity across states, a phenomenon also known as convergence.[6] Therefore, even if we detect that convergence is induced by globalization, we do not need to interpret this as an unambiguous sign that states give up their policy autonomy. Instead, convergence can epitomize the adaptivity that states exhibit when their policy space keeps shrinking. Substitution serves as a major mechanism through which strategic policy convergence under globalization transpires.[7] In other words, the core argument in this book is that globalization can induce interstate policy convergence through states' strategic policy substitution in single or multiple issue areas and at either domestic or international levels, or across these two levels. This process involves policy changes not categorically dictated by globalization but those attributable to states' strategic choices.

Substitution is possible because there often exists a set of policy options that allows states to pursue the same policy goal. These policies differ from each other in their effectiveness, political costs, or both. In practice, however, the functional similarity among them makes political costs the primary criterion by which to determine what kind of policies to pursue (Genovese et al., 2017, p. 238). The literature on policy substitution frequently focuses on policy tools at the same level of analysis (e.g., Carnegie, 2015; Clark & Reed, 2005; Clark, 2001; Genovese et al., 2017; Greffenius, 1986; Shin, 2017). Nonetheless, substitution can occur between policies that are seated at different levels of analysis—that is to say, between domestic and international tools (see Davies, 2016). Additionally, mutually substitutive policies do not need to affect the same issue area. They can operate across multiple issue areas as well. As Carnegie (2015) has shown, foreign aid becomes a major tool of coercion when the WTO removes tariffs as an effective means of foreign policy.

More importantly, policy substitution produces convergence. Genovese et al. (2017) have demonstrated that states substitute internationally diffused policies with more politically beneficial alternatives. Although states' policies deviate from convergence on an international instrument, they do converge on feasible domestic ones. Furthermore, policy tools that are used as substitutes can be compatible with or even driven by globalization. For example, leftist governments in some developed nations substitute opaque probusiness policies for transparent pro–welfare tax policies (Shin, 2017). This point will be explored in more detail later.

As a sign of states' policy adaptivity, convergence can logically occur via substitution within or across levels of analysis and issue areas. Tables 1.1–1.3 summarize these possibilities. First, let's examine the scenario in which states practice policy substitution only within particular issue areas. When states seek to avoid a domestic policy in Issue Area I, they can substitute for that policy with a domestic alternative or an international one in the same issue area, and vice versa. Substitution that occurs within Issue Area II follows the same logic. For example, if a state refuses to improve the rule of law as a means to attract foreign capital, then it can either encourage joint partnership between state-owned enterprises and foreign investors—a domestic policy tool—or it can make bilateral investment treaties—an international policy instrument. Substitution leads to convergence within issue areas at either a domestic or an international level. The thick arrowhead lines represent substitution that occurs at the same analysis level, while the thin ones indicate substitution that occurs across different levels of analysis.

Now, we turn to cross-issue substitution, which is more complex. When states seek to avoid a domestic policy change in Issue Area I, they can choose a domestic policy or an international one from Issue Area II. Both choices lead to convergence. In a symmetrical fashion, states that intend to avoid a domestic policy change in Issue Area II can select a domestic policy or an international one from Issue Area I. For example,

Table 1.1. Substitution-Induced Convergence within Issue Areas

	Issue Area I	Issue Area II
Level of Analysis		
Domestic	Avoidance ➤ Convergence	Avoidance ➤ Convergence
International	Avoidance ➤ Convergence	Avoidance ➤ Convergence

Source: Author-created image.

when a state finds it hard to comply with its economic competitors' pressure to degrade labor protection—a policy change in Issue Area I—then that state can provide extra tax credits—a domestic policy in Issue Area II. Alternatively, the state could sign a preferential trade agreement—an international policy in Issue Area II. In both scenarios convergence is produced. Likewise, convergence results if states attempt to avoid certain international policy changes in either Issue Area I or Issue Area II. As in Table 1.1, Table 1.2's thick arrowhead lines denote cross-issue substitution that occurs at the same level of analysis. Table 1.3's thin lines signify cross-issue substitution across different levels of analysis.

These possibilities are grouped into four larger types in Table 1.4. The first one is convergence through within–issue area substitution that occurs at the same analytical level. The second type is convergence through within–issue area substitution that occurs across analytical levels. The third one is convergence through across–issue area substitution that occurs at the

Table 1.2. Substitution-Induced Convergence across Issue Areas (at the Same Level of Analysis)

	Issue Area I	Issue Area II
Level of Analysis		
Domestic	Avoidance ⟶	Convergence
	Convergence ⟵	Avoidance
International	Avoidance ⟶	Convergence
	Convergence ⟵	Avoidance

Source: Author-created image.

Table 1.3. Substitution-Induced Convergence across Issue Areas (across Levels of Analysis)

	Issue Area I	Issue Area II
Level of Analysis		
Domestic	Convergence	Avoidance
	Avoidance	Convergence
International	Convergence	Avoidance
	Avoidance	Convergence

Source: Author-created image.

same analytical level. The fourth type is convergence through across–issue area substitution that occurs across analytical levels. I examine three of these four types of convergence—the second, third, and fourth[8]—in relation to four policies. These policies are: bilateral investment treaties (BITs), preferential trade agreements (PTAs), corporate taxation, and central bank independence (CBI). These policies are selected because they allow states to more competently participate in a globalized economy and therefore help to sustain the deepening of globalization.

First, BITs as a bilateral commitment device are used to avoid costly domestic policy changes. In practice, foreign investors, who often fall prey to the policy whims of host states (Li, 2009), need an assurance of the security of their assets in host states. By delegating investment dispute settlement to a third party, BITs credibly convey the commitment demanded by FDI carriers. In so doing, BITs bring in more investment for a state employing such instruments (Kerner, 2009). States are therefore strongly motivated to form these treaties (Elkins et al., 2006a; Jandhyala et al., 2011). More importantly, because states believe that concluding BITs can promote capital inflows, they tend to form more BITs to avoid difficult domestic legal reforms designed for the same purpose, that is, those promoting judicial independence, as these domestic reforms often prove politically unstable and thus less credible to investors. For leaders of host states, BITs, in the meantime, also enable and even encourage greater political control over judiciaries, thus maximizing the chances of political survival (cf., Ginsburg, 2005; Massoud, 2014). Therefore, despite the almost uniform preference that capital-exporting states show for BITs, the convergence on BITs does not indicates the oppressive power of globalization. To the contrary, host states purposefully employ BITs as a feasible solution to thorny domestic problems.

Convergence applies to trade policy tools as well. Here, it follows a logic slightly different from that of investment protection. Like capital flow, trade is another significant aspect of globalization. It is of vital importance that a state maintains its advantages in trade. States seeking

Table 1.4. Types of Convergence through Substitution

Substitution-Convergence	Same Analytical level	Across Analytical levels
Within issue area	Type 1	Type 2
Across issue areas	Type 3	Type 4

Source: Author-created image.

to minimize trade costs resort to a variety of methods, including the policy of reducing labor protections. Policy moves by economic peers pressure their competitors to adopt similar policies (Wang, 2018). To avoid yielding to this pressure, states can adopt alternative policies. To sign a PTA is one such policy. PTAs can generate considerable economic gains, such as trade promotion and job creation. Furthermore, they can do so in a less politically costly way than policies compelled by globalization—for instance, the policy of reducing legal protections for labor. As a result, a pair of states is more likely to form a PTA in the face of policy pressure to downgrade labor laws. The fact that states sign PTAs does not necessarily constitute evidence that globalization forces them to do so. Policy convergence may result from states' desire to avoid costly policy changes in a different issue area.

States can also prioritize one domestic policy change over another, the costlier one; this equally leads to policy convergence. For instance, taxation affects economic flows. Political parties prefer separate tax policies based on their ideological positions. Leftist governments tend to tax corporations heavily, while rightist governments do not. Nevertheless, whether leftist governments can enact their preferred tax policy depends on the policy environment in which they operate (Plümper et al., 2009). When leftist governments are pressured by their economic competitors to diminish protections for labor rights, they lighten corporate tax burdens instead. This is because one policy is more politically harmful than the other, but both are effective in achieving the same goal, that is, reducing potential costs to investors and encouraging flows of FDI. Leftist governments facing globalized economic competition make strategic compromises by adopting market-oriented policies in issue areas that deviate from their ideological preferences, but prove less costly than yielding to the pressure to alter policies in areas that directly hurt their core constituencies.

Finally, states can employ CBI to substitute for the abandonment of capital control. This gives rise to convergence in polices that sustain highly autonomous central banks. Capital control is an important policy tool to maintain macroeconomic stability. To compete for scarce capital, however, states are pressured to open their financial markets to foreign investors. To avoid losing such a vital policy tool, states can increase CBI to signal to investors that governments will refrain from intervening in the economy. In turn, this signal works to stabilize prices and thus to tame inflation. CBI can fulfill these functions because it solves the time inconsistency problem. In a state where the central bank is largely independent of governmental control, politicians can rarely pursue expansive fiscal policies without worrying that the central bank will use its monetary policy to offset the potentially adverse impact of a politically driven fiscal expansion (Bodea & Hicks, 2015b; Bodea & Higashijima, 2015). Compared to a policy of relaxing capital control, CBI incurs lower costs in terms of effective economic management; at the same time, it adds significant economic benefits. Therefore, CBI is a better policy alternative than forfeiting the control of capital flows.

Given the same constraining environment, policy divergence is unquestionably an important indication that states preserve their policymaking autonomy under globalization. Nonetheless, extant literature unreflectively assumes that convergence automatically constitutes the evidence of the constraining power of globalization. I argue that convergence can be the result of states that actively avoid the costly policy changes caused by domestic institutional barriers or imposed by globalization. Substitutive policies that lead to convergence can be either international instruments, as in the cases of BITs and PTAs, or domestic ones, as in the cases of corporate taxation and CBI. Moreover, such policy substitution can operate within particular issue areas, as is true of the case of BITs. Alternatively, the substitution can occur across issue areas, as will be demonstrated in the investigations of PTAs, corporate taxation, and CBI. Therefore, policy substitution-induced convergence is a hallmark of state adaptivity. Table 1.5 exhibits the four policies examined in this

Table 1.5. Convergence through Substitution in Four Policies

Substitution-Convergence	At the Same Analytical Level	Across Analytical Levels
Within issue areas		**BITs** (implementing judicial independence reforms)
Across issue areas	**Corporate taxation** (weakening labor protection) **CBI** (relaxing capital control)	**PTAs** (weakening labor protection)

Note: The policies in parentheses are substitutes for those listed above them.

Source: Author-created image.

study alongside their corresponding categories of convergence through substitution.

Conclusion

To conclude, states can substitute feasible policies for undesirable ones. Unlike the literature showing that states tend to maintain their policy independence and therefore foster policy diversity despite globalization's pressure for convergence, I argue that divergence is not the only symbol of policy autonomy and that convergence can be emblematic of policy adaptivity too. In other words, states do not respond to globalization in one uniform fashion as frequently assumed. Rather, they do so through a variety of means as will be revealed in the following chapters. In addition, IPE scholars often hold that it is necessary to consider systemic factors in order to understand domestic policy processes and outcomes (Chaudoin et al., 2015; Gourevitch, 1978; Weinberg, 2016). My approach demonstrates that system-level factors do constrain states and that such constraints can lead to new system- and state-level changes both within and across issue areas. This challenges the expectation that system-level factors only compel changes in one direction within individual issue areas.

Throughout the following four chapters, I will illustrate the empirical validity of the proposed substitution-induced convergence. Each chapter will focus on a specific convergent policy change. I will begin with investigating convergence in BITs, which will be followed by a successive examination of policy convergence in PTAs, corporate taxation, and CBI.

2

The Proliferation of
Bilateral Investment Treaties
and Judicial Independence

In this chapter, I will examine one type of convergence that is caused by within–issue area substitution across analytical levels. I will do so by investigating how developing countries use bilateral investment treaties (BITs) to substitute for domestic judicial reforms. At the core of these two policy tools is the magnitude of power that national judiciaries exercise: whereas BITs restrict this power, judicial reforms reinforce it. The substitution that occurs between BITs and judicial reforms ultimately leads to the diffusion of BITs and the erosion of political independence for the domestic courts of the treaties' developing members.

Rapid capital flows constitute one significant aspect of globalization. Many factors affect where capital goes; in particular, the safety and security of the capital that is invested in host countries are major concerns (Biglaiser & Staats, 2012; Li & Resnick, 2003; Staats & Biglaiser, 2012). Host governments can use either domestic or international means to protect property rights. Governments can grant more independence to their judiciaries in order to check the executive power that preys on investors. Alternatively, governments can use BITs to signal their commitment to property rights. As encouraged by the World Bank, many countries have engaged in reforms for the rule of law. Nevertheless, the progress of these reforms remains slow across the developing world; occasionally, a reversal even occurs. Investment into developing countries has grown rapidly since the 1990s. How is it possible that decreasing levels of judicial independence are accompanied by growing capital inflows to developing host states? I argue that the decline in judicial independence is an intended result of host governments' strategic choice to substitute BITs for costly processes of pursuing domestic judicial reforms.

As stated in chapter 1, policy convergence is strategically pursued under two conditions. First, the policy changes that the state is being pressured to implement are costly. Second, policy substitutes are available. Investors prefer locations where economic opportunities abound and the rule of law supersedes the rule of man (Beazer & Blake, 2018; Staats & Biglaiser, 2012). In such locations, investors will not need to worry that their assets might be subject to arbitrary confiscation—or, if such confiscations do occur, investors can rest assured that they will be properly compensated. An independent judiciary is the cornerstone of the rule of law (World Bank, 2003). It constrains executive power (North & Weingast, 1989). Without an independent judiciary, the rule of law would be an empty promise.

Improving judicial independence is politically costly, however. As I will show in this chapter, highly independent courts pose serious threats to political leaders. This is especially true in non-democracies. Therefore, political leaders must devise policies that promote foreign capital invest-ment and minimize potential political risks. BITs serve as one viable option. They are among the most popular instruments used to protect foreign direct investment (FDI). Many studies have revealed that BITs effectively promote investment flows. Furthermore, in contrast to domestic judicial reforms, BITs address only investment-related matters, but not other subjects that could jeopardize existing regimes or governments. In other words, the political costs of BITs are comparatively lower than the costs of implementing domestic reforms. The perceived effectiveness of BITs and the low political costs that they incur affect politicians' calculus in regard to which institutions they should employ to protect investors and attract investment. Therefore, politicians in host states tend to deem BITs to be a competent substitute for costly domestic reforms.

Nonetheless, it is unrealistic to expect that merely a few BITs will increase investment flows. Hence, politicians in host states will improve judicial independence in tiny increments when there are only a small number of BITs in force. Once the number of BITs substantially increases, these politicians have fewer incentives to continue improving judicial independence. Consequently, we should expect that host states will often experience a decline in judicial independence when they have more BITs in force. In other words, a curvilinear relationship is posited between the two. Using the dose response function to deal with the continuous treatment—that is, the number of BITs in force—and to create comparison groups based on generalized propensity scores, I find evidence supporting the theoretical conjecture.

In the following discussion, I briefly review the literature on the politics of judicial independence. I then address the difficulty in providing and securing judicial independence. Following that, I discuss the mechanism through which BITs may substitute for costly domestic reforms. I present empirical evidence afterward. The following case study of Egypt shows how the mechanism that I have described functions in the real world. The final section of this chapter summarizes the argument and findings, and then draws policy implications.

The Politics of Judicial Independence

Scholars consider the politics of judicial independence as largely being domestically driven. The literature reflects this underlying assumption. Despite variations among previous studies, they appeal to a common theoretical framework: political competition (Aylin, 2013; Epperly, 2017; Ginsburg, 2003; Helmke, 2002; Jodi, 2005; Landes & Posner, 1975; Ramseyer, 1994). Political competition—primarily regularized competition—produces uncertainty in times of power transfer. When the political factions that occupy an incumbent government fear to lose power, they tend to use independent courts to prevent the incoming opposition government from monopolizing power or abolishing their legislative legacy (Landes & Posner, 1975; Ramseyer, 1994). This tendency appears in both democratic and non-democratic settings (Epperly, 2017; Hayo & Voigt, 2003; Landes & Posner, 1975; Ramseyer, 1994). It does, however, occur less often in states whose electoral process is not well institutionalized or internalized (Popova, 2010; Smithey & Ishiyama, 2000). To that end, intense political competition implies a greater number of constitutionally sanctioned veto players, which helps to increase the possibility that courts will maintain their independence (Julio, 2007).

Some studies have begun to investigate how the demand for FDI shapes judicial independence and the rule of law. Moustafa (2007) shows that the Egyptian government established a Supreme Constitutional Court (SCC) in 1979 to signal its sincere dedication to protecting investors' assets. Over subsequent years, this court has mostly maintained its independence. Several cross-sectional studies similarly find that legal reforms are executed for the purpose of attracting foreign capital (Biglaiser & Staats, 2012; Lee et al., 2014b; Staats & Biglaiser, 2012). Wang (2014) demonstrates that competition for FDI has improved the rule of law in Chinese provinces, where economic reform has deepened since the 1990s. Smith and Farrales (2010) document the Chilean and Filipino judicial reforms initiated in the 1970s and afterward; these reforms accorded more power and autonomy to courts as a way to attract FDI.

Other scholarship examines the evolution of judicial independence from the perspective of policy diffusion. Ginsburg and Versteeg (2014) analyze whether the global spread of constitutional review can be attributed to policy diffusion among culturally similar states. They obtain no evidence of such a relationship. Instead, they conclude that the adoption of constitutional review is driven purely by domestic electoral politics. In contrast, Stroh and Heyl (2015) contend that institutionalized domestic political uncertainty and international norm diffusion among states with cultural affinities both help to explain the dissemination of constitutional courts. By focusing on West Africa, these scholars find that the Gallic diffusion is persistent among Francophone states in Africa.

Extant literature, however, misses an exploration of how international policy tools can affect the decision whether to deepen domestic judicial independence. As an important means of protecting investment in foreign jurisdictions, BITs should exert some impact on the political calculation of costs and benefits from pursuing domestic judicial reforms. Although such potential impact is rarely investigated, two notable exceptions are worth our attention. Ginsburg (2005), focusing on investors, acutely observes that BITs remove pressure on host states to improve domestic governance; this is because capital carriers can resort to BITs in order to protect their assets. Hence, host states are discouraged from advancing difficult domestic reforms. Ginsburg's pioneering study emphasizes the calculations of investors but excludes those of host governments. Because executing judicial reforms is politically costly, it requires sustainable political support to maintain momentum. Therefore, when host governments can rely on external legal means to promote investment, they see no need to pursue domestic judicial reforms.

In contrast to Ginsburg, Massoud (2014) places host states' calculation where it belongs. By conducting a case study of Sudan, Massoud (2014) aptly demonstrates that authoritarian leaders use international arbitrations to avoid the political risks associated with domestic judicial reforms while simultaneously reaping the benefits of increased investment via the credibility-signaling mechanism of the arbitrations. Massoud's study, however, does not specifically discuss how or whether convergence on BITs will undermine judicial independence. Building on Massoud's work, I seek to show that the substitution of BITs for political reforms can prove consequential in terms of judicial independence. Moreover, I argue that this kind of strategic thinking exists in democracies and non-democracies alike. Because judicial reforms can be inherently unstable, they lack credibility to investors. Additionally, policy substitution only occurs when a certain threshold is crossed. I will elaborate on both of these theoretical points as follows.

The Difficulty of Sustaining Domestic Judicial Reforms

Judicial effectiveness requires the political independence of courts. Although such independence is necessary to maintain the legitimacy of courts, it threatens the executive branch. This political threat underlies the inherent difficulty of sustaining judicial independence (Ginsburg & Moustafa, 2008, pp. 6–7).

Judicial independence encourages political opposition in authoritarian states. Relying on courts to create a legitimate facade for the authoritarian rule backfires whenever courts seek to expand their power beyond the scope that autocratic leaders permit. This expansion can facilitate mobilization against the existing regime and even cause its demise. In Pakistan, the fall of military rule under President Pervez Musharraf illustrates this point (Ghias, 2010). Even if authoritarian leaders merely use courts to pursue restricted goals—such as attracting investment and spurring economic growth—the judiciary can use its legally uncompromised power to pursue agendas that authoritarian executives deem menacing. This occurred in Egypt, when President Hosni Mubarak granted the SCC independence and the authority to check governmental actions (Moustafa, 2007). Judicial independence also hurts authoritarian leaders whenever the benefits of economic growth create societal interests orthogonal to those of the ruling elites (Root & May, 2008).

Knowing this, authoritarian governments have no incentive to institute a truly independent judiciary that might threaten the regime's stability; instead, they merely maintain the deceptive appearance of judicial independence (Solomon, 2015). This deception can hardly add much credibility to the policies that these governments implement for economic gains. As Solomon (2015) has aptly stated:

> In addition to needing law as a source of legitimation at home, authoritarian leaders often faced international pressures, if only to encourage trade and investment. It is difficult for authoritarian leaders to find a comfortable balance between their aspirations for control and the need to allow courts to rule against their interests, and most of the solutions to this dilemma involve contradictions and conflict. As a result, the administration of justice tends to be less stable and predictable in authoritarian states than in democratic ones. Rarely does it meet the standards of ROL (rule of law) even in its least demanding form. Rule by law remains the best description of its role. (p. 433)

Judicial independence not only encourages political opposition but also fails to sustain itself. Because it can be reversed, it is not inherently stable. This is true in autocracies for the reasons detailed earlier. Even in democracies, however, judicial independence is not free from challenges. The commitment to an independent judiciary can be retracted under a democracy (Widner & Scher, 2008). This is particularly true if the level of uncertainty during times of power transfer is significantly reduced— for instance, as occurred in democratizing Bulgaria (Magalhães, 1999). Moreover, unlike what conventional wisdom has suggested (Aylin, 2013; Epperly, 2017; Ginsburg, 2003; Helmke, 2002; Jodi, 2005; Landes & Posner, 1975; Ramseyer, 1994), political competition does not automatically perpetuate judicial independence. Under certain circumstances, a greater degree of political competition diminishes judicial independence because fierce electoral fights can magnify the benefits of compliant courts (Popova, 2010). Judicial independence will also be retrenched when leaders fear to lose office or when courts make decisions that challenge incumbents (VonDoepp & Ellett, 2011).

Finally, like many important political institutions, the judicial system is highly path-dependent. Even if leaders hope to promote judicial independence, the lack of well-trained professionals and an effective judicial tradition will compromise such hopes in practice. This is what has occurred in Russia after the Cold War (Solomon, 2008). Additionally, the degree to which high levels of legality prove conducive to a real, sustainable, and autonomous judiciary depends on the level of repression that a dissolved authoritarian regime can implement. In Chile, Brazil, and Argentina, different configurations of legality and repressive structures have led judicial independence to three very different fates (Pereira, 2003). Similarly, in Eastern Europe, "institutions that allowed high degrees of judicial independence emerged in countries where the legacies of the past entailed high levels of totalitarian politicization of the judiciary"; in contrast, the relatively permissive rule in ex-communist countries produced stronger liberal and conservative parties that "often struggled to impose institutions that would permit a stricter political control of judiciaries and increase their responsiveness to political authorities" (Magalhães, 1999, pp. 58–59).

Facing difficulties in executing a politically sound and credible judicial reform, political leaders in these capital-importing countries have to turn to other policy tools to convey the same commitment to protecting investment. BITs serve as a desirable policy substitute. I will explain why in the following section.

BITs as a Policy Substitute

The belief that BITs might constitute an effective instrument to convey the credibility of states' commitment to investors' property rights lies in their mechanism of settling disputes. Most BITs contain provisions stipulating that a third-party arbiter will resolve disputes between investors and host states (Vandevelde, 1998). This third party is intentionally kept out of any state's jurisdiction (Schreuer, 2011). For investors concerned about the fairness of local courts whose independence from host governments is questionable, third-party arbitration is certainly an optimal way to settle disputes. Furthermore, as Schreuer (2011) states: "Even if there is no intervention, a sense of judicial loyalty to the forum State is likely to influence the outcome of proceedings especially where large amounts of money are involved. In addition, in many countries domestic courts are bound to apply the local law even if it is at odds with international legal rules protecting the rights of investors" (p. 71). Finally, third-party arbitration allays corruption and transparency concerns (Vinuesa, 2002).

This third-party arbitration is in the interest of host states as well. As Schreuer (2011) rightly contends: "Public proceedings in the domestic courts are likely to exacerbate the dispute and may affect the host State's investment climate. Once the host State's highest court has made a decision, it may be more difficult for the government to accept compromise or a contrary international judicial decision" (p. 73).

Moreover, unlike domestic judicial reforms that aim to empower the judiciary at the risk of facilitating social mobilization, international third-party arbitration does not cultivate political opposition against existing regimes. Arbitration deals only with investment disputes (Franck, 2007; Schreuer, 2011). Although these disputes are not unambiguous, they are narrowly defined. Such a limited jurisdiction constitutes the basis of the arbitration body's power. More importantly, however, it also restricts that body's power. In contrast to arbitration, domestic judicial reforms cannot be pursued so selectively. At least on the surface, judicial empowerment is often widespread. As previously noted, such a broad pattern of empowerment is very likely to put leaders in a precarious position and make them recalculate the benefits of judicial independence vis-à-vis the possible political risks. Because of this calculation, developing host states eager for foreign investment are willing to conclude BITs (Allee & Peinhardt, 2010; Guzman, 1998) that allow them to continue using courts as a tool of social control (Massoud, 2014).

This by no means suggests that BITs are not costly. To the contrary, BITs carry both ex ante and ex post costs (Kerner, 2009), including the substantive and procedural concession of regulatory space to investors. Nevertheless, it is precisely because of these costs that BITs successfully communicate a credible commitment to property rights (Dolzer, 2004; Kerner, 2009). For host states, losing sovereign regulatory power is therefore a cost worth paying. To attract investment and stimulate the economy, leaders must prepare to pay costs. The question is which policy measure will be less costly, but equally effective. Domestic judicial reforms can be politically harmful and unsustainable in the long run. Compared to these reforms, which generate dubious gains, BITs incur lower political costs while also generating the benefit of credibility that such costs can produce.[1]

Furthermore, by providing arbitration clauses, BITs significantly limit the role that domestic courts can play in settling investment disputes. Losing judicial sovereignty to international arbitration bodies is a cost that leaders are willing to pay in exchange for higher levels of investment. However, it should be noted that only a few BITs would hardly suffice to fulfill the intended function of credibly conveying the commitment to protecting property rights and maximizing the attractiveness of a developing country signatory to investors. Therefore, states would not immediately cease the judicial reforms as soon as they start making BITs. They will only do so when they believe that there are enough BITs in place to attract foreign investors. In other words, there is a rough threshold in decision-makers' minds when it comes to the sufficiency of BITs.

In addition, since the cost of making BITs is sacrificing domestic judicial autonomy, leaders have a strong incentive to make judiciaries more dependent on or accountable to executives after a sufficient number of BITs are concluded. In other words, leaders prefer courts to be beholden to them when states surrender much of their judicial control over disputes with foreign investors. It is, therefore, expected that leaders will use BITs to substitute for or even reverse domestic judicial reforms when they perceive that a threshold is reached in the making of BITs. Massoud's (2014) research heuristically revealed this political calculation in the case of Sudan.

Overall, the use of BITs helps political leaders to avoid political trouble, signal policy credibility, and provide a political justification to rein in the judiciary. Such political calculations can only be explained by assessing how BITs affect judicial independence. In other words, political motivation is embodied in the outcome. In terms of rational calculation, this outcome *precedes* the making of BITs; in terms of manifestation, it *follows* them. This relationship is similar to the one between trade and war. The fact that war is reduced by higher levels of trade is attributed to policies that are designed to encourage trade to suppress the likelihood of war in the first place. Therefore, changes in the level of judicial independence cannot be interpreted as the unintended consequences of BITs. Rather, they are precisely intended by the capital-craving developing nation members. Moreover, if the act of making BITs is merely competition driven, then host states should strive to improve judicial independence. Doing so would reduce the need for BITs—or, put differently, it would reduce the pressure from peer states to form more BITs. Hence, an underlying rationale of making BITs can be identified in the changes to judicial independence that occur after the BITs enter into force.

Because states make BITs to avoid costly domestic reforms, it is reasonable to expect that BITs will, in the long run, decrease judicial independence around the world. This is an unintended consequence for the designers of BITs, but it is a consequence that domestic policymakers strategically pursue. This is why general support for BITs and the International Centre for Settlement of Investment Disputes (ICSID) in investment disputes remains strong despite the legal losses suffered in a few Latin American countries (Vinuesa, 2002).

The Highly Restricted Role of Domestic Courts in Investor-State Disputes

Scholars, however, argue that although BITs focus on investment, they can still exert a positive effect on the overall judicial conditions in host states. In other words, from the perspective of host states' political leaders, BITs may be as risky as domestic judicial reforms. Franck (2007) identifies the following causal factors for this phenomenon: forum shopping or a fork in the road, enforcement, the recognition and ex post review of arbitration awards, and contract-based disputes. In a similar vein, Guthrie (2013) suggests fair and equitable treatment, effective means, and a publication requirement as the channels through which BITs enhance the rule of law. Unfortunately, it is unlikely that the mechanisms through which BITs might strengthen the rule of law will materialize. Therefore, BITs will be unable to incentivize host states to improve their judicial quality as envisioned. The reasons go as follows.

First, when it comes to investment disputes, international arbitration tribunals take precedence over domestic courts (Schreuer, 2011). Article 26 of the ICSID Convention reads, "Consent of the parties to arbitration under this Convention shall, unless otherwise stated, be deemed consent to such arbitration to the exclusion of any other remedy." Since the 1990s, ICSID arbitration has risen to domination in BITs. Out of 2,576 mapped treaties, 2,186 identify the ICSID as the dispute-settlement mechanism. Moreover, 2,442 of 2,576 mapped treaties have investor-state dispute clauses (UNCTAD, 2019b). Even where parties can choose from multiple dispute-settlement options, there is no guarantee that investment-related disputes will be definitively resolved by domestic courts in the future. International investment law largely overturns the notion that local remedies have been exhausted as a general principle of international law (Schreuer, 2011). Moreover, if most BITs only allow domestic courts to hear disputes, then it becomes unnecessary for states to produce such an agreement in the first place. Studies in South Asia show that domestic courts have played little in settling investment disputes (Saravanan & Subramanian, 2017).

Second, enforcement assistance only applies to non-ICSID awards, which account for merely a fraction of the total number of arbitration awards. Nevertheless, the 1958 New York Convention on the Recognition and Enforcement of Foreign Arbitral Awards requires signatory states to enforce extraterritorial judicial decisions. Therefore, in these limited cases, domestic courts do not have as much influence as assumed when it comes to enforcing arbitration awards. Furthermore, the distinction between contract-based disputes and treaty-based disputes is not immediately clear, especially when umbrella clauses are involved (Schreuer, 2011). Hence, there is no reason we should conclude that such a blurred line between the two types of disputes necessarily prioritizes domestic courts over international arbitration tribunals. As to Guthrie's (2013) proposed mechanisms, they are merely de jure requirements that host states can fulfill without impacting how domestic judicial systems actually work.

More importantly, international arbitration helps to develop global legal standards concerning the treatment of investors (Schreuer, 2016). This can constrain the behavior of domestic judicial bodies as well. As two scholars have commented, "Investment jurisprudence requires their actions to be legal, with reference to both domestic and international law, and 'effective' with reference to an objective international standard" (Ranjan & Raju, 2014, p. 837).[2] By relegating domestic courts to the confines delimited by existing international legal rules, this requirement further eclipses these courts' significance in settling investment disputes. In addition, judicial independence is not necessary in some circumstances—that is to say, governments can rely on or employ joint ventures to utilize foreign capital. This also provides political protection to the investors (Betz & Pond, 2019).

To summarize, states conclude BITs to avoid the pressure of implementing costly domestic judicial reforms in response to the globalized competition for capital. Compared to these reforms, BITs are perceived to be not only less politically challenging but also equally effective in attracting investment. In other words, states know that two policy instruments may yield similar results when it comes to attracting foreign capital. Therefore, they substitute more feasible BITs for the difficult process of implementing widespread domestic judicial reforms. This substitution occurs when states feel that it is impossible to further improve their judiciaries and when they have concluded a sufficiently large number of BITs to signal that potential investors' assets will be protected. The asset protection that these BITs provide allows host states to tighten social controls by making courts less independent. Overall, the empirical expectation will be that *making BITs is nonlinearly correlated with the dynamics of judicial independence*. Therefore, we can draw the following hypothesis:

In the early stage of BITs' making, states will incrementally improve judicial independence as they increase the number of the treaties. When crossing a threshold of BITs, states will reverse the judicial independence reform and the level of judicial independence will hence fall.

Research Design

DATA

I take judicial independence data from Linzer and Staton (2015). They focus on "the power concept of de facto independence," which "requires not only that an independent judge be autonomous but that she can expect her decisions to be implemented properly, especially by sitting governments" (Linzer & Staton, 2015, p. 225). This is because it is "difficult to measure the autonomy of a court without simultaneously measuring its power" (p. 225). Applying a Bayesian bounded graded response model to a series of indicators of judicial independence drawn from the current literature, Linzer and Staton "construct a unified measure of latent judicial independence that is available for 200 countries from 1948 to 2012" (p. 224).[3] This measure has many advantages over existing scores, as it addresses measurement errors prevalent in these scores, solves temporal data missingness, captures both smooth trends and abrupt shifts across time, and increases the certainty of the measure. Due to these merits, it has been employed by the latest research (Beazer & Blake, 2018; Crabtree & Nelson, 2017; Epperly, 2017). I focus on developing nations because these states face pressure to attract foreign capital by sending investors credible signals of their commitment to protecting foreign capital. Developed countries, however, are not subject to the pressure to make such commitment openly credible.

The key independent variable is the number of BITs in force that a state has concluded (UNCTAD, 2019b). It is a cumulative value on a state-year basis. I then include a series of variables considered in the current literature. I first account for the impact of the level of democracy, which is found to induce and sustain judicial independence (Epperly, 2017; Hayo & Voigt, 2003). I also control for the durability of the regime. Political elites in a long-standing regime feel more secure and are less reluctant to allow political veto players to exist (Tsebelis, 2002), such as a politically independent court. Data on these two variables are from the Polity IV project (Marshall & Jaggers, 2012).

In addition, economic development also exerts positive impact on judicial independence (Epperly, 2017; Hayo & Voigt, 2003; LaPorta et al., 2003; Rigobon & Rodrik, 2005). I use income (GDP per capita) to control for the effect of economic development. A state receiving smaller FDI inflows should have a greater incentive to improve judicial independence to increase such capital inflows. I then include FDI inflows (% of GDP). Trade has an ambiguous effect on governance outcomes (Greenhill et al., 2009; López-Cariboni & Cao, 2015; López-Córdova & Meissner, 2011; Mosley, 2011). Trade openness (% of GDP) is thus taken into consideration to address this possible confounding relationship. Large endowment of natural resources tends to reduce the incentive to protect property rights for the purpose of economic development (Ross, 1999; Wright, 2008), so I control for the rents from natural resources (% of GDP).

A populous society normally demands more public goods and is thus prone to more disputes and conflict. This poses significant challenges to the government in providing such goods efficiently and fairly. As expected, the government does not see it in its interest to have its deficiencies and/or unfairness in providing public goods exposed in an independent court. Hence, a larger size of population should be correlated with a lower level of judicial independence. Similarly, civil conflict is also likely to discourage a government from adding more veto players into a contemporaneous political chaos. Data on income, FDI inflows, trade openness, and population are taken from the World Development Indicators (World Bank, 2016). Data on civil conflict are obtained from the Armed Conflict Dataset (Gleditsch et al., 2002). All independent variables are lagged one year to deal with the potential endogeneity problem.

ESTIMATION

I use the dose response function to gauge how concluding BITs relates to judicial independence, which allows accurate causal inference when treatment is potentially endogenous and continuous. This estimation involves three steps. First, it will estimate the generalized propensity score (GPS) for each observation using the generalized linear model. Second, it will calculate the conditional expectation of the outcome for a given level of treatment based on the estimated GPS. Third, it will estimate the average effect on the outcome of each level of treatment (Bia & Mattei, 2008). In contrast, the conventional ordinary least squares model is not suitable for drawing reliable causal inference embedded in the hypothesis due to its inability to deal with continuous and endogenous treatment.

FINDINGS

Results are plotted in Figure 2.1. The left panel exhibits the overall results from the dose response function estimation, and the right panel displays the results from the treatment effect function estimation. Mathematically, the latter is the first-order derivative of the former, representing the slope of the former. First, let's examine the left panel. Initially, states increase judicial independence while they are making an increasing number of

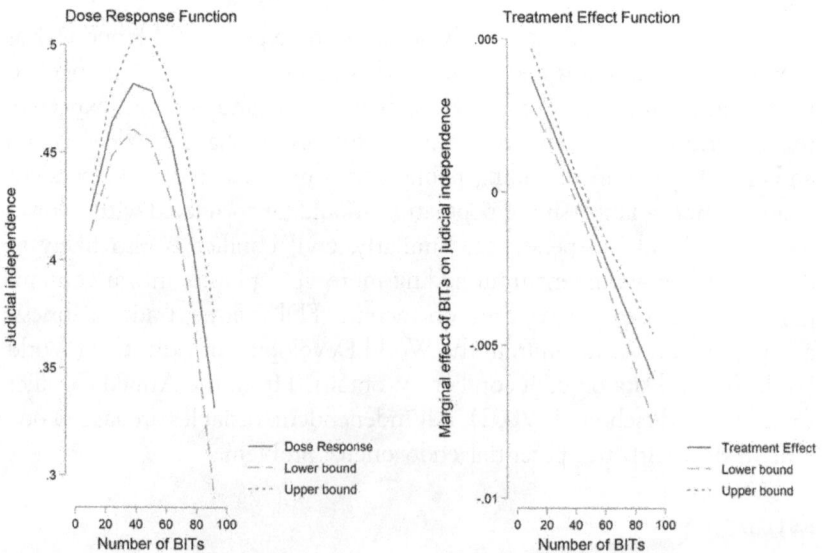

Figure 2.1. How Judicial Independence Changes with BITs. *Source:* Author-created image.

BITs. However, after the number of BITs reaches 50 (slightly higher than one standard deviation [20] above the mean [26]), states start to reduce judicial independence. This provides strong evidence in support of the hypothesis. Then, let's turn to the right panel. Again, the graph in the right panel illustrates the marginal effect of one BIT on judicial independence. As we can see, when the number of BITs is smaller than 50, the marginal effect is positive but shrinks, corresponding to the positive effect of BITs on judicial independence shown on the left panel. When the number of BITs is greater than 50, the marginal effect becomes negative, echoing the negative effect of BITs on judicial independence under the same circumstance.

When I split the sample into democracies and non-democracies, some more interesting findings emerge (Figures 2.2 and 2.3). The policy substitution between BITs and judicial independence is more pronounced in democracies than in non-democracies. In democracies, BITs is invariably correlated with decline in judicial independence. By contrast, in non-democracies, such substitution only appears when the number of BITs reaches 60. However, this is not really surprisingly. Relatively speaking,

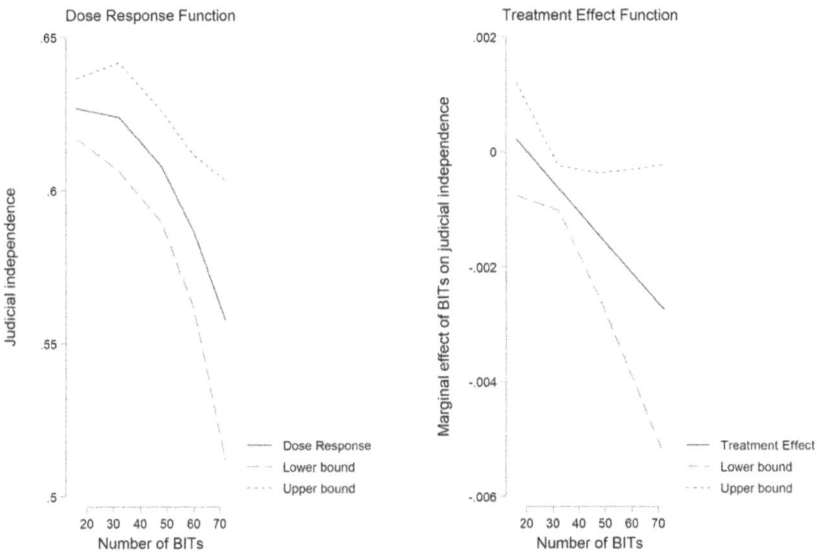

Figure 2.2. How Judicial Independence Changes with BITs: Democracies. *Source:* Author-created image.

Dose Response Function

Treatment Effect Function

Judicial independence

.3

.28

.26

.24

Marginal effect of BITs on judicial independence

.002

.001

0

-.001

-.002

-.003

Dose Response
Lower bound
Upper bound

Treatment Effect
Lower bound
Upper bound

0   20   40   60   80
Number of BITs

0   20   40   60   80
Number of BITs

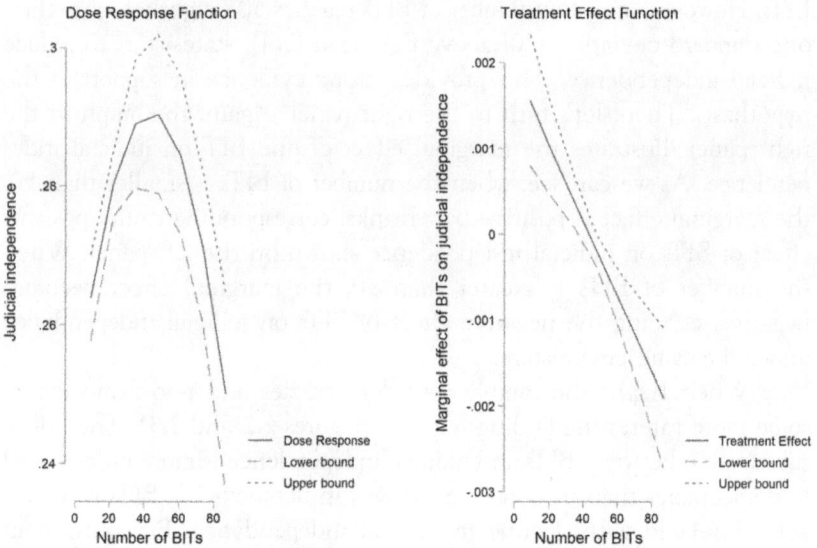

Figure 2.3. How Judicial Independence Changes with BITs: Non-democracies. *Source*: Author-created image.

democratic developing countries protect property rights better than their non-democratic counterparts (Li & Resnick, 2003), therefore, failing to maintain high judicial independence will not considerably detract from their attractiveness in the eyes of foreign investors. Non-democratic developing nations that are not reputed for high judicial independence are strongly incentivized to enhance judicial independence, even if they have already begun to make BITs. Only when the number of BITs they have concluded can put them in a perceivably safe spot in terms of attracting investment can they stop deepening judicial reforms.

ROBUSTNESS CHECKS

I run a series of robustness checks to ensure that the main findings are not sensitive to the construction of dependent variable, model specifications, or the choice of time lags. First, I use the rule of law from the Worldwide Governance Indicators (World Bank, 2015) to replace the judicial independence as the dependent variable. The rule of law is dependent on judicial independence. Improving judicial independence ultimately contributes to the realization of the rule of law. But the rule of law is also contingent on controlling corruption and crime. Changes in the rule of law, therefore, cannot be mainly understood through the logic proposed in this chapter. Moreover, the measurement provided by the World Bank is not an objective one but based on selected experts' subjective evaluations. These are the reasons why I do not focus on the rule of law in this chapter. The results are displayed in Figure 2.4. As it shows, despite the conceptual distinction and operationalization shortcomings, the findings using the rule of law largely match what the main analysis reveals.

Second, I control for the regional diffusion of judicial independence. I calculate the yearly regional averages of judicial independence less that of a state at issue. Again, the results are consistent with the findings from the main analysis (Figure 2.5).

Third, it might be the case that because judicial independence changes slowly, what the main analysis captures is merely the contemporaneous correlation between the number of BITs and static judicial independence. I thus employ a longer time lag for the key independent variable, lagging the number of BITs by three years. Once more, the main results remain almost unaltered (Figure 2.6).

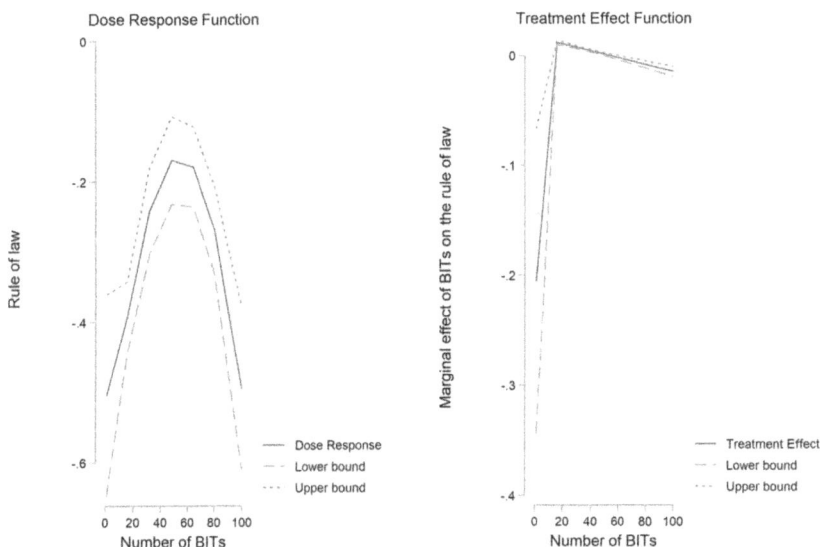

Figure 2.4. Alternative Dependent Variable: The Rule of Law. *Source:* Author-created image.

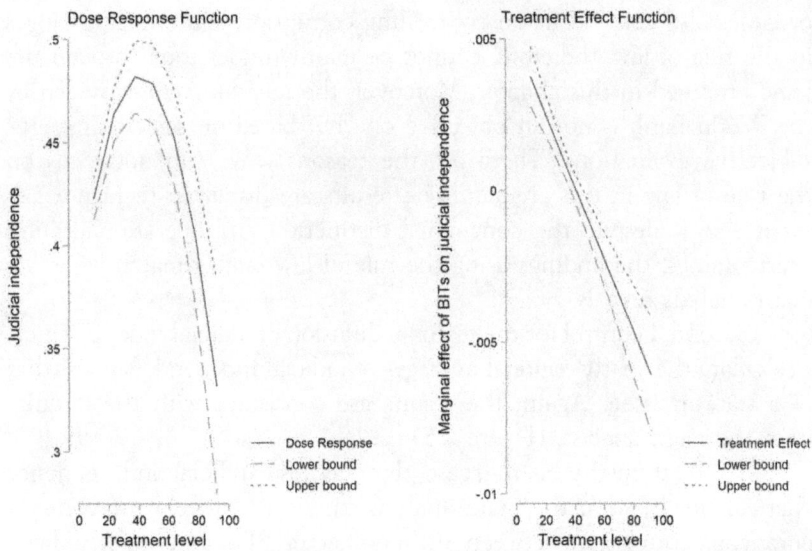

Figure 2.5. Controlling for Regional Diffusion. *Source*: Author-created image.

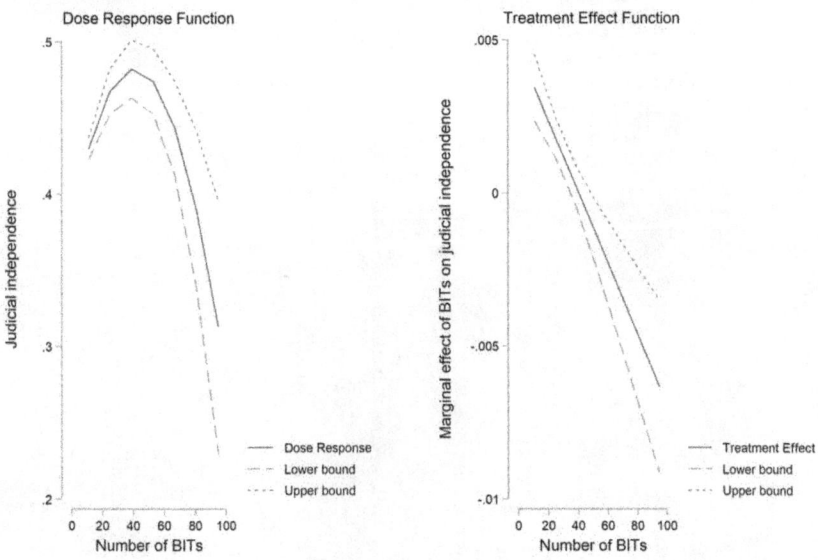

Figure 2.6. The Number of BITs (t–3). *Source*: Author-created image.

Fourth, to confirm that the dose response function is an appropriate estimator, I perform the analysis on a fixed effects estimator. However, in this environment, the number of BITs is only negatively signed but achieves no statistical significance at conventional confidence levels (Table 2.1), corroborating that the nonlinearity assumed in the dose response function fits with the data.

Table 2.1. Judicial Independence and BITs: A Fixed Effects Estimation

DV = Judicial independence	(1)
Number of BITs	−0.007
	(0.006)
Level of democracy	0.017***
	(0.001)
Regime durability	0.001*
	(0.000)
FDI inflows (% of GDP)	−0.000
	(0.000)
Trade openness (% of GDP)	0.000
	(0.000)
GDP per capita	0.038**
	(0.015)
Natural resources rents	−0.011
	(0.008)
Population (ln)	0.002
	(0.025)
Civil conflict	−0.009
	(0.009)
Constant	0.079
	(0.404)
Observations	2,699
R-squared	0.531
Country FE	yes

Robust standard errors in parentheses

***p < 0.01, **p < 0.05, *p < 0.1

Source: Author-created image.

I will use the case of Egypt to demonstrate the political logic proposed in the next section of this chapter.

The Case of Egypt

The example of Egypt precisely illustrates the argument advanced in this chapter. Over the past fifty years, the dynamics of judicial independence and BIT-making in Egypt mirror this theoretical postulate. The number of BITs has kept increasing since the 1970s. As of 2011, Egypt had 74 BITs in force, and it had concluded 103 BITs (UNCTAD, 2019b). In contrast, the judicial reforms experienced ebbs and flows. As Brown (2002) put it, "After 1979, especially after the mid-1980s when the new appointment procedure had begun to seriously affect the composition of the Constitutional Court, the Court rapidly distinguished itself as the boldest and most independent judicial actor in Arab history" (pp. 151–152). This growing independence reversed in the late 1990s, however, when the vacancy left by the retirement of Awad al-Morr, the president of the SCC, "was used to pressure the Court into accepting a diminution in its authority to issue retroactive judgments" (p. 152).

The Egyptian government started to pursue economic liberalization in the early 1970s. Over the next 20 years, it made a series of legislative efforts to promote foreign investment; these efforts included laws that encouraged the investment of non-Egyptian capital in real estate and infrastructure. Many similar reforms were planned to unify corporate laws, establish national treatment for business entities, reduce red tape, improve the protection of minority shareholder rights, and optimize corporate taxes (Louis et al., 2004). In particular, Article 9 of the Egyptian Constitution and Article 9 of Law No. 8 both ban nationalization. Additionally, Law No. 8 "offers guarantees against seizure, requisition, blocking, confiscation, and placing under custody or sequestration and against full or partial expropriation of real estate and investment project property" (UNCTAD, 1999a, p. 26).

Notwithstanding these reforms, the Egyptian government's commitment to property rights was still questionable for the following reasons. First, mutual references between laws created considerable obscurity and uncertainty. Second, many laws lacked legal validity due to their unconstitutionality. Third, too many laws were passed within a short period of time, which seriously weakened their credibility (El-Mikawy

& Handoussa, 2002). Foreign investors therefore showed little interest in investing in Egypt. For example, almost no US firms would willingly invest in Egypt without insurance. Moreover, most of these US firms received "medium and long-term financing for projects from the United Agency for International Development under their 'Private Investment Encouragement Fund'" (Moustafa, 2003, p. 892).

According to an official statistic published by the Egyptian government, the laws passed during the 1970s were not as effective as expected, contributing "a total of only 74,946 jobs" (Moustafa, 2003, p. 892). Put in perspective, "From the total Egyptian workforce of nearly 11 million, law 43 projects accounted for only .7% of total employment in the country. With the Egyptian population growing at a rate of approximately one million per year by the end of the 1970s, law 43 projects were not generating nearly enough new employment to address Egypt's population explosion" (Moustafa, 2003, p. 892). In the meantime, the 1970s witnessed Egypt's debt reach "$15.4 billion, and debt servicing consumed a full 51% of all export earnings" (Moustafa, 2003, p. 892). The meager effectiveness of commercial law changes and the deteriorating debt issue compelled Sadat to finally "strengthen institutional guarantees on private rights through the establishment of an independent constitution with powers of judicial review" (p. 892).

Judicial reforms granted significant autonomy to the new SCC. To name one important change, professionalism prevailed. Although the Egyptian president legally holds the final authority to decide who will occupy the chief justiceship, a new norm emerged saying that the most senior judges would be promoted to that position. For the next two decades, the president would always choose the chief justice in this fashion. Furthermore, other measures were implemented to ensure that judges would exercise their power independently from government interference. For example, only the general assembly of SCC can make disciplinary decisions regarding the behavior of the court's members. The reform also prevented the government from using lucrative legal consulting work to purchase justices' compliance in specific cases. Finally, according to Law 48 (1979), the SCC enjoys financial and administrative independence (Moustafa, 2003).

In substantive terms, the newly granted judicial independence would not be meaningful if the SCC did not have the power to issue consequential decisions. To that end, the SCC had three functions that were exclusive of other agencies: "(1) to issue binding interpretations of existing legislation when divergent views emerge; (2) to resolve conflicts of jurisdiction between different judicial bodies; and (3) to perform judicial review of legislation" (Moustafa, 2003, p. 894). Its judicial review powers are particularly strong.

> Article 29 of law 48/1979 specifies that the SCC is empowered to perform judicial review only when it receives cases transferred from courts of merit. If any court, in the course of deciding a concrete case, finds that a law being applied may be unconstitutional, it can suspend the proceedings and transfer the case to the Supreme Constitutional Court for review. In most cases, a petition for judicial review in front of the SCC is initiated at the request of litigants themselves. However, judges also have the right to initiate a petition in front of the SCC if they find the constitutionality of a particular law they are applying questionable. After a ruling is issued by the SCC on the constitutionality or unconstitutionality of a law in question, it is returned to the court of merits, and the case proceeds with the new clarification provided by the SCC. (Moustafa, 2003, p. 894)

Nevertheless, reform that focuses on judicial independence is far from sufficient to attract investors, as it cannot solve the low efficiency problem that plagues Egyptian courts. It is difficult to make much progress in that regard within a short period of time. The commercial legal system is characterized by slowness and corruption. During the 1990s, more than 60 percent of cases could not be cleared, and it usually took six years to secure a decision. The poor performance of the courts is largely ascribed to personnel deficiencies and low financial incentives (Louis et al., 2004).

Setting aside the matter of insufficient judicial reforms, Egypt had many other problematic institutions as well. To a considerable degree, these institutions prevented capital from entering the country. For instance, the taxation system was ineffective and distorted. Because tax incentives often invalidated each other, they achieved no effect. Bureaucratism in the tax administration worsened this situation. Moreover, due to the strict regulations on investment, the costs of doing business became unreasonably high. Civil service was an understaffed, disincentivized, corrupt, and conservative bureaucracy that staunchly defended its parochial interests by resisting any reforms that might improve public welfare (Louis et al., 2004).

Reverting to international instruments could mitigate the deficiencies of Egypt's domestic reforms. For example, Egypt signed and ratified the Convention on the Settlement of Investment Disputes between States and Nationals of Other States (1966) in 1972. This convention allows contracting states—or a national of these contracting states—to request arbitration. It also establishes a standing institution to provide arbitration services to disputing parties. More conspicuously, Egypt has, since the 1970s, intensified its efforts to make BITs. Egypt signed many BITs with major source countries/economies of FDI, such as Germany (1974), France (1974), the United Kingdom (1975), the Netherlands (1976), Japan (1977), the Belgium–Luxembourg Economic Union (1977), Sweden (1978), Finland (1980), the United States (1986), Italy (1989), Spain (1992), Greece (1993), South Korea (1996), Canada (1996), Singapore (1997), and Portugal (1999). From the 1970s to the 1990s, Egypt signed 91 BITs (UNCTAD, 2019b). These made up approximately 81 percent of its total such treaties.

These treaties have proven practical and impactful. Owing to the ineffective and corrupt justice system in Egypt, most commercial disputes were actually settled through arbitration. According to one estimate, "Eighty per cent of investment disputes were settled through arbitration since the Egyptian judicial system is considered slow and its procedures cumbersome" (UNCTAD, 1999a, p. 27).

Maintaining judicial independence becomes more politically costly as time passes. In 2000, the SCC directly challenged the Mubarak regime's interests by issuing two decisions; one declared the unconstitutionality of an NGO law, and the other called for electoral supervision (Moustafa, 2007). In response to this political threat, Mubarak broke the aforementioned norm pertaining to chief justice appointments and instead chose a chief justice who paid homage to the authoritarian government. This newly designated chief justice then exploited the legal vacuum regarding the SCC's size; he added five more justices to the court, all of whom exhibited absolute loyalty to the regime (Moustafa, 2007). Since 2001, the SCC has once again been relegated to complete subjugation to the regime, which it has provided with the facade of legitimacy (Lombardi, 2009). In 2005, the chief justice certified that a fraudulent election under its oversight was essentially free and fair. In addition, by performing a priori reviews of presidential election laws, the SCC essentially renounced its unique, and most important, function: the judicial review of legislation (Moustafa, 2007). Figure 2.7 displays the trends of BITs and judicial independence in Egypt from 1960 to 2012.

Mubarak was able to subject the court because he thought that the SCC served no economic function as a quasi-independent institution. Rather, the SCC's economic significance had been replaced by other policy instruments, mainly BITs. In practice, a decline in judicial independence does not deter FDI inflows. An UNCTAD report regarding FDI inflows to Africa documents:

> As in previous years, two countries were by far the most important FDI recipients in 1998: Egypt and Nigeria, which together accounted for about one third of FDI inflows. In the case of Egypt, a significant increase in FDI inflows to $1.1 billion was directly due to increased flows into manufacturing (accounting for almost 50 per cent of all FDI inflows in 1998). Beneficiaries were especially chemicals, building materials, engineering, food, metals and textiles, as well as the tourism

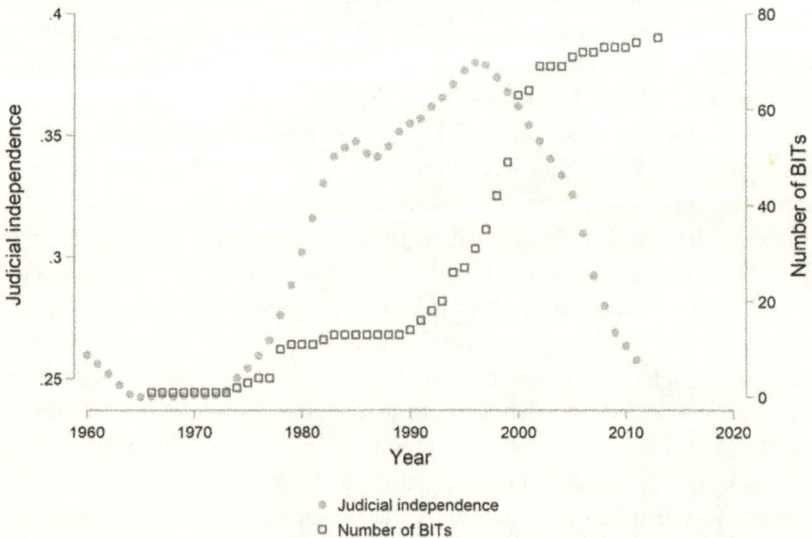

Figure 2.7. Judicial Independence and BITs in Egypt: 1960–2012. *Source:* Author-created image.

industry—in the upgrading of which foreign investors were actively involved through privatization programmes and various forms of non-equity investment. Nigeria, which has ranked first for many years, received slightly lower FDI inflows than in 1997. The growth in inflows registered by Egypt, combined with that registered in Tunisia, and to a lesser extent Zimbabwe and Gabon, helped to maintain a relatively high level of FDI inflows, at least compared to the early 1990s. (UNCTAD, 1999b, p. 46)

If FDI continues to enter a country, then there is no reason to sustain judicial independence, especially when political opponents increasingly take advantage of such institutional arrangement to challenge the existing regime. Figure 2.8 shows that, compared to the late 1970s, FDI in Egypt continued to grow throughout the 1980s and 1990s. This phenomenon precisely correlates with the increase in judicial independence and the number of BITs. When Egypt's judicial independence was seriously undermined in the early 2000s, FDI was barely disrupted.

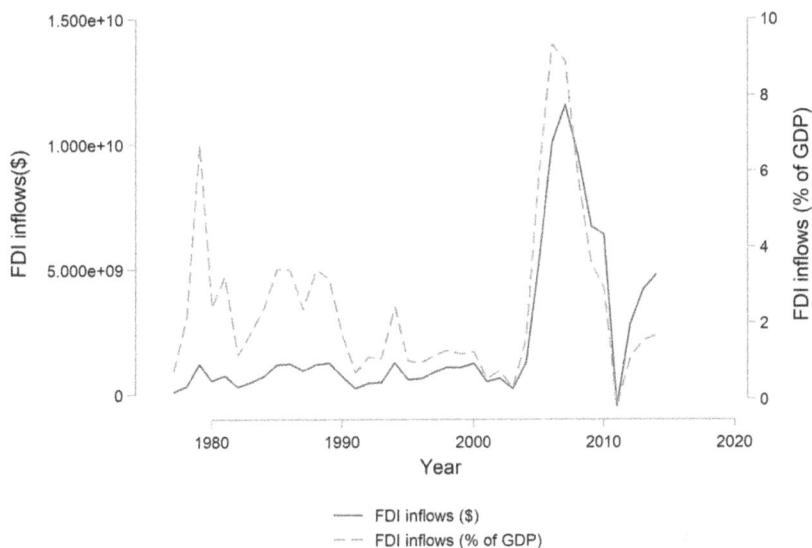

Figure 2.8. FDI in Egypt: 1977–2014. *Source*: Author-created image.

At that time, BITs had already been concluded with most of the major source countries of capital flowing to Egypt. The Egyptian government successfully substituted costly domestic judicial reforms with the making of BITs. In doing so, it not only maintained its attractiveness to foreign investors by enhancing the credibility of its commitment to protecting foreign assets but also tightened its control of the country by keeping political opposition at bay through an obedient judiciary.

Conclusion

The world has witnessed the rapid proliferation of BITs over the past 50 years. BITs are now considered to be the foremost method of governing and protecting FDI. One important reason why states converge on this new norm is the fact that many developing nations view BITs as a policy substitute for costly domestic reforms. In consequence, BITs replace these states' domestic institutions and become the primary instrument by which to regulate FDI. Accordingly, these states cease to deepen their judicial independence; in some cases, they even reverse it. This political calculation produces the expectation that a small number of BITs correlates with moderate improvement in judicial independence in the short term. In the long term, the absence of these treaties weakens judicial independence. Utilizing the dose response function to deal with the continuous treatment—that is, the number of BITs in force—and to create comparison groups based on generalized propensity scores, I find evidence supporting these conjectures. This substitution effect is present in developing democracies and non-democracies alike. The proposed nonlinear relationship between BITs and judicial independence, however, exists solely in the case of non-democracies. The case of Egypt clearly illustrates the logic of strategic substitution.

This chapter's emphasis on the strategic substitution that occurs between BITs and domestic judicial reforms suggests that the diffusion of BITs gains momentum from domestic political considerations. As an emergent approach, the strategic interaction between international and domestic policy tools has only received a very limited degree of attention (Ginsburg, 2005; Massoud, 2014). Ginsburg does not consider the strategic calculation behind the making of BITs in relation to the costliness of executing judicial reforms. Although Massoud demonstrates the possibility that strategic substitution between BITs and domestic judicial reforms might occur, he leaves untouched the systemic consequences of this substitution. By uncovering a nonlinear substitution between BITs and judicial independence, this chapter enriches our understandings of the convergence on BITs and the dynamics of judicial independence in developing nations. This substitution between domestic governance and international policy instruments reveals that states use means that are both economically and politically efficient to adapt to new policy environments imposed by globalization. Ultimately, this adaptation leads to convergence on policy tools.

This chapter explores the within-issue convergence that occurs across analytic levels. In the next chapter, I will turn to another type of policy convergence, one that not only occurs across analytic levels but also across issue areas. I will show how states that face the pressure to deregulate their labor markets deflect this pressure by resorting to preferential trade agreements.

3

Labor Rights and the
Making of Preferential Trade Agreements

In the last chapter, I showed how states substitute for costly domestic policies with feasible international treaties that belong to the same issue areas. This substitution leads to convergence on international policy instruments. In this chapter, I will demonstrate that cross-analytical-level substitution that occurs across issue areas can also produce policy convergence. I will do so by exploring how states use preferential trade agreements (PTAs) in order to resist the pressure to diminish labor rights laws.

As shown in previous chapters, a race to the bottom in domestic regulations deeply concerns many globalization scholars. Labor rights protection is one issue area where such concern is grave and widely shared. In this chapter I maintain that scholars' worry is warranted that globalization places an increasing pressure on states to pursue social dumping in labor market institutions. However, states do not invariably follow the dictates of globalization. They are able to avoid pressured costly policy changes, and keep their socially preferred labor standards instead. In other words, states can fend off unpopular policy pressure imposed by globalization. The condition for this resistance is that states turn to an effective but politically acceptable policy substitute, signing PTAs. As I will demonstrate later, making PTAs mitigates the losses that might result from refusing to accede to economic competitors' deregulation initiatives. Meanwhile, PTAs generate numerous efficiency gains from which workers can benefit, and these gains keep the political costs of making PTAs low.

Consequently, resisting the pressure to diminish the protection of labor rights results in policy convergence on concluding PTAs.

In addition, I argue that states are more likely to include stringent labor provisions in PTAs. These protections assure the better-protected workers that their rights will not be unduly restricted under the agreed-upon liberalization. The protections thereby facilitate the conclusion of PTAs. This further suggests that substitutive policies can not only be employed to replace undesirable domestic policy changes but also be designed to preventing these changes from being made. Put differently, domestic labor regulations are locked in the design of PTAs that protect labor. Convergence on labor-friendly PTAs thus sets up a new barricade to block the initiation of a downward trajectory in labor market institutions as globalization intensifies. However, I also posit that the extent to which the policy pressure facing a dyad to downgrade labor rights laws affecting the likelihood of signing PTAs is weakly constrained by states' ability to repress workers in practice. When states can more easily diminish the practical protection of labor rights, they see less utility in forming PTAs, although such diminishment has its own limitations. In other words, when the costs of altering domestic policies are institutionally kept low, states only have a weaker incentive to seek alternative policies. In this circumstance, we observe convergence on exclusively market-oriented deregulation that is detrimental to labor and that states with high domestic policy costs strive to avoid through convergence on less harmful but equally effective policies.

By taking advantage of a newly compiled data set on global labor rights, I identify whether a pair of states faces the policy pressure to reduce legal protections for labor. I then find that policy pressure renders a dyad more likely to form a PTA and that it tends to contain stronger labor provisions. I also find that, when a dyad is more capable of repressing labor in practice, it proves somewhat less likely to form a PTA despite the policy pressure that it faces. Fortunately, such conditional effect is as weak as expected.

The remainder of this chapter proceeds as follows. The next section briefly discusses what extant literature understands to be the determinants of PTA formation. In order to demonstrate a pressing need to alter domestic labor policies, I then show how globalization has externalized the economic implications of national labor regulation. Next, I explain why forming PTAs is a better alternative than reducing legal protections for labor. Afterward, I lay out the study's theoretical expectations and provide details on its research design. I then discuss the results and check their robustness. This is followed by a case study of the making of the China–New Zealand Free Trade Agreement to further corroborate the causal narrative that I have advanced. The chapter's last section concludes by summarizing the findings and exploring their broad implications.

Why States Form PTAs

States form PTAs for a variety of reasons. Extant scholarship has shown that states may do so to manage possible trade disruptions that result from hegemonic decline and global recessions (Mansfield, 1998), to secure access to larger markets (Perroni & Whalley, 2000), to occupy a better position in subsequent multilateral trade negotiations (Mansfield & Reinhardt, 2003), to deepen vertical trade specialization (Manger, 2009, 2012), to protect exporting industries from trade diversion (Baccini & Dür, 2011), to stabilize political trade dependence (Manger & Shadlen, 2014), to provide desired public goods (Mansfield & Milner, 2012; Mansfield et al., 2002), to ameliorate the discriminative effects on investment from competing states' PTAs (Baccini & Dür, 2015), to seek political survival (Hollyer & Rosendorff, 2012), and to promote economic reform (Baccini & Urpelainen, 2014; Whalley, 1996). The literature, however, has overlooked one motive behind the making of PTAs: they constitute viable policy substitutes for costly policy changes in other issue areas.

In this chapter, I will show that states facing policy pressure to diminish legal protections for labor have a greater tendency to sign PTAs. This is because PTAs constitute desirable policy alternatives that suitably substitute for the pressured reductions in domestic labor protection. Later, I will demonstrate that, as globalization deepens, states exhibit a real need for policy changes in the field of labor protection. Having done this, I will explain why the act of forming PTAs is a better choice than joining the race to lower legal protections for labor.

Globalization and Labor Protection

To remain competitive in a globalized economy, states enact policies that can provide them with economic advantages. The protection of labor rights is among these policies owing to its substantial economic implications. Rigid labor regulations—including strong protections for labor rights—have been shown to be economically inefficient because they exert distortive effects on production costs, demand for labor, and productivity (Besley & Burgess, 2004; Botero et al., 2004; Fialová & Schneider, 2009; Heckman & Pages, 2000; Nickell, 1997). These effects adversely impact exports and investment (Belderbos & Zou, 2006; Rodrik, 1996; UNCTAD, 2014). The case of South Korea provides a recent example. From 2014 to 2017, the labor-cost ratio of South Korea's top 500 companies rose by 0.5 percent; during the same period of time, their sales declined by 1.9 percent (Kwack, 2017). Meanwhile, soaring labor costs were one factor that prompted GM to close a large plant in South Korea (White & Park, 2018). The fact that the cost of labor continues to climb is attributable primarily to the bargaining power of Korean workers (Lee, 2019), which has been growing steadily since the late 1980s (Compa, 1993).

As the example of South Korea shows, states have strong incentives to lessen protections for labor rights whenever they can. When some states seek a competitive edge by opportunistically rejecting their commitment to labor rights, states that continue to adhere to this commitment face a disadvantage. In other words, the poor protection of labor rights generates cross-border negative policy externalities, which lock states into strategic complementarity (Franzese & Hays, 2008) and thus compel them to engage in deregulation, or a race to the bottom. Recent studies have found that states are drawn into this policy race by choosing to repress labor more severely (Davies & Vadlamannati, 2013; Wang, 2017a).

These negative policy externalities should matter mostly among economic competitors. This is because competitors have similar economic profiles that effectively channel these externalities into direct adverse impacts. Research has demonstrated that a state's economic competitiveness is largely immune to deregulation by the state's noncompeting peers (Cao, 2010; Cao & Prakash, 2010). Hence, when a particular state's economic competitors pursue deregulation in labor institutions by scaling back protections for labor rights, that state will face a higher degree of pressure to follow suit (Wang, 2017a).

Some scholars suggest that a climb to the top might exist in the realm of labor regulation. They argue that stringent labor protections can increase productivity by incentivizing workers to work harder; therefore, labor protections are economically attractive to businesses (Kucera, 2002). Although this might be true under certain circumstances, there is little evidence that rigid labor institutions are generally conducive to economic activities. As shown earlier, the opposite is more likely to be true. The lack of a worldwide climb to the top in labor regulation also testifies to this point (Mosley, 2011). Additionally, the economic logic that says that labor market rigidity is inefficient can hardly be reversed by diffusing trade-based policies from export destinations with high levels of labor protection to states with low levels of labor protection.[1] Unfortunately, this very economic logic may actually help to explain why such policy diffusion is weak and limited (Distelhorst & Locke, 2018; Greenhill et al., 2009). More importantly, policy diffusion will likely create or even amplify the pressure on states to deregulate, thus making it imperative for them to seek substitutive policies rather than accept the political costliness of deregulating.

PTAs as Viable Substitutes
for Reductions in Labor Protection

In this section, I establish that PTAs are viable substitutes for reductions in labor protection. First, I show that it is politically costly to lower legal protections for labor. Second, I demonstrate that PTAs generate substantial economic gains that also benefit workers and therefore incur comparatively lower political costs when states adopt them.

THE POLITICAL COSTLINESS OF REDUCING LABOR PROTECTION

As previously discussed, states are pressured to lower labor standards when they deepen their involvement in global production. For two reasons, however, simply submitting to this pressure is not an effective policy response. First, it is domestically politically costly to downgrade labor rights laws (Bhagwati, 2004, chap. 12). From a domestic perspective, weakening the legal protection of labor rights harms all workers by undermining their bargaining position vis-à-vis employers and the state. It has been widely shown that workers can only ensure better bargaining outcomes when they are able to organize themselves to prevent potentially harmful policies from being enacted (e.g., Dean, 2015; Owen, 2015; Pond, 2017; Robertson & Teitelbaum, 2011). There is no doubt that workers vigorously oppose debilitating policy moves by the state (Madrid, 2003). This opposition is more possible and more effective in states that are equipped with more inclusive institutions (Mosley, 2008; Wang, 2017a). In such states, workers are politically empowered, and they exercise a greater degree of policy influence, which makes it difficult to pass policies that are unfriendly to labor. In practice, politicians do face punishment if they ignore workers' demands (Margalit, 2011). Therefore, based on domestic political calculations, downgrading labor rights laws cannot be a wise policy move.

Moreover, enacting laws that loosen labor regulations can tarnish a state's international reputation—in other words, it can result in international naming and shaming (Murdie & Davis, 2012). Bad reputation can subsequently produce real economic impacts, such as the dampening of FDI and foreign aid (Barry et al., 2013; Dietrich & Murdie, 2016). This is why states even ratify human rights treaties in order to actively seek both reputational and other potential gains (e.g., Hafner-Burton & Tsutsui, 2005). Likewise, states should have similar incentives to make or to maintain satisfactory domestic laws in order to give international audiences a false, but positive, impression that they care about labor rights.

Consequently, the legislative diminishment of labor rights among a particular state's economic competitors should produce little impact on that state's policy choices (Wang, 2017a). This is true even if a state is fully aware that resistance will put it in a position of economic disadvantage in global competition. This partly explains why there is little to no downward policy convergence on labor rights laws (Mosley, 2011; Wang, 2017a). Although states must face the negative economic consequences of stringent labor regulations, it is too politically risky for them to pursue the opposite. Therefore, they must resort to more viable alternatives, such as PTAs.

It should be noted that this chapter does not argue that states will only seek to make PTAs when they face the pressure to diminish legal protections for labor. Rather, it merely contends that such pressure strengthens states' motivation to make these treaties.

The High Economic Benefits and hence Lower Political Costs of Making PTAs

PTAs generate considerable economic gains. First, they promote trade between members. They can do so because PTAs grant preferential tariffs on goods from members. For example, the US-Korea Free Trade Agreement (2007) sets out to eliminate 95 percent of each party's tariffs on goods within five years of its entering into force. This goal is hardly feasible under existing multilateral trade regimes such as the WTO, to which both the US and Korea are parties. The reduced tariffs enhance the competitiveness of one member's goods in the other's market. This helps to secure market access for the exporting state. By stabilizing the commitment to free trade, PTAs also suppress export volatility; in turn, this facilitates production and exports (Baccini & Dür, 2011; Behar & Cirera-i-Crivillé, 2013; Lambert & McKoy, 2009; Lee et al., 2008; Mansfield & Reinhardt, 2008). One widely cited study finds that free trade agreements approximately double bilateral trade between members 10 years after taking effect (Baier & Bergstrand, 2007). Moreover, PTAs boost FDI flows to their signatories. They do so by implementing various compliance mechanisms to generate a credible commitment to liberal economic policies (Büthe & Milner, 2008) and by increasing the size of the market through integration (Jaumotte, 2004). Such effects can be incredibly large. For example, it is estimated that PTAs among North African states can increase FDI stock by 62 percent in Algeria, 85 percent in Morocco, and 165 percent in Tunisia (Jaumotte, 2004, p. 15). Therefore, by encouraging trade and investment, PTAs can produce economic gains comparable to—if not greater than—those that lowered labor standards are intended to generate. As a result, the pressure that a state faces to reduce labor protections will be mitigated when it enters into a PTA.

More importantly, PTAs' ability to promote trade and investment can benefit workers significantly by expanding employment opportunities and boosting wages. For example, one report estimates that US free trade agreements "increased total employment by 159.3 thousand full-time equivalent employees (0.1 percent) and increased real wages by 0.3 percent in 2012" (United States International Trade Commission, 2016, p. 124). This effect is not limited to PTAs that involve developed nations. Developing-developing PTAs can generate remarkable economic gains for workers as well. For instance, according to UNCTAD's estimation (Saygili et al., 2018), Africa will expect to see employment grow by an extraordinary 1.17 percent under a fully free trade arrangement. Clearly, workers could be better off under PTAs.

Therefore, whereas workers might oppose a state's decision to reduce protections for labor rights, they should have little reason to oppose the formation of PTAs. Workers can receive substantial gains from these trade agreements without weakening their bargaining positions. Moreover, workers in import-competing industries—who are likely to be adversely affected by the liberalization policies that states negotiate—do not insist on preventing the making of PTAs; this is because PTAs can shield these industries from being impacted (Grossman & Helpman, 1995). PTAs often focus on vertical specialization (Manger, 2009; Manger & Shadlen, 2014), which limits the potentially negative impacts of negotiated liberalization. Additionally, trade adjustment assistance programs can be instituted to help ill-fated workers (Hays et al., 2005; Nooruddin & Rudra, 2014). This explains why a broad degree of public support exists across Latin America for trade agreements with the US (Baker, 2009).[2]

In retrospect, the fast growth of PTAs around the world indirectly attests to the low political costs of forming them. According to the latest statistic available (World Trade Organization, 2022), 355 such agreements are in force now. This would be impossible if workers felt that these agreements would seriously harm them; after all, organized labor often successfully prevents international agreements from being concluded when workers perceive that these agreements could be detrimental to their interests (Caraway et al., 2012).

In addition, states can use labor provisions to further induce workers to support PTAs. Workers worry that further liberalization policies may lead to the restriction of their rights. Because governments are tempted to deregulate the labor market to gain a competitive edge, they can then trigger a race to the bottom in labor regulations among PTA members. Including labor provisions in PTAs helps to mitigate this uncertainty by assuring workers that states will neither preemptively compromise their rights to seek unfair gains nor respond to similar behavior from others. Empirical research finds that states do strategically incorporate labor provisions in PTAs to increase the domestic approval of proposed agreements (Kim, 2012). Moreover, in states where labor rights are well protected, the demand for labor provisions in PTAs is stronger. This is not only because workers are more politically powerful in such states (Raess et al., 2018) but also because such states are perceived to have more room in which to downgrade their labor laws. Therefore, when two states are pressured to lower the legal protections for labor, they are likely not only to employ a PTA as a substitutive policy but also to design it in a way that protects workers more effectively than when such pressure is absent.[3]

To summarize, states in a globalizing world face the ever-growing pressure to lessen protections for labor. Doing so, however, is barely politically feasible, as it harms most workers. Making PTAs is a viable alternative because they produce substantial economic benefits for workers. These treaties can also be designed to mitigate possible negative impacts. Together, these two factors render it more politically acceptable to conclude PTAs. As a result, we can expect that, whenever states are pressured by their competitors to reduce labor protections, they will have a greater incentive to choose a more realistic policy, such as signing a PTA. Moreover, states tend to sign PTAs that include substantive provisions that protect workers. Therefore, the following hypotheses can be elicited:

> *Hypothesis 1 (H1): When two states are faced with policy pressure to lower the legal protection of labor rights, they are, ceteris paribus, more likely to sign a PTA.*

> *Hypothesis 2 (H2): When two states are faced with policy pressure to lower the legal protection of labor rights, they are, ceteris paribus, more likely to design a PTA that includes stringent labor provisions.*

Furthermore, the causal relationship summarized in H1 is likely to be weakly constrained by a state's ability to repress workers. As previously argued, it is difficult to downgrade labor rights laws, but it is relatively easy for states to protect labor rights less actively in practice (Davies & Vadlamannati, 2013; Moran, 2002, chap. 4; Mosley, 2011; Wang, 2017a). They do this to avoid the domestic and international costs incurred by the act of diminishing legal protections for labor. In fact, the gap between law and practice in the protection of labor rights is always glaring (Stallings, 2010). Moreover, repressing labor is, in practice, procedurally easier than forming PTAs, an act that entails interstate collaboration. Therefore, it is possible that when states have a greater ability to repress labor practically, they will exhibit a lower inclination to form a PTA in the face of the policy pressure to lower the legal protection of labor rights. However, such constraining effect should not be too large to offset the impact of the policy pressure. First, states could not entirely abolish the practical protection to maximize economic gains. Law constrains the practical diminishment in labor rights protection to varying degrees, and there is only so much room for states to maneuver. Meanwhile, states' domestic labor rights practices are linked to their competitors' policy choices (Davies & Vadlamannati, 2013; Mosley, 2011; Wang, 2017a), suggesting that states will not deviate from their own labor rights laws too far in enforcement as long as their competitors' policy choices permit doing so. Second, the efficiency gains from restricting workers' rights in practice are declining at the margin and can be limited in some sectors (Blanton & Blanton, 2007, 2009; Distelhorst & Locke, 2018). These decreasing marginal and limited gains might not be worth the high political costs of severely repressing workers.[4]

Hypothesis 3 (H3): When two states are more able to repress labor in practice, they will be, ceteris paribus, less likely to sign a PTA in the face of the policy pressure to lower the legal protection of labor rights.

Research Design

The dependent variable for H1 and H3 is whether a (undirected) dyad signs a PTA in year t.[5] The PTA data are drawn from the Design of Trade Agreements Dataset (Dür et al., 2014) for the period 1994–2012. Setting the start year of this chapter in the mid-1990s is because PTAs have only increased rapidly and stably since 1994 (World Trade Organization, 2022, which therefore ably provides meaningful and sufficient variation to evaluate the mechanisms previously depicted.[6] For H2, the dependent variable is the level of legalization of labor provisions in PTAs, data on which is taken from Content of Deep Trade Agreement, a data set made by the World Bank (Hofmann et al., 2017), which codes labor provisions in three categories: regulation of the national labor market; affirmation of International Labour Organization (ILO) commitments; and enforcement. I sum values for these three categories, resulting in a new variable ranging from 0 to 3.[7] An absence of labor provisions is represented by 0, while 3 denotes the highest level of legalization of labor provisions.

The key explanatory variable is policy pressure to reduce legal labor protection facing a dyad. To construct this variable, it is necessary to first create a measure of competitors' policy regarding labor rights. Previous literature on policy diffusion has employed structural equivalence to calculate competitors' policy, which allows the construction of a matrix that captures the similarity in economic competition between two states (Baccini & Koenig-Archibugi, 2014; Cao, 2010; Elkins et al., 2006b). Using the identical concept and technique, in this chapter, competitors' policy is calculated as a mathematical product of the weighting matrix, $\omega_{i,j,t}$, which captures the competitive distance between a state under observation and its competitors, and a vector of labor rights scores for all states for a given year, *Labor Rights*$_{k,t}$. The weighting matrix is produced using the product-level bilateral UNCTAD trade data (2012).[8]

$$Competitors'\ policy_{i,t} = \sum_{k} \omega_{i,j,t} labor\ rights_{k,t}$$

Labor rights data are taken from a new data project developed by Colin Barry, David Cingranelli, and Chad Clay (2022). In this new data set, they code information on labor protection recorded in annual human rights reports by the US State Department. This new data set has two major advantages over the existing data on labor protection: longer temporal and geographical coverages, and nuanced coding. It contains information on labor protection for both developed and developing states over the period examined in this chapter: 1994–2012.[9] It also distinguishes law from practice as well as collective labor rights from substantive labor rights. Earlier data either focus on a shorter period of time: 1993–1997, such as Kucera's (2002), or cover solely developing states, such as Mosley and Uno's data. Neither data makes distinctions between law and practice or between the two types of labor rights. Therefore, in terms of assessing the proposed hypotheses in this chapter, Barry et al.'s data set is more suitable.

Collective labor rights are comprised of freedom of association and collective bargaining rights, which together shape substantive labor rights (Langille, 1997), such as maximum working hours, minimum wage, freedom from forced labor, and occupational health and safety. For this reason, I employ collective labor rights as a proxy of labor protection in this chapter.[10] In Barry et al.'s data, freedom of association and collective bargaining rights are coded on a three-point scale (0 = complete lack of protection, 1 = partial protection, 2 = full protection), respectively for law and practice. Law refers to the legislative protection of collective labor rights, that is, whether they are recognized in national legislation and the extent to which they are protected, and practice denotes the actual protection provided by the government (Barry et al., 2022). As my argument is partly built on the costliness of lowering legal labor protection, I use labor rights in law to perform the main analysis. An index of collective labor rights laws is created by adding together the scores for these two collective rights in law, ranging from 0 to 4, and is employed to calculate a competitor's policy on labor protection using the formula specified in the beginning of this section.

With the competitor's policy, I then calculate policy pressure to lower legal labor protection. I consider a state to be under such pressure if its score in the collective labor rights index is higher than its competitor's policy score in a given year, or the difference between the two is greater than zero. Because I argue that the policy pressure to lower legal labor protection facing a dyad increases the likelihood of singing PTAs, this argument implies three possible scenarios: common pressure (both states in a dyad under pressure), partial pressure (only one state in a dyad under pressure), and no pressure (no state in a dyad under pressure). Accordingly, I assign 2 to common pressure, 1 to partial pressure, and 0 to no pressure. For example, India's labor rights score is 0.44 and Chile's is 0.4 higher than their respective competitors in 2005. They are hence considered as under common pressure (or policy pressure = 2) in that year. A free trade agreement between them was signed in the following year. Another example will be Canada and Peru. Both were under common pressure with differences in labor rights score being 0.5 and 1.5, respectively, in 2007, one year before their free trade agreement was concluded. In the case of the Singapore–Costa Rica free trade agreement that was made in 2010, only the latter state (score difference being 0.5) is under pressure in the previous year but not the former (–0.4). Hence, for the Singapore–Costa Rica dyad the policy pressure is 1 in 2009. I lag this variable by one year to account for the potential delay in its effect.[11] It is expected to be positive and statistically significant. Figure 3.1 displays the percentages of dyads signing PTAs and those not signing PTAs across different levels of policy pressure. As it shows, as the policy pressure grows greater, the percentage of dyads signing PTAs becomes higher and eventually surpasses that of those not signing PTAs.

$$
\begin{cases}
\text{Policy pressure}_{i,j,t} = 2 \text{ (common pressure), if competitors' policy}_{i,t} - \\
\quad \& \text{ competitors' policy}_{j,t} - \text{labor rights}_{j,t} > 0 \\
\\
\text{Policy pressure}_{i,j,t} = 1 \text{ (partial pressure), if competitors' policy}_{i,t} - \\
\quad \text{labor rights}_{i,t} > 0 \text{ or competitors' policy}_{j,t} - \text{labor rights}_{j,t} > 0 \\
\quad\quad\quad\quad \text{(but not both)} \\
\\
\text{Policy pressure}_{i,j,t} + 0 \text{ (no pressure), otherwise}
\end{cases}
$$

To capture the constraining effect of the ability to practically repress workers, I create an interaction term: *policy pressure* × *domestic violation*

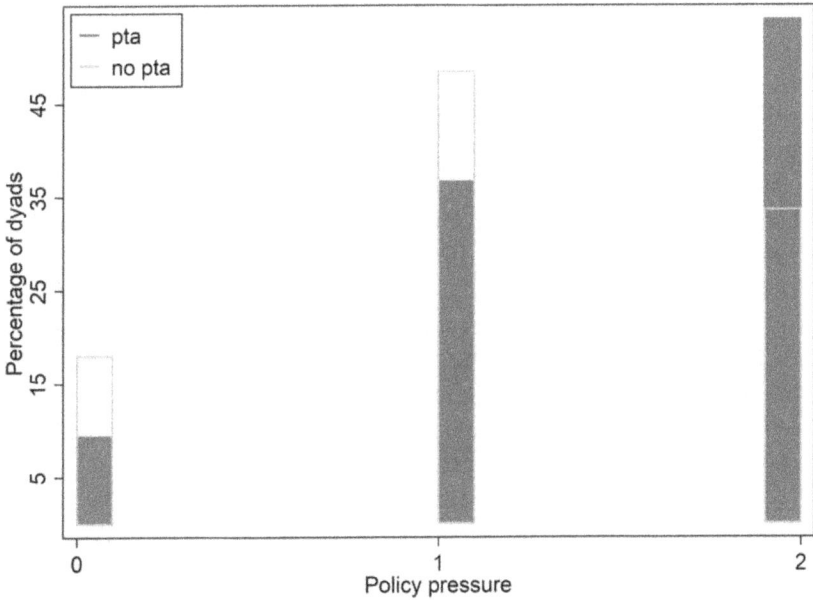

Figure 3.1. Policy Pressure and PTA Formation. *Source*: Zhiyuan Wang, "Thinking Outside the Box: Globalization, Labor Rights, and the Making of Preferential Trade Agreements," *International Studies Quarterly* 64 (2020): 343–355.

of labor rights. I define *domestic violation of labor rights* as the difference between labor rights law and labor rights practice in a given state/year. A larger difference indicates the greater ability of a state to reduce its practical labor protection, and therefore the greater constraining effect that it may exert. For a dyad, the observation with a lower value on this variable is selected. The interaction term is expected to be negative and not highly statistically significant.

I control the following confounding factors considered in extant scholarship that might affect a dyad's decision of making a PTA. First, following the literature (Baccini & Dür, 2015; Haftel & Thompson, 2013), I use the "weakest link" criteria to select state-level variables, including economic significance of trade, the sum of imports and exports of a state in a dyad over its GDP; reliance on foreign direct investment, measured as the ratio of FDI flows over GDP; the size of economy, GDP; income level, GDP per capita; economic growth (World Bank, 2016); and the level of democracy (Marshall & Jaggers, 2012).

The previous literature also suggests that PTAs help to reinforce bargaining positions of members in multilateral trade negotiations (Mansfield & Reinhardt, 2003). I therefore include three relevant variables such as the common WTO membership, whether in an ongoing WTO-sponsored multilateral trade negotiation round, and whether engaging in a trade dispute. I also consider the following dyad-level variables: military alliance (Gibler & Sarkees, 2004) and geographical distance (Stinnett et al., 2002), which have proved to be influential in economic treaty making (Baccini & Dür, 2015; Elkins et al., 2006a; Manger, 2012). Further, cultural affinity is also found to be consequential in economic treaty formation (Baccini & Dür, 2015; Elkins et al., 2006a); I therefore include three broadly used variables: colonial legacy (Hensel, 2014), linguistic similarity (taken from Baccini & Dür, 2015), and religious commonality (Maoz & Henderson, 2013).

I then control for difference in labor laws and labor law shock. The former deals with a possibility that two states with dissimilar labor standards will be less likely to enter into a PTA, as one may fear that it will be taken advantage of by the other in complying with the agreement. The latter, which is defined as the change of one standard deviation below the mean in competitors' labor laws, helps to further remove potential exogenous influences.

Finally, I take into account the smaller number of PTAs that two states under observation have formed with the third states respectively in year t–1, which is expected to capture learning and ceiling effects (Mansfield & Reinhardt, 2003).

As for the estimator, I employ a probit model for H1 and H3 and an ordered probit model for H2 with Huber-White standard errors, which mitigate potential heterogeneity and within-panel serial correlation problems. I also use a three-way clustering (on dyad and two constitutive states) to address the additional error correlation issue present in dyadic data. I finally employ cubic polynomials to account for time dependence when applicable (Carter & Signorino, 2010).

$$H1: P_{ij,t} = \alpha + \beta \text{ policy pressure}_{ij,t-1} + \gamma X_{i,j,t-1} + \Gamma Z_{i/j,t-1} + \varepsilon_{i,j,t}$$

$$H2: LP_{ij,t} = \alpha + \beta \text{ policy pressure}_{ij,t-1} + \gamma X_{i,j,t-1} + \Gamma Z_{i/j,t-1} + \varepsilon_{i,j,t}$$

$$H3: P_{ij,t}\alpha + \beta \text{ policy pressure}_{ij,t-1} + \Psi \text{ common pressure}_{ij,t-1} \times \text{Domestic violation of labor rights}_{ij,t-1} + \Phi \text{ domestic violation of labor rights}_{ij,t-1} + \gamma X_{i,j,t-1} + \Gamma Z_{i/j,t-1} + \varepsilon_{i,j,t}$$

In the preceding equations, $P_{ij,t}$ is whether a PTA is signed between state i and state j in year t. $LP_{ij,t}$ is the level of legalization of labor provision in PTAs. $X_{i,j,t-1}$ is a group of dyadic variables, $Z_{i/j,t-1}$ monadic variables, and $\varepsilon_{i,j,t}$ is the error term.

Results

The results for *H1* are reported in Table 3.1. As expected, *policy pressure* is positive and statistically significant at the 99 percent confidence level,

Table 3.1. How Policy Pressure to Reduce Legal Labor Protection Affects PTA Formation

DV: Signing PTAs = 1	(1)
Policy pressure	0.134***
	(0.013)
Trade	0.001*
	(0.000)
FDI	0.014***
	(0.002)
Total GDP	0.033***
	(0.007)
GDP per capita	0.018**
	(0.009)
GDP growth	0.009***
	(0.002)
Alliance	−0.099***
	(0.023)
Level of democracy	0.020***
	(0.001)
Distance	−0.245***
	(0.009)
WTO membership	0.195***
	(0.048)
WTO round	0.183***
	(0.031)
Trade dispute	−0.329***
	(0.092)

continued on next page

Table 3.1. Continued.

DV: Signing PTAs = 1	(1)
Colonial legacy	−0.218***
	(0.032)
Linguistic similarity	0.230***
	(0.034)
Religious commonality	0.237***
	(0.019)
Difference in labor laws	−0.124***
	(0.006)
Labor laws shock	0.494***
	(0.159)
No. of signed PTAs	0.039***
	(0.004)
Constant	−3.188***
	(0.193)
Observations	318,178
Cubic polynomials	yes
Log-likelihood	−12656
χ^2	2949

Robust standard errors in parentheses

***$p < 0.01$, **$p < 0.05$, *$p < 0.1$

Source: Zhiyuan Wang, "Thinking Outside the Box: Globalization, Labor Rights, and the Making of Preferential Trade Agreements," *International Studies Quarterly* 64 (2020): 343–355.

strongly supporting it. Because the interpretation of the coefficients from maximum likelihood estimations (MLE) is not as straightforward as that of those from ordinary least squares (OLS) models, I calculate the marginal effects of the independent variables using Model 1's results and plot them in Figure 3.2. We can see that *policy pressure* exerts a substantial positive impact on the probability of signing PTAs. In other words, when two states are under the policy pressure to reduce labor protection, they are more likely to sign a PTA.

I also plot the predicted probabilities for three groups of dyads (Figure 3.3): one subject to common policy pressure (dark gray), one under partial policy pressure (light gray), and the third one under no pressure (lighter gray). The contrast is sharp. The group under the policy pressure is significantly more likely to sign a PTA than one that is

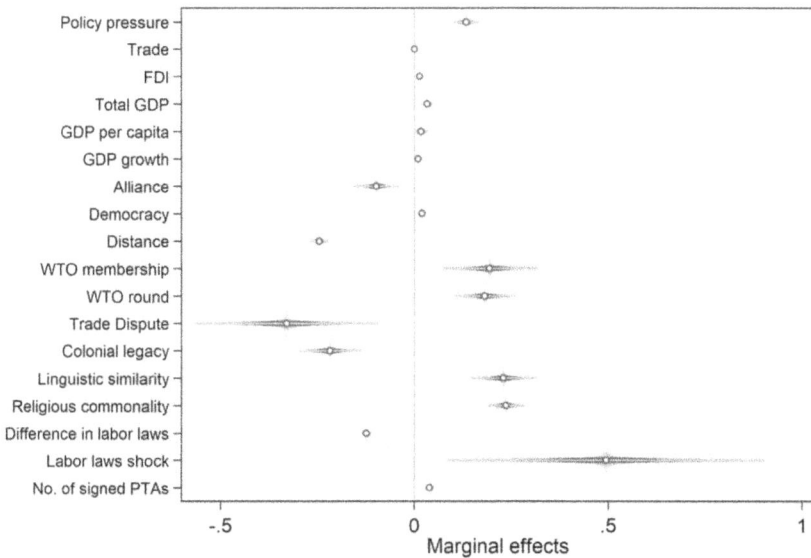

Figure 3.2. Marginal Effects of Independent Variables on the Probability of Signing PTAs. Note: Figure 3.2 is created based on the results of Model 1. The hollow circle denotes the marginal effect of each independent variable. The shortest darker line indicates the 90 percent confidence interval, while the longest lighter line indicates the 99 percent confidence interval. *Source*: Zhiyuan Wang, "Thinking Outside the Box: Globalization, Labor Rights, and the Making of Preferential Trade Agreements," *International Studies Quarterly* 64 (2020): 343–355.

not. The controls behave largely similar to those in existing literature. Economic openness increases the likelihood of making PTAs (Baccini & Dür, 2015; Manger, 2012; Mansfield & Reinhardt, 2003). The economic performance of states within a dyad, especially the size of the economy, exhibits a much larger predictive power in PTA formation than other control variables (Baccini & Dür, 2011; Manger, 2012). Democracy also contributes to the formation of PTAs, consistent with the literature that finds that democracy enhances international cooperation (Mansfield et al., 2002). Contrary to the expectation, alliance does not improve the probability of PTA formation but decreases it, although the magnitude is quite small, which likely results from its varying effects across different state pairs and mirrors the mixed findings in the literature (Baccini & Dür, 2015; Manger, 2012; Manger et al., 2012; Mansfield & Reinhardt, 2003).

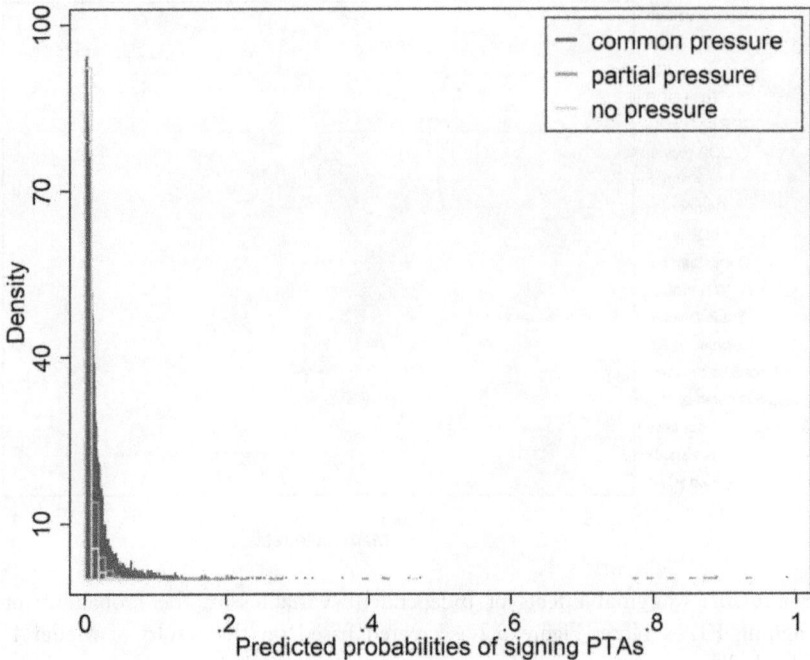

Figure 3.3. Predicted Probabilities of Signing PTAs across Two Groups of Dyads. *Source:* Zhiyuan Wang, "Thinking Outside the Box: Globalization, Labor Rights, and the Making of Preferential Trade Agreements," *International Studies Quarterly* 64 (2020): 343–355.

Two geographically distant states are much less likely to form a PTA, in line with the previous findings (Baccini & Dür, 2011, 2015; Manger, 2012; Manger et al., 2012). WTO membership expectedly increases the likelihood of forming a PTA as research has shown (Baccini & Dür, 2011, 2015; Mansfield & Reinhardt, 2003). The multi-round negotiation is positive but gains no statistical significance at a conventional confidence level. Echoing the literature, trade disputes generally reduce the tendency of signing a PTA within a dyad (Baccini & Dür, 2011, 2015). Regarding the cultural factors, both linguistic similarity and religious commonality raise the likelihood of forming a PTA, confirming the cultural influence in international policy diffusion found in the extant scholarship (Baccini & Dür, 2015; Simmons & Elkins, 2004), whereas the colonial legacy seems to prevent a PTA from forming, which partly matches the existing findings (Baccini & Dür, 2011). As expected, when two states differ greatly in their labor laws, the likelihood of signing a PTA is lower. But the labor laws shock in competitors makes it more possible to enter into a PTA. In congruence with the literature (Manger, 2012; Manger et al., 2012; Mansfield, 1998; Mansfield & Reinhardt, 2003), the larger number of PTAs signed with third states in previous year by states within a dyad renders it more likely to form one in the current year.

Table 3.2 presents results for H2.[12] Again, *policy pressure* is positive and statistically significant at the conventional levels, suggesting that when two states are both pressured to downgrade labor rights laws, they

Table 3.2. How Policy Pressure to Reduce Legal Labor Protection Affects Labor Provisions in PTAs

DV: Signing PTAs = 1	(1)
Policy pressure	0.121*
	(0.072)
Trade	–0.000
	(0.002)
FDI	–0.011**
	(0.005)
Total GDP	–0.223***
	(0.030)
GDP per capita	0.463***
	(0.048)
GDP growth	0.004
	(0.026)
Alliance	0.336***
	(0.107)
Level of democracy	0.030***
	(0.008)
Distance	0.141***
	(0.044)
WTO membership	5.252***
	(0.160)
WTO round	1.380***
	(0.251)
Trade dispute	–0.086
	(0.180)
Colonial legacy	–0.470**
	(0.194)

continued on next page

Table 3.2. Continued.

DV: Signing PTAs = 1	(1)
Linguistic similarity	0.315***
	(0.105)
Religious commonality	–0.159***
	(0.036)
Difference in labor laws	–0.165
	(0.121)
cut1	
Constant	6.974***
	(1.012)
cut2	
Constant	7.086***
	(1.011)
cut3	
Constant	7.192***
	(1.015)
Observations	1,392
Cubic polynomials	yes
Log-likelihood	–819.1
χ^2	.

Robust standard errors in parentheses

***$p < 0.01$, **$p < 0.05$, *$p < 0.1$

Source: Zhiyuan Wang, "Thinking Outside the Box: Globalization, Labor Rights, and the Making of Preferential Trade Agreements," *International Studies Quarterly* 64 (2020): 343–355.

are more likely to insert more stringent labor provisions into a PTA, in support of the hypothesis. This finding echoes a recent treaty-level study that concludes that politically powerful workers make stronger labor provisions in PTAs (Raess et al., 2018). Figure 3.4 displays how policy pressure affects the possibility of including different levels of labor provisions in PTAs based on the results in Table 3.2. As it shows, the presence of policy pressure (dark triangle) is positively and strongly associated with the likelihood of incorporating stronger labor provisions into PTAs, whereas its absence (hollow square) is not.

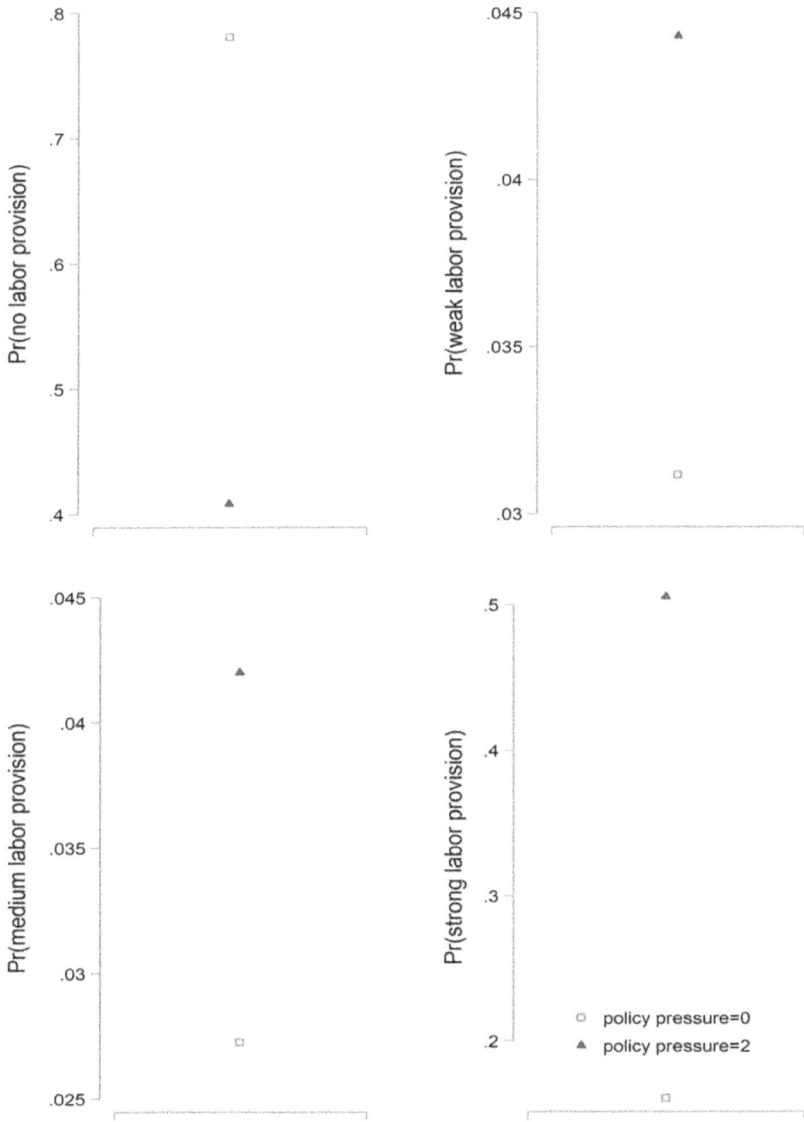

Figure 3.4. Predicted Probabilities for Different Levels of Labor Provisions in PTAs. *Source*: Zhiyuan Wang, "Thinking Outside the Box: Globalization, Labor Rights, and the Making of Preferential Trade Agreements," *International Studies Quarterly* 64 (2020): 343–355.

Table 3.3 presents results for H3. *Policy pressure* is positive and statistically significant at the 99 percent confidence level while the interaction term is negative and only achieves significance at the 90

Table 3.3. How the Ability to Violate Labor Rights Moderates the Effect of Policy Pressure on PTA Formation

DV: Signing PTAs = 1	(1)
Policy pressure	0.148***
	(0.013)
Policy pressure × domestic violation of labor rights	−0.052**
	(0.020)
Domestic violation of labor rights	−0.025
	(0.026)
Trade	0.001**
	(0.000)
FDI	0.014***
	(0.002)
Total GDP	0.035***
	(0.007)
GDP per capita	0.013
	(0.009)
GDP growth	0.010***
	(0.002)
Alliance	−0.097***
	(0.023)
Level of democracy	0.020***
	(0.001)
Distance	−0.243***
	(0.009)
WTO membership	0.177***
	(0.048)
WTO round	0.184***
	(0.031)
Trade dispute	−0.347***
	(0.092)

Colonial legacy	−0.211***
	(0.032)
Linguistic similarity	0.233***
	(0.034)
Religious commonality	0.241***
	(0.019)
Difference in labor laws	−0.124***
	(0.006)
Labor laws shock	0.487***
	(0.159)
No. of signed PTAs	0.039***
	(0.004)
Constant	−3.199***
	(0.192)
Observations	318,178
Cubic polynomials	yes
Log-likelihood	−12638
χ^2	2953

Robust standard errors in parentheses

***p < 0.01, **p < 0.05, *p < 0.1

Source: Zhiyuan Wang, "Thinking Outside the Box: Globalization, Labor Rights, and the Making of Preferential Trade Agreements," International Studies Quarterly 64 (2020): 343–355.

percent level, as expected. However, interpreting the marginal effect of a constituent variable in an interaction term in MLE is not immediately as clear as that in OLS environments (Brambor et al., 2006). I employ graphical visualization to do so. Figure 3.5 displays the graph. As *domestic violation of labor rights* becomes greater, meaning a dyad is more able to repress labor in practice, the probability of its forming a PTA declines. However, this constraining effect only exits when *domestic violation of labor rights* is not substantially large, such as being smaller than 3, and is effectively close to 0. Hence, we may conclude that a dyad is some-what less motivated to form a PTA only when the states maintain the practical protection of labor rights slightly lower than the labor rights laws. In other words, repressing workers beyond certain point would no longer be perceived economically beneficial and therefore does not further diminish the likelihood of signing PTAs.

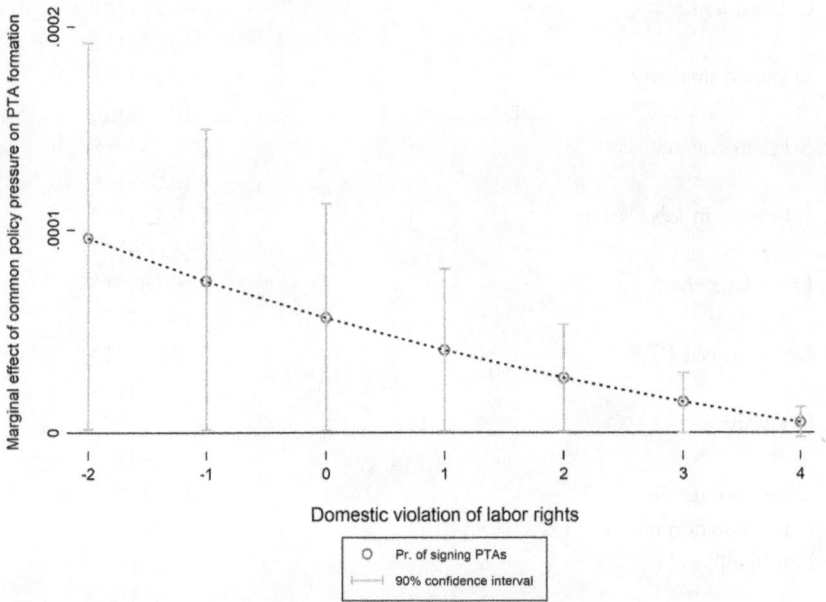

Figure 3.5. Marginal Effect of Policy Pressure to Reduce Legal Labor Protection on the Probability of Signing PTAs Conditional on the Ability to Repress Labor in Practice. *Source:* Zhiyuan Wang, "Thinking Outside the Box: Globalization, Labor Rights, and the Making of Preferential Trade Agreements," *International Studies Quarterly* 64 (2020): 343–355.

Robustness Checks

First, the literature suggests that PTAs diffuse due to investment discrimination (Baccini & Dür, 2015).[13] This discrimination results from tariff differentials on intermediary goods and relaxed investment restrictions prescribed in PTAs. Hence, states confronted with this discrimination have a stronger tendency to form PTAs to mitigate the possible negative effects due to such discrimination. Using sophisticated techniques, Baccini and Dür construct a variable to capture the discrimination. I borrow this variable from them, add it to the main models, and rerun the analysis. Because the time period examined in their study ends in 2007, the sample shrinks quite a bit. However, the results remain largely unchanged.

Furthermore, because it may take more than a year to negotiate a PTA, I try the following time lags: two, three, four, and five years. The results are virtually identical to the main findings.

Next, I reconstruct the key explanatory variable—*policy pressure*—by recalculating competitors' policies with an FDI-based weighting matrix. The results are in line with the main findings.

Additionally, a state's dependence on resources might also affect its likelihood of signing a PTA. I therefore use the rents from natural resources to control for such a possibility. The results echo the main findings. Due to the misbehavior of the MLE models that consider fixed effects (Greene, 2004), I did not control for the time- and region-specific effects in the main analysis. In order to see whether the inclusion of these effects impacts the study's results, I reestimate the models when considering different fixed effects. The results are consistent with the main findings. I also run a monadic estimation, which is largely in agreement with the dyadic analysis for H1 and H2, but less so for H3.

Finally, I adopt a Cox proportional hazards model to reanalyze the data for H1 and H3. Once again, the results are congruent with the main findings.

The Case of the China–New Zealand Free Trade Agreement

The argument advanced in this chapter can be illustrated by the case of the China–New Zealand Free Trade Agreement. In June 2007, China passed a new Labor Contract Law to improve the protection of workers' rights. This law was the fruit of a long legislative effort that had begun at the end of 2004. It accorded workers a greater degree of collective bargaining power, and it made it more difficult for employers to fire them (Li & Freeman, 2015; Wang et al., 2009). The possibly negative consequences of this new law are, however, concerning. It constrains the flexibility of employers to hire and hence rigidifies the labor market; in the long run, this will likely increase the cost of labor and undermine China's economic competitiveness (Chen & Funke, 2009). These negative consequences are particularly worrying because many of China's economic competitors—such as Vietnam, Bangladesh, and Brazil—have historically maintained low protection for labor rights.

Nevertheless, China could not reduce legal labor protections by reversing the law. This is because the new Labor Contract Law constitutes the least harmful way for the Chinese government to manage a looming legitimacy crisis. Workers have been marginalized during the country's reform years (Gallagher, 2004), which leads to the surge of labor protests (Elfstrom & Kuruvilla, 2014). Unless it meets workers' demands for better treatment, the Chinese Communist Party will seriously undercut its legitimacy as a party of the working class (Wang et al., 2009). Therefore, this new law—which is a favorable response to workers' persistent cry for more protections—is not open to reversal. The Chinese government must turn to alternative policies to ameliorate the potential economic disadvantages that it causes.

In New Zealand, the 2001 labor law restored the rigidity of the labor market (Rasmussen, 2009). A highly regulated labor market, however, can incur high costs to productivity (Margaritis et al., 2005), especially in an open economy such as New Zealand's (Kang, 2015). Consequently, trade suffers: the ratio of exports over the GDP of New Zealand has remained almost stagnant for the past decades (Iyer, 2010). Meanwhile, New Zealand—which is a major exporter of dairy products, meat, wood, wool, and fish—has been facing fierce competition from the US, Belarus, Turkey, Vietnam, and Chile, which all have more flexible labor regulations. Given New Zealand's political climate, there was no indication that the country could once again deregulate the labor market as it had done in the 1980s (Rasmussen, 2009). It is, therefore, imperative for New Zealand to seek viable policy alternatives in order to maintain its economic competitiveness.

Because China and New Zealand were similarly motivated to substitute more viable policies for politically unfeasible ones, they signed a free trade agreement in April 2008. Both parties believe that the agreement would significantly improve trade and investment between them. Moreover, this agreement includes several provisions—such as Article 113 and Article 126—that aim to protect labor in each party. These provisions, however, were intentionally made weak, as they include no effective enforcement mechanisms.

Conclusion

In this chapter, I have sought to illustrate the possibility of how policy convergence can result from cross-issue substitution across the levels of analysis. Focusing on a frequently cited case in the race to the bottom thesis, labor rights protection, I contend that states do not always engage in such a race by willfully following the dictates of globalization. Rather, they turn to trade agreements to compensate for resisting the deregulation pressure unleashed by globalization. PTAs generate considerable economic gains in a less politically costly way than lowering legal labor protections. Whereas diminishing labor protections proves universally harmful to workers, the benefits that emanate from PTAs improve welfare and benefit both businesses and labor. Specifically, I hypothesize that when a pair of states face policy pressure from their competitors to reduce legal protections for labor, then they are more likely to form a PTA. Moreover, I posit that states facing policy pressure are inclined to include substantive labor provisions in PTAs. These provisions appease their better-protected workers and thus facilitate the making of these treaties. Finally, I also expect that, even in the face of the policy pressure to lower legal protections for labor, states may feel less inclined to sign a PTA if they are already capable of repressing workers. The empirical analysis lends strong and robust support to these theoretical postulates.

These findings defy the belief that globalization does nothing else but induce and intensify states' policy convergence on deregulation. The race to the bottom in labor market institutions does not materialize as widely held, especially in labor rights laws, as shown in more recent literature (Greenhill et al., 2009; Malesky & Mosley, 2018; Mosley, 2011; Wang, 2017a). The mechanism depicted in this chapter helps to explain why this might be the case. States appeal to more effective alternatives that are capable both of avoiding the high political costs associated with publicly undesirable policies and of maintaining—or even enhancing—economic competitiveness. More importantly, substituting politically desirable policies for undesirable ones leads to convergence in practice too. This convergence does not stem from the surrendering of policy autonomy. Instead, it results from strategic choices.

Overall, these findings demonstrate the core theoretical assertion in this book that convergence can be evidence of states' policy adaptivity under globalization. Convergence in one issue area goes side by side with divergence in another. In this very sense, it can be said that convergence renders possible divergence.

In addition, this chapter also shows a carefully designed PTA that protected labor can further prevent deregulation. Therefore, we may conclude that convergence on a certain design of a strategically chosen policy tool increases the costs of deregulation, sustaining divergence in policy areas of direct and strong distributional consequences. Finally and however, when the costs of deregulating as imposed by globalization are low due to domestic institutional arrangements, the incentive to sub-stitute unpopular policies is weaker, likely leading to more convergence on deregulation as the race to the bottom thesis claims.

Focusing on the substitution that occurs across issues and analytical levels, this chapter depicts a mechanism through which policy conver-gence is generated. The next chapter follows the same political logic to explore the convergence that is engendered by another type of mecha-nism: cross-issue substitution that occurs at the same level of analysis.

4

Partisanship, Labor, and Corporate Taxation

In this chapter, I will turn to a third mechanism of convergence: cross–issue area substitution at the same analytical level. To demonstrate this mechanism, I investigate the conditions under which leftist governments cut corporate tax rates. I focus on the leftist governments because they provide a useful scenario in which substitution between domestic policies is politically imperative and practically feasible and such substitution is what globalization causes and eventually leads to convergence as demanded by it as well. As in the last chapter, the pressure to deregulate the labor market is central to this investigation. Lessening the corporate tax burden allows leftist governments to substitute for their political inability to succumb to such pressure. The convergence on downward fiscal policy adjustment shields them from the possible political backlash that would emanate from implementing unpopular labor deregulation.

Leftist governments prefer higher corporate tax rates. However, the current scholarship provides only inconclusive and mixed empirical evidence for this policy preference (Basinger & Hallerberg, 2004; Devereux et al., 2008; Garrett, 1998; Hays, 2003; Inclan et al., 2001; Kumar & Quinn, 2012; Quinn & Shapiro, 1991; Shin, 2017; Swank & Steinmo, 2002; Williams & Collins, 1997). As a matter of fact, worldwide corporate tax rates have downwardly converged for the past three decades (Devereux et al., 2002; Grubert, 2001; Rodrik, 1997; Slemrod, 2004; Tanzi, 1995). Paradoxically, this trend seems to go hand in hand with the global rise of leftist governments since the 1990s (Figure 4.1). If we consider individual countries, leftist governments across the globe have witnessed cuts in corporate tax rates, from Denmark, France, and South

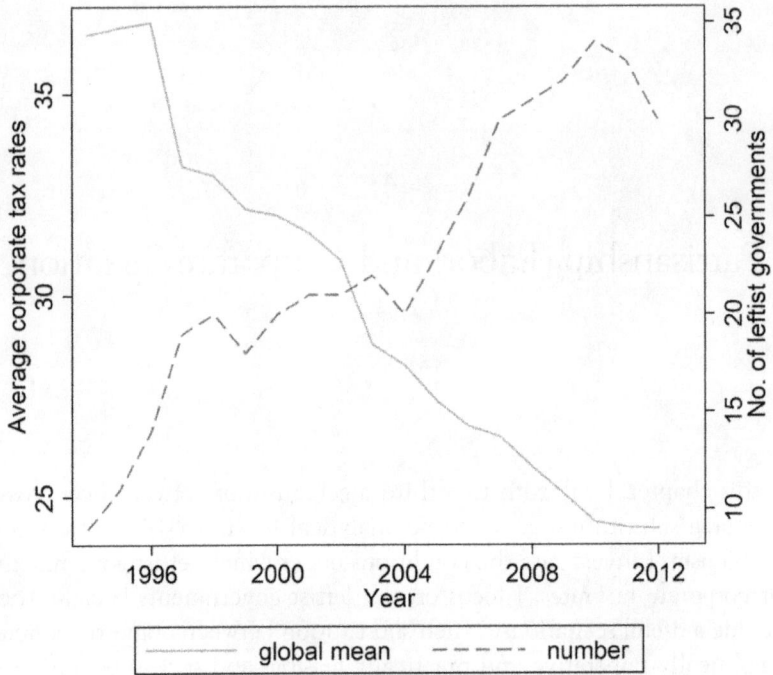

Figure 4.1 Global Trends in Statutory Corporate Tax Rates and Leftist Governments: 1993–2012. Data on statutory corporate tax rates are taken from KPMG (2006, 2015) Global Tax Rate Surveys. Data on leftist governments are taken from the Database of Political Institutions (Cruz et al., 2016). *Source:* Zhiyuan Wang, "Choosing a Lesser Evil: Partisanship, Labor, and Corporate Taxation under Globalization," *Political Research Quarterly* 74 (2021): 571–586.

Africa, to Sri Lanka, India, China, Uruguay, and Canada. What, then, explains this puzzling occurrence? In this chapter, I intend to explore answers to this question.

As elaborated in previous chapters, globalization accelerates downward policy convergence among states, as it significantly externalizes the effects of domestic policy changes (e.g., Basinger & Hallerberg, 2004; Cao, 2010; Lee & Strang, 2006; Swank, 2006). As one constitutive feature of globalization, capital flows at the global level profoundly affect a state's economy (International Monetary Fund, 2000). States partake in a fierce competition for this scarce resource. Capital-friendly policies that help states survive this competition force their convergence across borders. For example, when states that compete for capital restrict labor rights to lower the cost of labor in the hope of attracting and retaining investment, others competing for the same investment feel pressured to follow suit (Davies & Vadlamannati, 2013; Mosley, 2011).[1] However, not all governments can make this type of policy move because for some of them the political costs of doing so are unbearably high, as discussed in chapter 3. This is especially true for leftist governments: reducing labor rights protection has a direct negative impact on their constituencies. Therefore, in the face of this downward pressure, leftist governments will seek policy alternatives that can achieve the goals that diminished labor rights protection is expected to accomplish. Among these alternatives, lowering corporate tax rates is a competitive option. Specifically, I argue that when it is politically unfeasible for leftist governments to restrict labor rights to maintain economic competitiveness, they seek to spur investment by allowing investors to keep a greater share of the return to their investment through levying lower corporate taxes, which is demonstrably effective and less politically costly. This policy substitution ultimately gives rise to convergence on low corporate taxation.

To capture the pressure leftist governments face to restrict labor rights, I first use novel global panel data on labor rights and the structural equivalence technique to calculate yearly labor rights policies in a state's capital competitors, as I have done in chapter 3. Here these capital competitors are identified using bilateral foreign direct investment (FDI) stock data, a practice widely adopted in the extant literature (Baccini & Koenig-Archibugi, 2014; Cao, 2010; Elkins et al., 2006b). I then formulate policy pressure as the difference between a state's own labor rights score and its competitors' policies for a given year, which increases as the competitors' policies decrease (i.e., as competitors reduce labor rights protection) when it is unable to do the same. I find robust support for this theoretical conjecture. Although leftist governments do levy higher taxes on corporations than their partisan opponents, they can only do so when they do not face strong pressure from their competitors to restrict labor rights. As the pressure increases, they are forced to retreat from their declared policy positions by cutting corporate tax rates.

The rest of the chapter will unfold as follows: the following section reviews the literature on partisanship and capital taxation. I then present my theoretical argument. Specifics on data and estimation strategy are then provided. Next, the findings are discussed, and their robustness is subsequently checked. Two pieces of anecdotal evidence are offered to lend further support to the theoretical postulate. The conclusion sum-marizes the key findings and discusses their implications.

Partisan Governments and Corporate Taxation

Leftist governments pursue socioeconomic equality through redistribution (Bradley et al., 2003). Leftist governments' tax policies are therefore expected to rely more on capital than labor income taxation. Many studies support the notion that leftist governments set higher corporate tax rates (Angelopoulos et al., 2009; Garrett, 1998; Inclan et al., 2001; Kumar & Quinn, 2012; Osterloh & Debus, 2012; Quinn & Shapiro, 1991; Shin, 2017). However, other scholars have reached different conclusions, arguing that either leftist governments lower statutory corporate tax rates (Swank & Steinmo, 2002; Williams & Collins, 1997) or partisanship has no statistically significant impact on tax policy enactments (Basinger & Hallerberg, 2004; Devereux et al., 2008). These conflicting findings appear to suggest that leftist governments do not pursue their preferred policy unconditionally.

However, there is little research on the conditions that constrain leftist governments' choices regarding corporate tax rates. Plümper et al.'s (2009) study is a notable exception. They argue that a leftist government levies higher corporate taxes when the fairness constraints it faces are high. Another exception is Shin's (2017) recent article. It postulates that leftist governments can maintain high tax rates because they relax regulations on transfer pricing, allowing firms to transfer profits abroad with more ease and thus reducing their tax burden. These two studies demonstrate that the ability of leftist governments to adopt high corporate tax rates is not unconditional but largely contingent on the policy environment.

In addition, scholarship on partisanship and corporate taxation primarily focuses on developed countries (Swank, 2016). Meanwhile, the studies that have examined the developing world only pay scant attention to the impact of partisanship, let alone the conditions that shape unorthodox partisan tax policies (Genschel et al., 2016; Keen & Simone, 2004; Li, 2006, 2016).

Filling the gaps in the literature is particularly important, as the unrestricted partisanship proposition that leftist governments refuse to endorse lower corporate tax rates is incongruent with the fact that corporate tax rates have experienced downward convergence worldwide over the past three decades (Devereux et al., 2002; Grubert, 2001; Rodrik, 1997; Slemrod, 2004; Tanzi, 1995), including in developing countries (Devereux, 2007). Exploring the conditions that induce seemingly unconventional partisan tax policies, such as lowering corporate tax rates by leftist governments, will help us get a better sense of the inconsistency in the extant literature and the mismatch between the literature and political reality.

In this chapter, by focusing on the pressure economic competitors exert to diminish labor rights protection, I explore one major constraint that prevents leftist governments from maintaining their stated policy positions regarding corporate taxation in a global sample. More importantly, by showing the substitution of cutting corporate tax rates for relaxing labor regulations, I demonstrate a possibility that policy convergence can be an intended outcome of strategic choices, which are made across issue areas at the same analytical level.

Leftist Governments, Labor Rights, and Corporate Taxation under Globalization

LOWERING LABOR RIGHTS PROTECTION HURTS LEFTIST GOVERNMENTS' CONSTITUENCIES

Leftist governments draw substantial political support from workers. Leftist parties have historically grown out of workers' enfranchisement (Przeworski & Sprague, 1986). Workers are the core constituencies of leftist parties (Griffin et al., 1990). Labor rights, especially the rights to organize and bargain collectively, are of vital importance to workers, as they enhance the bargaining position of workers vis-à-vis employers and the state (also see Acemoglu & Robinson, 2008; Korpi, 1985). Where these rights are well protected, income inequality is lower (Kerrissey, 2015), wages are higher (Dean, 2015), FDI is more restricted (Owen, 2015; Pond, 2017), and workers are more likely to negotiate better deals with international organizations (Caraway et al., 2012). Undoubtedly, restricting these collective labor rights will weaken workers both politically and economically. Hence, workers have a strong interest in protecting these rights and have been successful in doing so (Cook, 2002; Korpi, 1989; Madrid, 2003).

Given that workers do care about their own rights, it would be unwise for leftist governments to enact policies against workers' key interests, such as legally restricting collective labor rights, which will certainly alienate their core constituencies. This is the cost leftist governments are unable to bear.[2] Research has shown that workers punish partisan politicians electorally when their interests are hurt (Margalit, 2011). In addition, leftist governments do not want to make workers feel betrayed by their party, as they also need workers' support to pass their preferred redistributive policies (Bradley et al., 2003; Esping-Andersen, 1985; Kristal, 2010). As a result, politicians on the left have strong incentives to secure workers' policy preferences. In non-democracies, leftist governments also exhibit a relatively high level of responsiveness to workers' political demands. In these states, workers are less likely to face a collective action problem than other groups due to their enormous size and organizational capacity and can therefore easily form mass mobilization, which threatens the authoritarian rule, especially that of single leftist-party governments (Ulfelder, 2005, p. 317). To appease and co-opt workers, these single-party authoritarian states often institute good labor rights laws (Cammett & Posusney, 2010; Caraway, 2009) and provide substantive protection and benefits to workers (Chen, 2016; Cook, 1993; Leung & Nann, 1995). Overall, leftist governments see it in their best interest to represent and favor the interests of workers (Korpi, 1989). Studies indeed show that leftist governments provide better protection of labor rights across regimes and despite globalization (Blanton et al., 2015; Mosley & Uno, 2007).

Therefore, leftist governments are reluctant to reduce labor protection, in particular the protection of collective labor rights, by downgrading relevant laws even when faced with pressure from their economic competitors to do so.

CUTTING CORPORATE TAX RATES IS ECONOMICALLY EFFECTIVE AND POLITICALLY ACHIEVABLE

The classic production function indicates that labor and capital are two essential factors that affect economic output. Increasing the input of either factor will be sufficient for increasing the output. Governments can use policies to influence the price of factors and thus the input and output levels. Specifically, governments can restrict collective labor rights to keep the cost of labor low and stimulate the demand for labor and its input, which enhances production. Governments can also grant investors more incentives to invest, such as allowing them to keep a higher proportion of their capital returns through lower taxation. As previously argued, when governments are politically constrained from restricting labor rights, turning to corporate tax policies could be a feasible alternative to expand production.[3]

In practice, corporate tax rates affect investment decisions. High taxation discourages and deters investors, who seek to equalize capital returns at the global level. As Zodrow (2007) has stated, "Any tax on capital income will drive out internationally mobile capital from the taxing jurisdiction, until its before-tax rate of return rises by enough to entirely offset the tax, so that mobile capital invested in the taxing country earns the same after-tax return that can be obtained elsewhere in the global economy" (p. 60). In contrast, reducing corporate tax rates promotes investment. The international capital market responds positively to tax reform; research has shown that investors will invest more in states where corporate tax rates are lower (Hines, 1999; Klemm & Parys, 2009; Wibbels & Arce, 2003).[4] That lower corporate taxation spurs economic growth (Lee & Gordon, 2005) also suggests that investment is indirectly promoted by such policy measures.

Growing investment in turn broadens the tax base (Swank, 2002) and raises national revenue from corporate taxation (Devereux & Keuschnigg, 2008).[5] For instance, the United States has derived more revenue from corporate taxation over the past two decades in the wake of the major corporate tax cuts of the late 1980s (Auerbach, 2006). In general, corporate tax revenue as the share of total revenue in OCED member countries has recently increased, following a prevailing reduction in corporate tax rates after a long period of stagnation since the 1970s (Devereux, 2007). Clearly, reducing corporate tax rates can generate broad and positive economic effects by encouraging investment.

In addition to the economic effectiveness of cutting corporate rates, the political costs are also lower than reducing labor standards. First, workers do not consider it particularly harmful or unacceptable when states cut corporate tax rates, as expanded investment contributes to job creation (Pinto et al., 2010) and boosts their income (Zodrow, 2007). Thus, in practice, voters electorally reward politicians who provide more tax incentives to businesses, as they believe that such policy measures create economic benefits they can enjoy (Jensen et al., 2014). This low resistance to cutting corporate tax rates should be more likely when workers' collective rights are well protected. For example, in 2007, Uruguay's then leftist government enacted a tax reform that reduced the corporate tax rate from 30 to 25 percent and registered low opposition, as workers have been guaranteed wide political and economic powers (Rius, 2013). As a matter of fact, workers' rights protection in Uruguay is among the best in Latin America and the world (International Trade Union Confederation, 2014).

Furthermore, states do not have to shift the tax burden from investors to labor in order to attract investment. Practically, only short-term investment reacts slightly positively to the tax burden–shifting strategy, while long-term investment, characteristic of FDI that states fiercely compete for, is unaffected by this policy (Wibbels & Arce, 2003). In other words, states can encourage long-term investment through levying lower corporate taxes without alienating workers by shifting tax burdens to them. Paradoxically, high corporate taxes overburden labor (Fuest et al., 2018), causing capital outflow that in turn adversely affects labor productivity and lowers wages (Zodrow, 2007, p. 60).

Moreover, voters can be aware of the policy constraints globalization imposes on their government and tend to appear "understanding" when the government adopts certain policies that are against its declared policy stances (Hellwig, 2008). They gradually assign lower weight to economic issues and yet higher weight to noneconomic issues in their evaluations of their government's performance (Hellwig, 2008; Ward et al., 2015). This change in attitude also helps to keep the political costs of cutting corporate tax rates tolerable.

Finally, leftist governments should encounter fewer hurdles from lowering corporate tax rates than their rightist counterparts since this policy is compatible with the opposing parties' ideological preferences. Research has demonstrated that leftist governments are more successful in implementing economic reforms mandated by the IMF than rightist governments because these reforms mirror the ideology of parties on the right, whose endorsement facilitates their implementation (Beazer & Woo, 2016).

The worldwide reduction in corporate tax rates over the past three decades attests to the relatively low political costs of doing so. For instance, the average statutory corporate tax rates in the European Union and the United States have experienced a remarkable decline from 48 percent in 1982 to 35 percent in 2001 (Devereux et al., 2002). In the meantime, in developing countries, the average statutory corporate tax rate dropped by 16 percent from the early 1990s to the early 2000s (Keen & Simone, 2004).

However, it should be noted that leftist governments will not reduce corporate tax rates if they lack strong reasons to do so. The ideological pursuit of leftist governments, a more equal society, necessitates higher government spending, which naturally requires greater tax revenue (Boix, 1997). In their view, lowering corporate taxes only serves to undermine this goal, thus making it an undesirable policy option for leftist governments to pursue even if the economic costs of rejecting it can be high (cf., Pinto et al., 2010). Therefore, under normal circumstances, leftist governments should value the egalitarian function of taxation more than its economic implications. Only when no better alternatives are available will leftist governments involuntarily reduce corporate tax rates.

Based on the preceding discussion, the following hypothesis is established:

> *Leftist governments are prone to cutting corporate tax rates, when they are faced with the pressure from international economic competitors to lower the protection of labor rights, ceteris paribus.*

Research Design

DATA

Following extant literature (Cao, 2010; Genschel et al., 2016; Slemrod, 2004), the dependent variable in this chapter is statutory corporate tax rate. This is because it is "the most visible component of the tax system" and "the statutory tax rate is the relevant factor shaping incentives for profit shifting activities of multi-nationals" (Osterloh & Debus, 2012, p. 196). The data are taken from multiple KPMG's Global Tax Rate Surveys (KPMG, 2006, 2015),[6] which cover the period 1993–2015.

The first key explanatory variable is leftist governments.[7] I obtain data on this variable from the Database of Political Institutions (Cruz et al., 2016), which measures the ideological leaning of the largest government party in a state's legislature and has been widely used in the literature.[8] It is expected to be positive and statistically significant.[9] Since

I propose a conditional relationship, an interaction term is necessary to capture this conditional effect. Before creating the interaction term, I need first to construct the policy pressure variable.

I define the variable *labor policy pressure* as the difference between a state's labor rights score and its FDI competitor's labor rights scores in a given year (equation 1). A positive value means that a state at issue provides better protection of labor rights than its competitors and therefore is under pressure to lower its own level of protection. A negative value or zero refers to the lack of such pressure.

$$\text{Labor policy pressure}_{i,t} = \text{labor policy}_{i,t} - \text{competitors' policy}_{i,t} \quad (1)$$

In order to construct this variable, it is necessary to first measure FDI competitors' policy regarding labor rights. Like in chapter 3, the structural equivalence technique is also employed for this task. To reiterate, competitors' policy is a mathematical product of a weighting matrix, which captures the competitive distance between a state under observation and its competitors, and a vector of labor rights scores for all states in a given year (the formula is given as follows). The weighting matrix is produced using bilateral FDI stocks (UNCTAD, 2019a).

$$\text{Competitors' policy}_{i,t} = \Sigma_k \omega_{i,j,t} \, \text{labor policy}_{k,t} \quad (2)$$

As in chapter 3, the labor rights data are taken from a new data set compiled by Barry, Cingranelli, and Clay (2022). Since the argument in this chapter is based on the political costliness of lowering legal labor protection, I use labor rights in law to perform the main analysis, as changing laws incurs higher costs than altering practices (Mosley, 2011). Therefore, additive collective labor rights scores, ranging from 0 to 4, are adopted to calculate the competitor's policy on labor protection using the formula specified earlier (equation 2).

Applying competitors' policy to equation 1, I generate *labor policy pressure*, which ranges from −2.7 to 4. For example, Canada had its labor policy pressure at 1.5 in 2001 before it reduced its corporate tax rate from 42.1 to 38.6 percent in the following year. In 1999, France's labor policy pressure was 1.1, and its corporate tax rates dropped from 40 to 35.33 percent one year after. Sri Lanka cut its corporate tax rate from 40 to 28 percent in 2003 while its labor policy pressure was 0.77 in the previous year. Figures 4.2a, 4.2b., and 4.2c plot both corporate tax rates

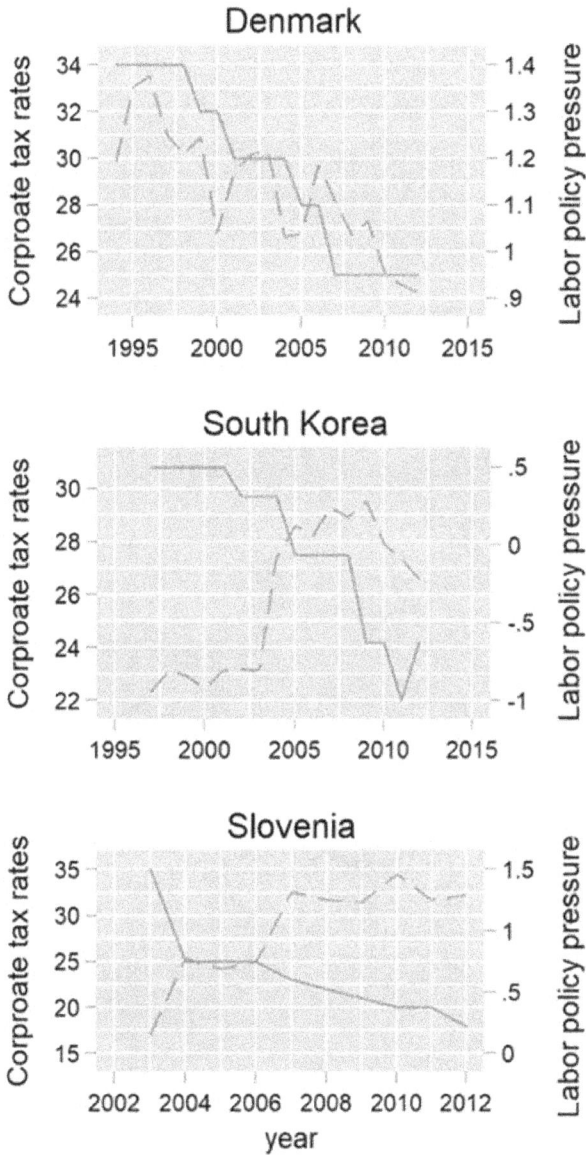

Figure 4.2a. Corporate Tax Rates and Labor Policy Pressure across Time in Select States. *Source*: Zhiyuan Wang, "Choosing a Lesser Evil: Partisanship, Labor, and Corporate Taxation under Globalization," *Political Research Quarterly* 74 (2021): 571–586.

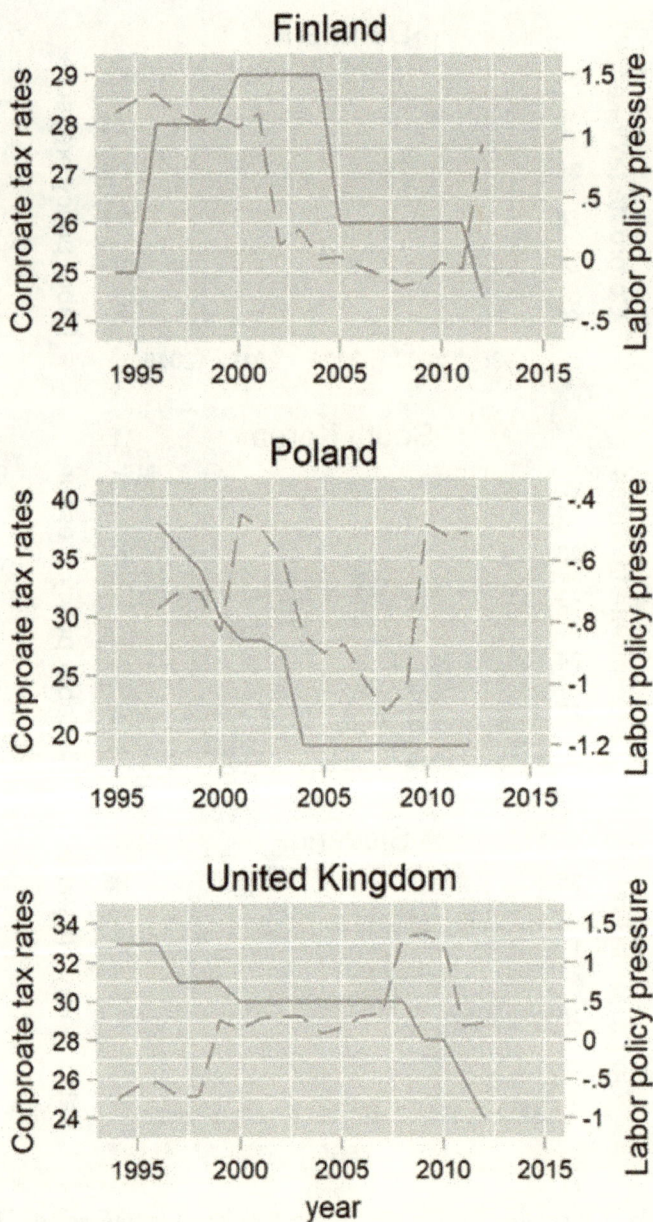

Figure 4.2b. Corporate Tax Rates and Labor Policy Pressure across Time in Select States. *Source*: Zhiyuan Wang, "Choosing a Lesser Evil: Partisanship, Labor, and Corporate Taxation under Globalization," *Political Research Quarterly* 74 (2021): 571–586.

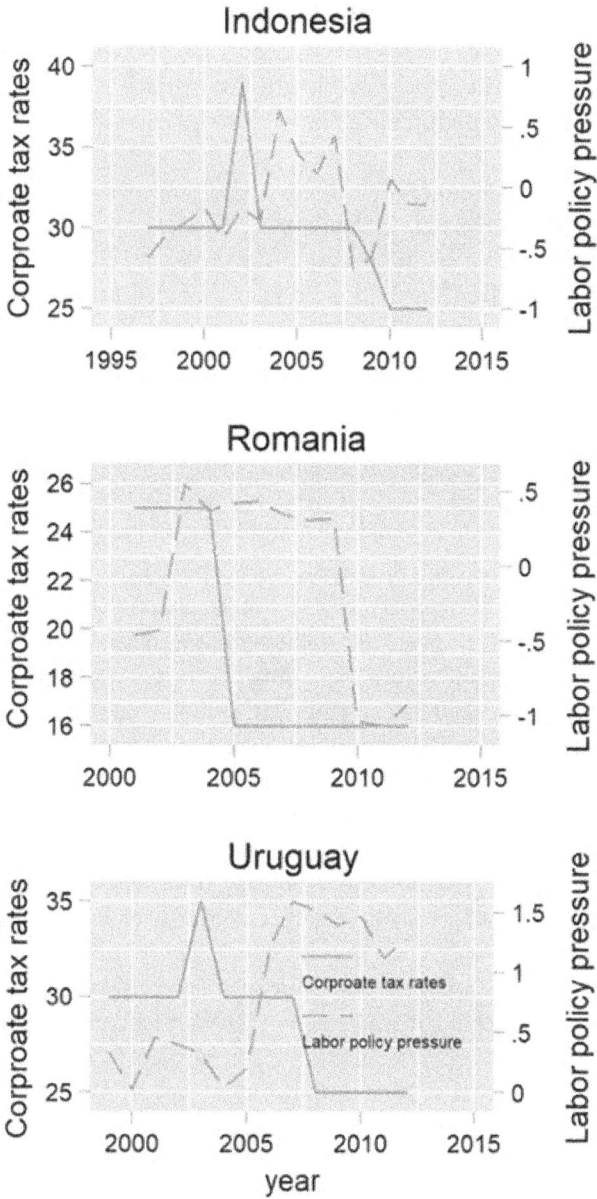

Indonesia

Romania

Uruguay

Figure 4.2c. Corporate Tax Rates and Labor Policy Pressure across Time in Select States. *Source*: Zhiyuan Wang, "Choosing a Lesser Evil: Partisanship, Labor, and Corporate Taxation under Globalization," *Political Research Quarterly* 74 (2021): 571–586.

and labor policy pressure for select countries across time. I then create an interaction term: *leftist government* × *labor policy pressure*, to help capture the conditional effect as proposed in the hypothesis. It is expected to be negative, suggesting high labor policy pressure forces leftist governments to lower corporate tax rates.

I control for a number of confounding factors considered in the existing literature (Basinger & Hallerberg, 2004; Cao, 2010; Genschel et al., 2016; Hays, 2003; Li, 2006; Shin, 2017; Swank, 2002). Using polity scores from Polity IV (Marshall & Jaggers, 2012), I first account for the possible impact of democracy on corporate tax choices, as democracy is believed to have a stronger extractive capacity (Cheibub, 1998) and to provide better public goods (Bueno de Mesquita et al., 2003). I then add a variable, *diffusion*, which is calculated as weighted averages of corporate tax rates based on geographical distance between states, as research finds that corporate tax rates tend to converge among geographically proximate states (Cao, 2010). I also take into account potentially influential economic factors, by including GDP per capita, GDP growth rate, the ratio of FDI inflows over GDP, and the trade share of GDP to tease out the effects of the macroeconomic environment and international integration. The expectations regarding these variables go as follows. When a state is richer on average, it should rely less on taxation. Similarly, higher economic growth should also reduce the incentive to use corporate tax rates to stimulate economy. Greater involvement in international economic transactions is expected to put downward pressure on corporate tax rates because capital seeks destinations where profits can be maximized. Additionally, I employ total labor force as a proxy for aggregate demand for jobs. A larger demand for jobs is expected to lead to lower corporate tax rates, as it is believed that lighter corporation taxation encourages job creation. Data on these variables are taken from the World Development Indicators (WDI) (World Bank, 2016). Finally, following the literature (Shin, 2017), I control for demand for public welfare spending, such as the unemployment rate and the proportion of people older than sixty-five, data on both which are from WDI (World Bank, 2016). It is expected that high unemployment rate and a larger percentage of seniors will force governments to levy higher corporate taxes to fund these welfare expenses. The resulting sample covers as many as 101 countries from 1994 to 2012.[10] All variables are lagged one year to minimize possible reverse causality.

ESTIMATOR

I use the Mundlak Approach (Mundlak, 1978) to adjudicate whether a fixed effects model or random effects model is an appropriate estimator. The Mundlak Approach, a robust estimator of the variance-covariance matrix, is more suitable than the Hausman test given the data structure, since it can deal with errors that are heteroskedastic and serially correlated. The results suggest that time-invariant unobservable factors are correlated with the predictors. Therefore, a fixed effects model fits the data better.[11] I also calculate White-Huber standard errors to tackle serial correlation and heterogeneity issues.

$$
\begin{aligned}
y_{ij,t} = {} & \alpha + \beta \; leftist \; government_{ij,t-1} \\
& + \Psi \; leftist \; government_{ij,t} \times labor \; policy \; pressure_{ij,t-1} \\
& + \Phi \; labor \; policy \; pressure_{ij,t} + \gamma X_{i,j,t-1} + \vartheta_i + \theta_t + \varepsilon_{i,j,t}
\end{aligned}
$$

In the preceding equation, y represents corporate tax rates. X are the control variables. The unobservable county-specific and year-specific factors are ϑ_i and θ_t, respectively. The error term is ε.

FINDINGS

Table 4.1 reports the results. Model 1 considers country fixed effects and Model 2 includes both country and year fixed effects. First, *leftist government* is positive and statistically significant at the 99 percent confidence level across models, indicating that leftist governments in general adopt higher corporate tax rates. Furthermore, consistent with the hypothesis, the interaction term, *leftist government* × *labor policy pressure*, is negative and statistically significant at the 95 percent confidence level, indicating that greater policy pressure from competitors to lower labor rights protection compels leftist governments to reduce corporate tax rates, against its entrenched policy stance in a situation where such pressure is absent. However, it is not immediately clear to what extent *labor policy pressure* constrains leftist governments' policy choice on corporate tax rates, or what the accurate marginal effects of *leftist government* are on the choice of corporate tax rates conditional on *labor policy pressure*. To obtain such information, I utilize graphical visualization.

Table 4.1. Leftist Governments, Labor Policy Pressure, and Corporate Tax Rates

DV = Statutory Corporate Tax Rate	(1)	(2)
Leftist government	1.360***	1.317***
	(0.329)	(0.330)
Leftist government × labor policy pressure	–0.725**	–0.695**
	(0.294)	(0.300)
Labor policy pressure	0.146	0.133
	(0.205)	(0.206)
Regime	–0.025	–0.016
	(0.080)	(0.082)
Diffusion	–0.022	–0.013
	(0.032)	(0.037)
GDP per capita	–0.000***	–0.000
	(0.000)	(0.000)
GDP growth rate	0.108***	0.092*
	(0.042)	(0.049)
FDI (% of GDP)	–0.049***	–0.041**
	(0.016)	(0.017)
Exports (% of GDP)	–0.016	–0.017
	(0.020)	(0.021)
Labor forces (ln)	–13.459***	–8.431**
	(2.723)	(3.660)
Unemployment rate	–0.040	–0.073
	(0.059)	(0.061)
Elderly population (ln)	–1.479***	–0.952***
	(0.206)	(0.214)
Constant	261.349***	177.110***
	(41.588)	(57.760)
Observations	1,142	1,142
R-squared	0.827	0.831
Country FE	yes	yes
Year FE		yes

Robust standard errors in parentheses

***p < 0.01, **p < 0.05, *p < 0.1

Source: Zhiyuan Wang, "Choosing a Lesser Evil: Partisanship, Labor, and Corporate Taxation under Globalization," *Political Research Quarterly* 74 (2012): 571–586.

Figure 4.3 plots the marginal effects. It shows that when the policy pressure builds up, corporate tax rates keep declining under leftist governments. A one-unit increase in labor policy pressure (e.g., from −1 to 0) is associated with a 3 percentage point decrease in corporate tax rates. This is about one third of the standard deviation of the corporate tax rates in the sample, suggestive of a nonnegligible effect. However, this relationship only holds when the policy pressure is lower than 1.2. When policy pressure is greater than 1.2, it no longer constrains leftist governments' policy choice in a statistically significant manner. This implies that when a leftist government is under great pressure to lower labor rights protection, it only partially appeals to the tax policy tool and is likely to use more diverse policy measures to address the challenge. We

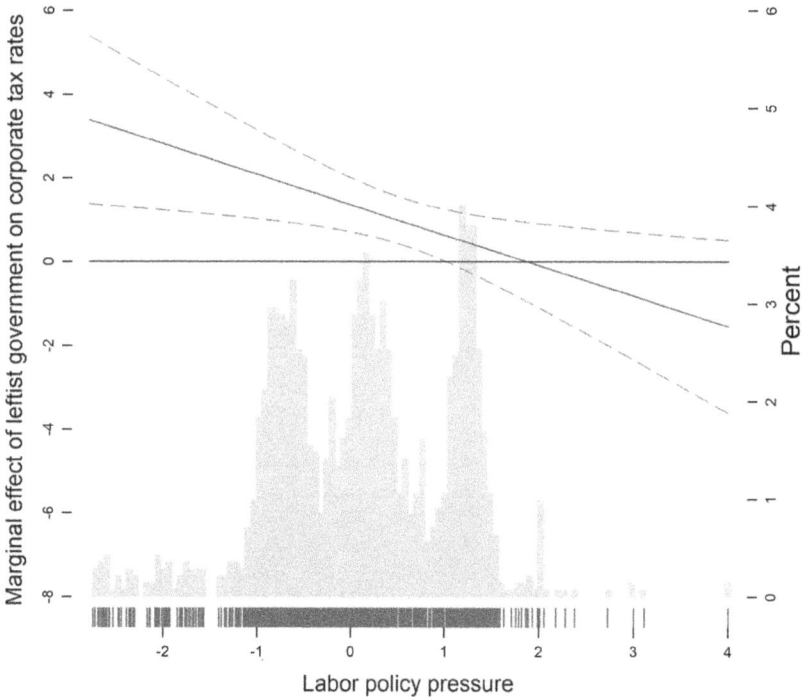

Figure 4.3. How Labor Policy Pressure Affects the Effect of Leftist Government on Corporate Tax Rates. Note: Figure 4.3 is created based on Model 1. *Source:* Zhiyuan Wang, "Choosing a Lesser Evil: Partisanship, Labor, and Corporate Taxation under Globalization," *Political Research Quarterly* 74 (2021): 571–586.

can also see that when the policy pressure is very low (when it is negative), leftist governments are more willing to maintain higher corporate tax rates, again in line with the theoretical expectation. Taken together, it demonstrates that for leftist governments, reducing corporate tax rates and restricting labor rights is mutually substitutable to a large extent.

Figure 4.4 plots leftist and non-leftist governments' choices on corporate tax rates as labor policy pressure increases. It shows that, as expected, higher labor policy pressure mitigates the policy difference in corporate tax rates between leftist and non-leftist governments. In other words, it suggests that increased policy pressure forces the leftist governments to revert to policies closer to those favored by parties on the right.

The results on the controls are in general consistent with those in the literature (Angelopoulos et al., 2009; Hays, 2003; Inclan et al., 2001; Kumar & Quinn, 2012; Osterloh & Debus, 2012; Shin, 2017; Swank & Steinmo, 2002). Regime is positive but achieves no conventional statistical significance, mirroring the mixed findings in the literature

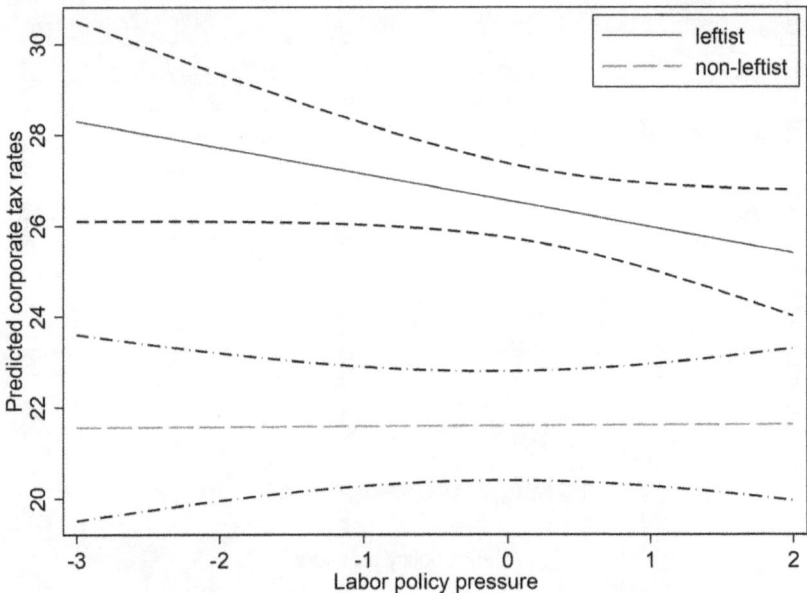

Figure 4.4. Predicted Corporate Tax Rates across Two Partisan Governments. Note: Figure 4.4 is created based on Model 1. The 95 percent confidence intervals are outlined. The original graph appearing in the published article is modified here. *Source*: Zhiyuan Wang, "Choosing a Lesser Evil: Partisanship, Labor, and Corporate Taxation under Globalization," *Political Research Quarterly* 74 (2021): 571–586.

(Jensen, 2013; Li, 2006, 2016). There is a negative correlation between neighbors' tax policy choices and a country's corporate tax rate, indicating that countries seek the first-mover advantage in tax competition with neighbors to gain capital and markets. Higher income (GDP per capita) is negatively associated with higher corporate tax rates, whereas faster GDP growth raises corporate tax rates. Increased reliance on FDI inflows lowers corporate tax rates. Exports are also negatively signed but not statistically significant at conventional confidence levels. Larger labor force drives down corporate tax rates, implying that a higher demand for jobs needs to be met with more investment, which can be achieved by lowering corporate tax rates. Unemployment does not affect corporate taxation, although a larger size of elderly population suppresses corporate tax rates, which seems to suggest that governments use tax policies to deal with an aging society.

Robustness Checks

To ensure that the main results are not induced by idiosyncratic measures, sample sizes, model specifications, or estimator choices, I have conducted multiple robustness checks. First, I utilize an alternative dataset to rerun the analysis. The CBR (Cambridge Business Research) Leximetric Datasets contain a fine-grained dataset on labor regulation laws (LRI) for 117 countries between 1970 and 2013 (Armour et al., 2016). Although the resulting sample is smaller than the main sample due to a narrower overlap between the corporate tax rates data and CBR's LRI, the results remain strongly supportive of the hypothesis. Furthermore, as previously noted, because leftist governments can mean different things in democracies than in non-democracies, I drop non-democratic state years from my sample. The new analysis yields similar results. Similarly, I drop coalitional governments from the sample as it might be the case that leftist parties do not necessarily have control over policies in these governments.[12] Again, the results comport to those in the main analysis. Third, since including a lagged dependent variable (DV) biases the coefficients in fixed effects models (Nickell, 1981), to appropriately address possible temporal dynamics I run a feasible generalized least squares model with a lagged DV. The results are in agreement with the main findings. Fourth, I add to main models extra controls that might also affect policy choices on corporate tax rates, that is, non-tax revenues, which have been shown to discourage governments from adopting growth-fostering economic policies (Bates, 2010; Wright, 2008). I consider two major types of these non-tax revenues: natural resource rents and foreign aid. Data on these two variables are taken from WDI (World Bank, 2016) and the AidData project (Tierney et al., 2011), respectively. The results are similar to the main findings. Fourth, I use an alternative measure of corporate tax rates, effective average corporate tax rates, which are collected by the Oxford University Centre for Business Taxation (2017). Although the resulting sample shrinks greatly, the analysis still supports the two hypotheses. Sixth, I re-perform the analysis with three alternative econometric estimators for panel data: a generalized moments model, random effects model, and pooled OLS with Driscoll and Kraay standard errors. The results are primarily consistent with the main findings.

Finally, I run an analysis on split samples: developed versus developing countries, and large versus small countries, respectively. The results comport with the main findings, only that the hypothesized effects are stronger in developing countries than in developed countries, and stronger in small countries than in large countries (Figure 4.5). They echo the current literature concluding that developing countries have a greater propensity to use tax incentives to attract investment (Garretson & Peeters, 2006; Keen & Simone, 2004; Kumar & Quinn, 2012; Mosley, 2003). In addition, recent research has revealed that small countries are more likely to reduce corporate tax rates, since they are more capital-reliant than large countries for economic development (Genschel et al., 2016). The split-sample results show that this is indeed the case. But more importantly, the split-sample analysis demonstrates that even if these confounding patterns are accounted for, the proposed hypothesis remains intact.

Some Anecdotal Evidence

There is some anecdotal evidence for the causal relationship proposed here. As discussed in the previous chapter, despite the anticipated adverse effects on its economic competitiveness, the Chinese government could not backtrack its promised protection for workers codified in the newly passed Labor Contract Law in 2007, fearing the possible negative impact of doing so on its rule. To resolve this dilemma, the Chinese government has turned to alternative policies. Seeking further trade liberalization through international agreements is one, as demonstrated in chapter

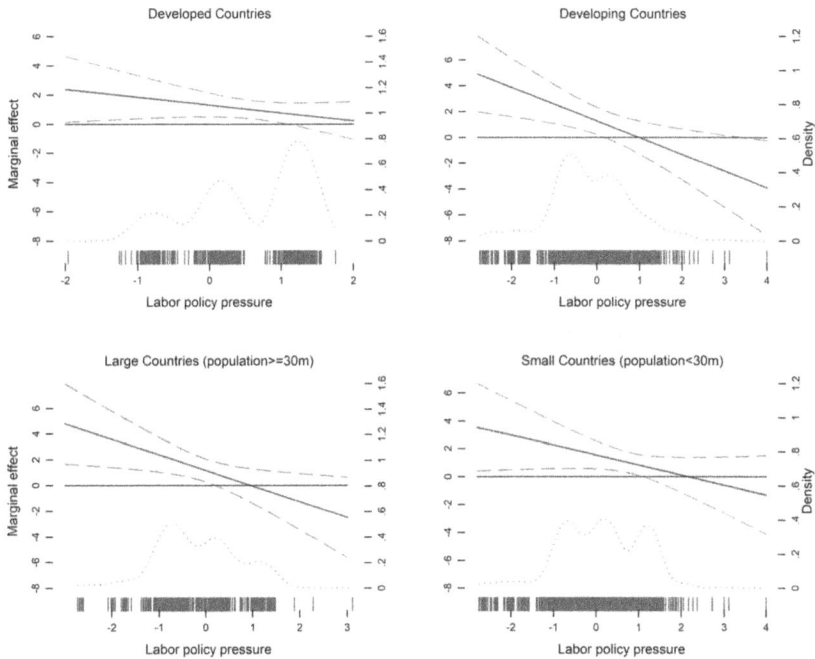

Figure 4.5. How Labor Policy Pressure Affects the Effect of Leftist Government on Corporate Tax Rates: Developed States versus Developing States, and Large States versus Small States. Note: Figure 4.5 is created based on Models 10, 11, 12, and 13 in Table A.8. The 95 percent confidence intervals are depicted. Source: Zhiyuan Wang, "Choosing a Lesser Evil: Partisanship, Labor, and Corporate Taxation under Globalization," Political Research Quarterly 74 (2021): 571–586.

3. Providing tax incentives is another. In 2008, the corporate tax rate decreased from 33 to 25 percent, which was clearly a calculated policy move and designed to maintain China's economic competitiveness. Although this is a significant drop, this new corporate tax rate is still higher than those in states with rightist governments, such as Romania (16%), Russia (24%), Saudi Arabia (20%), and Singapore (18%).

Another example comes again from New Zealand. The 2001 labor law restored the rigidity of the labor market (Rasmussen, 2009), which restricts its economic expansion. However, the country's political climate prevents any new attempt to deregulate the labor market, as occurred in the 1980s. As a result, the Labour Party decided to reduce the corporate tax rate, which dropped from 33 to 30 percent. While this reduction is not modest, this rate is still considerably higher than the rate of 25 percent in 2003, when the party had just defeated its opposition on the right.

Conclusion

Globalization erodes national policy autonomy in various ways. It can explicitly restrict the policy menu and compel policy convergence in the same issue area across states (chapter 2). It can also induce deregulation/liberalization in issue areas in one state that are different than those in its economic peers, just as this chapter and the preceding chapter have shown. In this chapter, I argue that leftist governments use corporate tax incentives as a substitute for engaging in a race to the bottom in labor rights protection. Concretely, I posit that leftist governments choose to reduce corporate tax rates, going against their preferred policy position in an attempt to effectively offset possible economic negativities emanating from their resistance to their economic competitors' strong pressure to lower the legal protection of labor rights, which would directly and seriously hurt their core constituencies (workers). Consequently, substituting lower corporate tax rates for deregulating the labor market leads to intended policy convergence across the states governed by leftist parties.

Although reducing corporate tax rates is also against leftist governments' preferred policy position, this strategy provides substantial economic gains and is less politically costly than outright diminishment in labor protection. Workers benefit from greater economic opportunities induced by lower corporate taxation. In addition, domestic audiences extend more sympathy to governments that are forced to pursue unwelcome policies owing to deepening globalization. Furthermore, leftist governments should meet little political opposition from the right to relaxing corporate tax control.

Taking advantage of novel global panel data on labor rights, I identify the pressure a state faces from its economic competitors to lower the legal protection of labor rights. The econometric analysis provides strong evidence for my argument. I find that leftist governments set higher corporate tax rates, which they cut when confronting the pressure to downgrade labor rights laws. These findings suggest that the race to the bottom prompted by economic globalization is more complicated and subtle than scholars have previously believed: policy convergence can be a result of cross-issue policy substitution rather than within-issue policy conformity. It suggests that when assessing the policy-constraining effects of globalization, we need to carefully distinguish one type of convergence from another, as it can be produced by discrete mechanisms.

This chapter, at a specific level, shows that partisan economic policy literature is not necessarily incompatible with business/investment literature. It proves that identifying the conditions under which leftist governments are able to pursue their preferred policies or the lack of such conditions reconciles these two strands of literature. It also echoes earlier studies on constraints on the effectiveness of partisan macroeconomic policies (Alvarez et al., 1991; Lange & Garrett, 1985). Meanwhile, this chapter, in a more general sense, helps us better understand leftist governments' coping strategies to manage decreased policy autonomy. It suggests that it is not merely that leftist governments adeptly refuse to succumb to the pressure imposed by globalization (Kwon & Pontusson, 2005; Swank, 2002). Rather, the source of resistance in one issue area is rooted in policy compromise in another. For scholars of labor rights and globalization, the findings in this chapter, along with those in the previous chapter, offer plausible explanations for why the race to the bottom is largely absent in labor rights laws (Greenhill et al., 2009; Malesky & Mosley, 2018; Mosley, 2011; Wang, 2018). States turn to feasible alternatives to secure efficiency gains that less labor rights protection is purported to achieve.

Policymaking in an era of deepening globalization has become increasingly complex. Now partisan governments have to maneuver within the confines delimited by both international pressure and their respective policy promises, in addition to other institutional and structural restraints. This chapter suggests that governments act strategically in dealing with challenges posed by globalization, seeking policy tools that are able to deflect international pressure to relinquish autonomous control over the policies that their constituencies value most, although this substitution is still conducive to policy convergence. This policy convergence is, however, fundamentally different from the one that torments many globalization scholars. In the next chapter, I will demonstrate that the convergence induced by domestic policy substitution across the issue areas shown here exists in central bank independence as well.

Diffused Capital Account Openness and Central Bank Independence

In this chapter, I will examine another case of cross–issue area substitution that occurs at the same level of analysis. In this case, governments substitute independent central banks for a more liberalized capital account, which leads to global convergence on the increased autonomy of monetary policy.

To allow free flows of capital and to institute an independent central bank are both desirable in the eyes of investors who seek global economic opportunities. As policy choices, however, these two practices incur different implementation costs. Liberalizing the capital account proves costlier than pursuing central bank independence (CBI), as it will introduce too much uncertainty and volatility. Therefore, when a state's competitors pressure it to relax capital controls, it can grant its central bank a higher degree of independence. As the Mundell-Fleming model predicts, doing so will generate economic advantages that allow the state to compensate for the decision to keep its capital account under tight control (Fleming, 1962; Mundell, 1961).

During the years after World War II, many states—including developed ones such as Germany and Japan—promoted CBI to maintain economic attractiveness, but they refused to liberalize their capital accounts simultaneously (Bernhard, 2002; Cohen, 1996; Goodman & Pauly, 1993). Nonetheless, few extant studies of international political economy pay close attention to the possible causal relationship between a restricted capital account and CBI. Rather, many believe that capital account openness accompanies CBI. This belief overlooks the sequence in which these two policies are implemented (Gupta, 2007; Quinn & Inclan, 1997). Contrary to what many scholars have suggested, they are not adopted side by side.

Echoing the findings in Tayssir and Feryel's (2018) research, this chapter uses statistical analysis and a case study to demonstrate that states employ CBI to substitute for costly financial liberalization. Such substitution results in interstate policy convergence on CBI.[1] The strategic substitution-induced convergence perspective expands existing literature on CBI (Bodea & Hicks, 2015a; Fernández-Albertos, 2015; Polillo & Guillén, 2005). Moreover, the investigation conducted in this chapter suggests that states enact these liberal policies sequentially—that is to say, they grant CBI first and then liberalize their capital accounts at a later point of time. It thus enriches academic understandings of how CBI diffusion connects to financial liberalization.

I first review the literature on the politics of CBI. I then discuss the costliness of liberalizing capital account. Afterward, I theorize why CBI and capital account openness attract foreign capital with equal efficiency. This is followed by a section that explains research design by detailing the data and estimation strategy. The results are discussed and their robustness is checked subsequently. Further, I illustrate the theoretical argument through examining the historical process of how the Philippines had pursued CBI. Finally, I conclude the chapter by summarizing the argument and findings.

Why CBI? Existing Studies

The current literature on CBI either analyzes domestic political factors and exchange rate systems or it focuses on international causes (Fernández-Albertos, 2015). Goodman (1991) argues that economic conservatives form coalitions to demand independent central banks. Politicians prove willing to relegate control over their countries' central banks because they have low expectations that their parties will hold power for a sufficiently long time. To preserve independence, however, central bankers must satisfy the demands of their supporting coalitions whenever the economic situation compels them to do so. Goodman finds support for these arguments by examining the cases of Germany, Italy, and France. Bernhard (1998, 2002) emphasizes political fragmentation to explain CBI. When cabinet ministers, legislators, and coalition parties exhibit divergent preferences over monetary policy, and when political support from legislators and coalition parties might be withdrawn at any time, governments are more likely to use CBI as a strategy to manage policy differences while maintaining political cohesion. Bernhard's statistical analysis of central banks in 18 industrial countries from 1970 to 1990 corroborates this theoretical conjecture.

Lohmann (1998) contends that federalism increases the costs of restraining a central bank's behavioral independence; this is because control over bank staffers is decentralized through staggered elections that occur across subnational entities and because the upper chamber, which is comprised of subnational representatives, is unlikely to move in concert with a federal government that wants to tighten control over the central bank for short-term political gains. Hallerberg (2003) further develops this argument by introducing a veto player framework. He posits that the number of veto players positively correlates with the adoption of monetary institutions that celebrate independence, as a great number of veto players increase the difficulty of claiming credit for macroeconomic policies. Expectedly, the delegation of monetary policies to politically dependent central banks tends to occur in places where multiparty or federalist governments exist.

Scholars have also explored the relationship between partisanship and CBI. Although CBI may limit the ability of leftist parties to pursue their policy goals (Bodea & Higashijima, 2015; Franzese, 1999; Way, 2000), it does not necessarily mean that leftist parties always prefer dependent central banks or their rightist counterparts will invariably prefer CBI. Leftist parties can strategically delegate monetary policy to central banks in order to enforce party cohesiveness. By delegating the power to make decisions about contentious issues to a third party, governments can focus on enhancing their effectiveness in other policy areas. Dellepiane-Avellaneda (2012) shows that this political calculation motivated the Labour government of Prime Minister Brown to grant independence to the Bank of England in 1998. Using a formal model, Burkovskaya (2019) demonstrates that CBI helps opposition parties win elections when a country's level of corruption is high. CBI is preserved because incumbents fear losing office if independence is rescinded. In other words, what matters most in sustaining CBI is not partisan ideology, but the struggle for political power. To answer the question of why the Conservative governments of Margaret Thatcher and John Major refused to accord the Bank of England more autonomy, Buller and

Whisker (2020) posit that these governments did not fully trust that the bank had the power to implement their desired monetary policies. They hoped to hold such power in their own hands. Hungin and James (2019), who focus on the Bank of England after the Great Recession, argue that the bank exploited the motivation of two major parties in order to avoid blame for the 2007 financial crisis and to maximize its own power. The bank did so through a two-pronged strategy: it sought a greater policy space while pursuing further delegation to minimize the possibility that it would damage its reputation in the potentially trying times of the future.

The second strand of literature turns to international factors to seek explanations for CBI reforms. Adopting the perspective of policy diffusion, Polillo and Guillén (2005) argue that learning and competition via the economic networks formed by global economic flows contribute to the cross-boundary spread of CBI. Similarly, Bodea and Hicks, who analyze a sample of 78 countries from 1974 to 2007, demonstrate that international capital flows work to channel the competition for and learning of CBI (2015a). By examining a dataset of 124 countries during the period 1998–2012, Reinsberg et al. (2020) find that the IMF also engages in promoting CBI through its loan conditionality. This is particularly true among countries where political power is more unchecked, public debt is more heavily monetized, and central banks are more politically dependent. De Haan and Eijffinger (2016) note that, despite the paradigmatic change that the Great Recession caused to central banks' policy approaches, CBI has been successfully maintained around the globe.

The third strand of literature revolves around the relationship between CBI and exchange rate systems.[2] It relies on policy interrelationality to understand the dynamics of CBI. This type of work constitutes the "second generation" of research on the determinants of monetary institutions (Bernhard et al., 2002). Broz (2003) advances an argument that monetary commitments are substitutive. The decision to utilize which commitment device depends on the macro-political environment. When a political regime encourages transparency about its policies, then the government will adopt an opaque monetary commitment—that is to say, it will pursue CBI—because political oppositions and private actors can easily detect and punish the government's interference with the central bank's independence. On the contrary, when a regime lacks policy transparency, then a government under it will make a highly visible monetary commitment—that is, it will opt for a fixed exchange rate system, which does not rely on political checks and balances.

In contrast to Broz, Bodea (2010, 2014) posits a complementary relationship between CBI and the fixed exchange rate regime. Puzzled by the fact that a substitutive relationship fails to explain why some countries adopt both monetary commitments, she contends that this kind of joint adoption occurs because neither commitment is deployed in a way that allows for an unambiguous assessment of its operations or effects. Making both commitments is a mutually reinforcing practice in places where one of them is weak and opaque.

There is no doubt that existing scholarship has significantly improved our understandings of how CBI is possible and how it varies across time and countries. It, however, overlooks an important relationship between globalization and CBI, that is, CBI as a practical policy tool substituting for costly policy alterations that globalization pressures states to adopt—the removal of capital controls. In the following section, I will discuss the costliness of liberalizing the capital account, a policy change that deepens globalization, but entails greater political risks than CBI.

Issues with Capital Account Openness

Capital account openness, or convertibility, refers to the removal of governmental restrictions on capital flows. Like the liberalization of trade (Eichengreen, 2001), liberalization of the capital account is believed to be welfare-improving (Obstfeld, 1994). Studies have shown that capital account openness is associated with low inflation rates (Gruben & McLeod, 2002), more FDI (Bartolini & Drazen, 1997; Sekkat & Veganzones-Varoudakis, 2007), faster economic growth (Henry, 2006; Quinn & Toyoda, 2008), and a lower likelihood of currency crisis (Glick et al., 2006). However, the findings in favor of capital liberalization are not conclusive. Far from that, the evidence against it is almost as strong (Eichengreen, 2001; Rodrik & Subramanian, 2009).

Other studies reveal that liberalizing the capital account only produces the expected gains if various conditions are satisfied. For example, Noy and Vu (2007) show that, among states with an open capital account, only those with lower levels of corruption and political risk attract FDI. In addition, Klein and Olivei (2008) find that the growth effect that follows capital account openness is primarily driven by developed countries; the effect disappears in developing countries. Similarly, Edwards (2001) demonstrates that, among emerging economies, capital account liberalization only promotes economic growth at a certain level of economic development. Arteta et al. (2001) conclude that states wishing to reap the growth benefits of financial liberalization must eliminate major macroeconomic imbalances prior to the policy change. Bussière and Fratzscher's (2008) research uncovers that financial liberalization only benefits growth in the short run. In the long run, economic growth depends more on factors like domestic institutions, the size of FDI inflows, and the sequencing of liberalization.

Therefore, it is impossible to confidently conclude that the benefits of financial liberalization outweigh its costs. For developing countries, liberalizing the capital account can be particularly risky, because it will cost macroeconomic stability. As Brooks (2004) has aptly explained:

> Because capital account openness directly transmits international shocks into domestic economies, countries with less fully developed financial sectors become vulnerable to the risk of massive capital outflows. To the extent that changes in international interest rates make investment abroad more attractive or that a decline in export revenue reduces the capacity for domestic borrowers to service debts, the risk of massive capital outflows increases. . . . For these nations, financial openness presents significant risks of disruptions in domestic production, consumption, and borrowing costs—and thus the credible threat of capital flight. (pp. 400–401)

In addition, sudden and heavy inflows of capital that likely follow the financial liberalization prove to be as dangerous as capital outflows. When governments are unable to sterilize them, they can increase inflationary pressure, cause currency appreciation, and undercut export competitiveness (Brooks, 2004).

According to Rodrik and Subramanian (2009), financial liberalization is essentially problematic because it is a solution to economic growth that does not attend to specific national conditions. Financial liberalization uniformly assumes that capital shortage is the primary reason why poor countries remain poor. In practice, however, this is often untrue. Rodrik and Subramanian show that the lack of demand for investment is the very reason why many countries fail to experience rapid economic growth even after liberalizing their capital accounts. When there is insufficient demand for investment in a country, the decision to allow free flows of capital will cause currency appreciation. This appreciation further hurts tradable sectors that are already experiencing limited profitability.

Because financial liberalization imposes heavy costs, it is reasonable to expect that capital mobility carries substantial distributional implications. Examining the data of 173 countries from 1960 to 2010, Furceri and Loungani (2018) obtain strong evidence for the argument that income inequality is exacerbated by opening capital markets: "The Gini index increases by about 0.8 percent in the very short term—1 year after the occurrence of the reform episode—and by about 1.4 percent in the medium term—5 years after the occurrence of the reform episode" (p. 130). They also find that the labor share of income falls in the wake of liberalization of the capital account: "Reforms have typically decreased the labor share of income by about 0.6 percentage point in the short term—1 year after the reform—and by about 0.8 percentage point in the medium term—5 years after the reform" (p. 139).

Overall, free capital flows fail to generate the benefits that they promise. Instead, they add new financial risks to the banking industry and to the society at large in the developing world. Governments are therefore cautious to promote such reforms. However, it does not suggest no governments should liberalize capital accounts. As a matter of fact, governments can do it only when they are competent to manage all the ensuing risks. As we already see, some developing states that have done so before they acquire such financial management competence ultimately reap more economic suffering than fruits. Nevertheless, as capital account openness promotes globalization by facilitating monetary flows, in the short run, financial liberalization initiated in a number of states will place pressure on their economic competitors to pursue similar policies. Being aware of the risks associated with this policy change, states under such pressure must seek alternative policies. Granting central banks political independence is one feasible option, to which I will now turn.

CBI, Credibility, and Foreign Capital Inflows

Many factors affect flows of capital (Blonigen & Piger, 2014; Li & Resnick, 2003; Schneider & Frey, 1985). General macroeconomic health is one of them. Central banks play a big role in maintaining a healthy macroeconomic environment, especially in terms of price stability. In order to control inflation effectively, states often delegate authority over monetary policy to an independent central bank. In principle, this bank can suppress inflation thanks to its ability to mitigate the time inconsistency problem in monetary policy (Barro & Gordon, 1983; Kydland & Prescott, 1977). The time inconsistency problem emerges when governments use expansionary policies to stimulate economic growth. This makes government promises to maintain price stability less credible. Independent central bankers, however, are more mission oriented than politicians, and they are much less vulnerable to political vagaries (Rogoff, 1985). By taking an important policy power away from conflicting political processes, independent central banks depoliticize monetary policy and lend it more predictability (Bernhard, 1998). Therefore, CBI is likely to induce among potential investors a more stable expectation of host states' economic performance.

Furthermore, in countries with political freedoms and the rule of law, independent central banks discourage the use of expansionary fiscal policies "through interest rate hikes and by refusing to lend to the government" (Bodea, 2013; Bodea & Higashijima, 2015, p. 48). In doing so, they lower the expectation of inflation.[3] A central bank's ability to independently set interest rates and to determine the quantity of the government securities that are bought and sold on secondary markets likewise lowers the expectation of inflation; in turn, this ensures a more robust monetary demand, and leads to stable prices (Bodea, 2014; Bodea & Hicks, 2015b). Additionally, credible displays of CBI ameliorate public concerns over price instability and thus make it possible to maintain stability in nominal wages without placing intensive demands on the monetary supply (Bernanke, 2010).

Therefore, inflation should generally be lower in countries with independent central banks. Empirical studies have found that independent central banks are successful at suppressing inflation in developed countries and in countries with a well-developed rule of law (Alesina & Summers, 1993; Bodea & Hicks, 2015b; Crowe & Meade, 2008; Cukierman et al., 2002; Franzese, 1999; Keefer & Stasavage, 2003). Expectedly, the capital market should view CBI as a strong signal of government's macroeconomic commitment. Indeed, Bodea and Hicks (2018) find that CBI is positively correlated with the ratings generated by leading credit-rating agencies.

Independent central banks have also become more transparent over the past three decades (Dincer & Eichengreen, 2009). Transparency means that central banks share more information about how they make monetary policy decisions. This process involves publicizing the formal objectives of monetary policy and the data and models used to make economic forecasts; it also entails disclosing policymaking rules and voting records, explanations, possible operational errors, and unanticipated influential macroeconomic disturbances (Eijffinger & Geraats, 2006). Transparency is important because it creates a public image that central banks as nonelectoral institutions are accountable to general constituencies. Transparency also sustains market stability; strengthens the flexibility, credibility, and predictability of policies; and contributes to stable expectations of markets (Dincer & Eichengreen, 2014).

In particular, "releasing forecasts of future rates, along with forecasts of future economic conditions to make those future-rate forecasts credible," enables "the central bank to influence long-term rates and associated private-sector decisions" (Dincer & Eichengreen, 2014, p. 120). This is important because fixed investment is heavily influenced by long-term interest rates, which result from a series of expected short-term interest rates in the future. Providing such information boosts the market's confidence in the ability and the willingness of central banks to adhere to their policy announcements. This is especially the case when banks have been faithful policymakers that have demonstrated to the public that they will stay within the constraints that they delimited for themselves. Enhanced predictability contributes to price stability and low inflation rates (van der Cruijsen & Demertzis, 2007).

Because transparency reduces the costs of monitoring whether central banks make policies prudentially and implement them faithfully, it increases the visibility of a central bank's performance in the same way that the fixed exchange rate system makes it easier to verify a government's adherence to its monetary commitments (Broz, 2003). Finally, "transparency has the potential to clarify who is the principal of the central bank and, in this sense, reduces the potential for corruption and undue influence from interest groups" (Bodea & Hicks, 2018, p. 347). Overall, transparency reinforces CBI.

Additionally, the fact that independent central banks possess the power to deny "the incumbent the opportunistic use of monetary policy" (Bodea & Hicks, 2015b, p. 41) makes these banks de facto veto players. An increase in the number of veto players multiplies checks on the policymaking power of other government agencies and thereby enhances policy stability (Tsebelis, 2002). It is in this sense that independent central banks facilitate the protection of investors' rights (Bodea & Hicks, 2018). Such protection undoubtedly attracts investors (Li & Resnick, 2003; Staats & Biglaiser, 2012). Empirical research shows that CBI does indeed promote private investment (Pastor & Maxfield, 1999). Historically, the British monarchy increased its fiscal power by chartering the Bank of England to independently manage monetary policy (North & Weingast, 1989). Giordano and Tommasino (2011) confirm that independent central banks reduce the likelihood that sovereign states will default on their debts.

Last but not least, CBI attracts capital because independent central banks do not dogmatically pursue monetary policy goals. A central bank's independence implies that the bank can exercise a substantial degree of policy flexibility whenever a need arises. In economically challenging times, "rather than apply very stringent monetary constraints, the monetary board allowed the currency to depreciate"; this contributes to economic stability by allowing output to recover via controlled inflation (Paderanga, 2013, p. 4). Moreover, independent central banks are less likely to deter expansionary fiscal policy when the economy is in trouble (Bodea & Higashijima, 2015). By easing emergency spending, central banks come to preserve the market's confidence and to discourage panicked capital flights. Investors will find consolation in such a move.

CBI's ability to attract capital without liberalizing the capital account is consistent with the precepts of the Mundell-Fleming model (Fleming, 1962; Mundell, 1961). According to this famous and influential model, states cannot have fully liberalized capital accounts without losing the autonomy of their monetary policies under the fixed exchange rate system (Obstfeld et al., 2005). Considering the fixed exchange rate regime stabilizes prices and mitigates uncertainty, it is more likely to be installed and maintained when states seek to expand trade and acquire advantageous positions in the world market (Ernesto López-Córdova & Meissner, 2003; Klein & Shambaugh, 2006). Also, because unrestricted financial openness can be economically and politically costly and because an autonomous monetary policy is desirable as well as economically and politically beneficial, as shown above, states have stronger incentives to maintain capital control while granting more independence to their central banks when their economies compete to take off and win more shares in the global economic arena under the aegis of fixed exchange rate systems.

The preceding theoretical discussion by no means suggests that only liberalizing the capital account incurs costs whereas enacting CBI is costless. Rather, these costs are higher than when a state can use an independent central bank to achieve the same economic purposes.

Therefore, we have the following hypothesis:

Facing the pressure to increase capital account openness, instead of pursuing such costly policy change, a state will grant more independence to its central bank, all other things being equal.

Research Design

DATA

The dependent variable is central bank independence reform: whether a developing nation experiences increase in CBI. It is a binary variable with 1 indicating observed increase in CBI and 0 otherwise. I take data on this variable from Garriga (2016). Garriga's dataset covers 182 countries for the period 1970–2012 (details are given later). Due to the wide spatial and temporal coverages, it has been used in an increasing number of recent prominent studies (i.e., Ballard-Rosa et al., 2019; Bodea & Hicks, 2015a; Henisz & Mansfield, 2019). I focus on the developing world because many developed countries already completed CBI reforms before the 1970s, which fall outside of the time frame of the dataset. The statistical distribution indeed reflects this historical trend. In the dataset, there are a total of 39 CBI reforms implemented in developed countries compared to 241 such reforms in their developing counterparts. Therefore, including developed countries in the analysis will put a downward bias on the magnitude of the proposed causal relationship.

Garriga (2016) codes detailed information on central banks, which comes from "over 840 documents—constitutions, laws, amendments, and decrees that directly refer to central banks, and central bank charters" (p. 853). Using online sources, she collects the relevant legislations that are available in English, Spanish, French, Portuguese, or Italian to ensure the comprehensiveness and thoroughness of the data (p. 853). Following the coding rules employed in Cukierman (1992) and Cukierman et al. (1992), Garriga codes each legislation on "16 dimensions related to four components of CBI, on a country-year basis: CEO's characteristics (appointment, dismissal, and term of office of the chief executive officer of the bank); policy formulation attributions (who formulates and has the final decision in monetary policy and the role of the central bank in the budget process); the central bank's objectives; and the central bank's limitations on lending to the public sector." Values for all 16 dimensions are then "combined into a single weighted index, ranging from 0 (lowest) to 1 (highest) CBI" (p. 854).

Garriga is careful to distinguish the partial amendments that affect any of these 16 dimensions of CBI and those that are not. Missing values are assigned when legislations are not available. But when she discovers mentions of reform in documents made publicly available by a central bank, she will include such information despite the fact the official laws are not located. She also includes "additional variables: central bank creation, a central bank reform that affects CBI in a given year, its direction (CBI increase or decrease), and whether the central bank is a regional entity." The data set finally has 6,786 observations and identifies 392 CBI reforms (p. 854), among which 294 increase CBI, 60 decrease CBI, and the direction of the remaining cases cannot be clearly identified. Figure 5.1 displays CBI reforms across the developing world from 1970 to 2012.

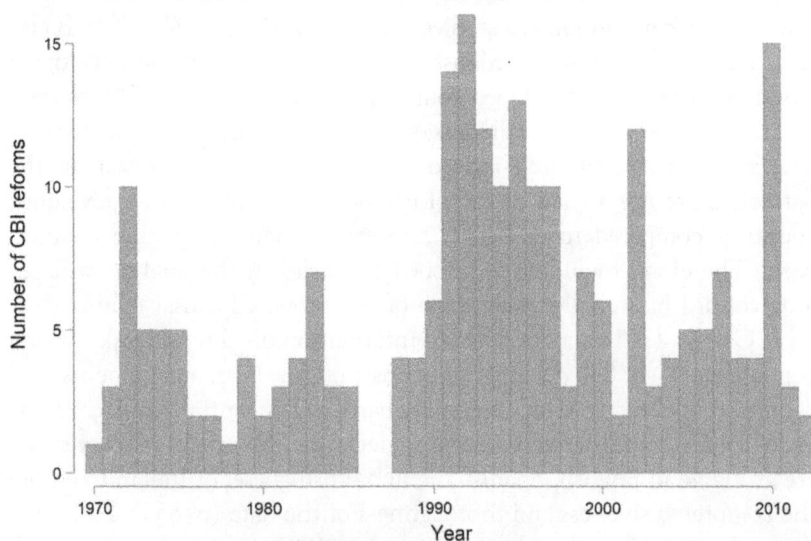

Figure 5.1. CBI Reforms across the Developing World: 1970–2012. *Source:* Author-created image.

The key independent variable is the difference between the level of capital openness of a state and the average level of capital openness of its neighbors in a given year. By constructing it this way, I hope to capture the pressure exerted by neighboring states on a state at issue in terms of liberalizing capital accounts. I use the Chinn-Ito index to measure capital openness, which was initially introduced in Chinn and Ito (2006). This index is created using "the information from the IMF's Annual Report on Exchange Arrangements and Exchange Restrictions (AREAER)" (Chinn & Ito, 2008). It is most comprehensive "for the time period of 1970–2018 for 182 countries" (p. 311). Up until 1996, they code four categories of restrictions on capital account: the presence of multiple exchange rates, restrictions on current account transactions, restrictions on capital account transactions, and the requirement of the surrender of export proceeds (Chinn & Ito, 2008, p. 311). However, in 1996 the IMF changed the classification method in the AREAER and further expanded the four categories, which better captured the "complexity of capital control policies." Their coding since 1997 therefore reflects this new categorization approach (Chinn & Ito, 2008, p. 311). The index ranges from −1.92 to 2.33 with larger values representing a higher level of openness.

I then calculate the annual average of capital account openness for a region (excluding the state at issue). To capture the policy pressure from competing neighbors to liberalize capital accounts, I take the difference between the average regional capital account openness and a state's level of financial openness in the same year such that a greater value denotes higher pressure from neighbors on a state to liberalize its capital account. The resulting variable spans from −3.7 to 3.48. Figure 5.2 plots the distribution of policy pressure to liberalize the capital account across the developing world. In Figure 5.3 using a bar graph I show how CBI reforms correlate with the policy pressure at issue here.

I take into consideration a battery of variables that have been used in the literature (Bernhard, 1998; Bodea & Hicks, 2015a; Polillo & Guillén, 2005). First, I consider the impact of political regimes. Current research demonstrates that a higher level of democracy promotes economic liberalization (Milner & Mukherjee, 2009). It is expected that democracy will be positively correlated with CBI. Data on political regimes are taken from the Polity IV project (Marshall & Jaggers, 2012). Second, I take into account the effect of GDP. More economically

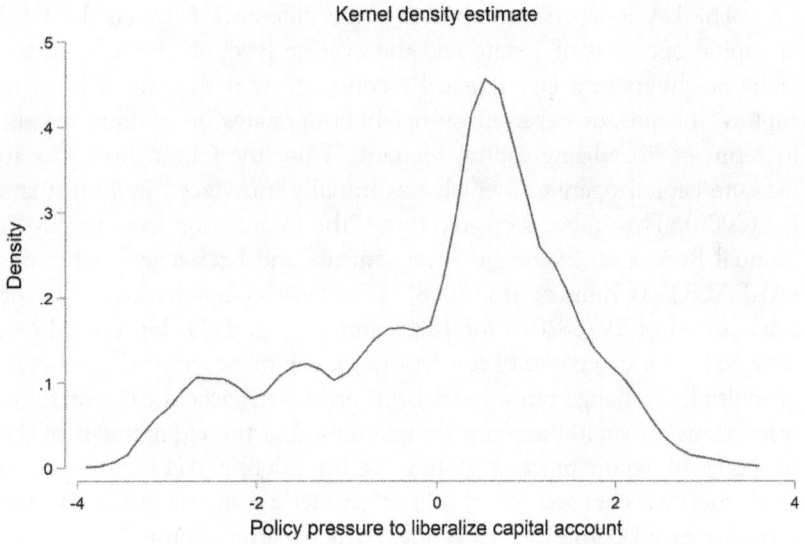

Figure 5.2. The Distribution of Policy Pressure to Liberalize Capital Account across the Developing World. *Source*: Author-created image.

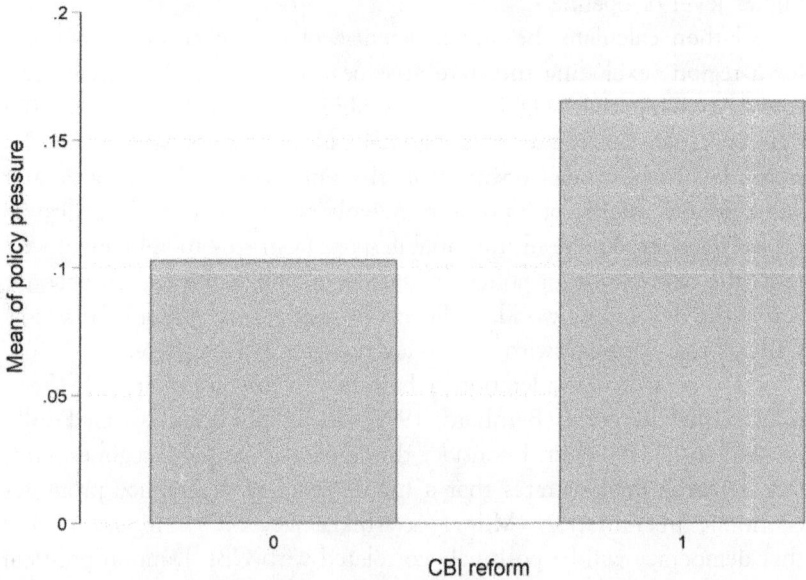

Figure 5.3. Policy Pressure by CBI Reform across the Developing World. *Source*: Author-created image.

advanced countries, especially those in the developing world, are more likely to attract more FDI and thus have stronger incentives to use CBI to maintain their attractiveness. Economically backward countries have very low dependence on FDI, and understandably, have little motivation to change domestic monetary institutions for the purpose of increasing FDI. Therefore, larger GDP should contribute to greater CBI. Third, I control for economic growth. Economic growth should work in a way opposite to that of GDP. If a state has experienced fast economic growth without high CBI, there is no reason for it to reform its central bank to attract foreign capital, as strong economic performance will constitute valid justification for investment decisions. Fourth, I isolate the impacts of inflows and outflows of FDI, respectively. Larger FDI inflows incentivize states to sustain credible monetary commitments through central bank reforms, whereas greater outflows dampen the enthusiasm for such reforms. Fifth, I include trade openness. When an economy is highly reliant on trade, the stability of price is of immense importance to the stability of trade. As a result, a state trading more with others will see it in its interest to reform the central bank. Finally, I add exchange rates (US dollars as base) into the right-hand side of the equation. When home currency is more expensive than the US dollar, it implies that a state may not care about economic flows as much as those with cheaper home currencies. Hence, it barely has any interest in improving CBI to encourage these flows. All economic variables are obtained from the World Development Indicators (World Bank, 2016) with the exception of exchange rates, which are from the Penn World Table 9.1 (Feenstra et al., 2015).

ESTIMATION STRATEGY

The estimation strategy is straightforward. Since the dependent variable is binary, I use the probit model. I cluster standard errors by country to deal with the temporal dependence among them. All independent variables are lagged one year to mitigate the possible endogeneity issue. Finally, to remove time dependence, I control for years since last reform and time splines (Beck et al., 1998). The following expression is the equation I estimate.

$$\Pr (\text{CBI } reform_{it} = 1) = \Phi(\alpha + \beta \text{ policy pressure}_{it-1} + \gamma \text{ controls}_{it-1})$$

Findings

Table 5.1 reports the results. The key independent variable, policy pressure to liberalize capital account, is positive and statistically significant at the 99 percent confidence level, strongly supporting the hypothesis. Based on the results, I then calculate the marginal effect on the probability of CBI reform, which is plotted in Figure 5.4. As it shows, for every one unit of increase in the policy pressure to open the capital account, the probability of CBI reform will increase by almost 0.01. This increase is substantial as it is equivalent to nearly 59 percent of one standard deviation of the overall probabilities of CBI reform.

Table 5.1. Policy Pressure to Liberalize Capital Account and CBI Reform

DV = CBI reform	(1)
Policy pressure	0.105***
	(0.035)
Level of democracy	0.014**
	(0.007)
GDP	0.002
	(0.041)
Economic growth	−0.003
	(0.007)
FDI inflows	0.005
	(0.007)
FDI outflows	−0.012**
	(0.005)
Trade	0.001
	(0.001)
Exchange rate	−0.000
	(0.000)
Constant	−1.910***
	(0.292)
Observations	2,460
Number of countries	114
Log-likelihood	−391.4
χ^2	22.81

Robust standard errors in parentheses

***p < 0.01, **p < 0.05, *p < 0.1

Source: Author-created image.

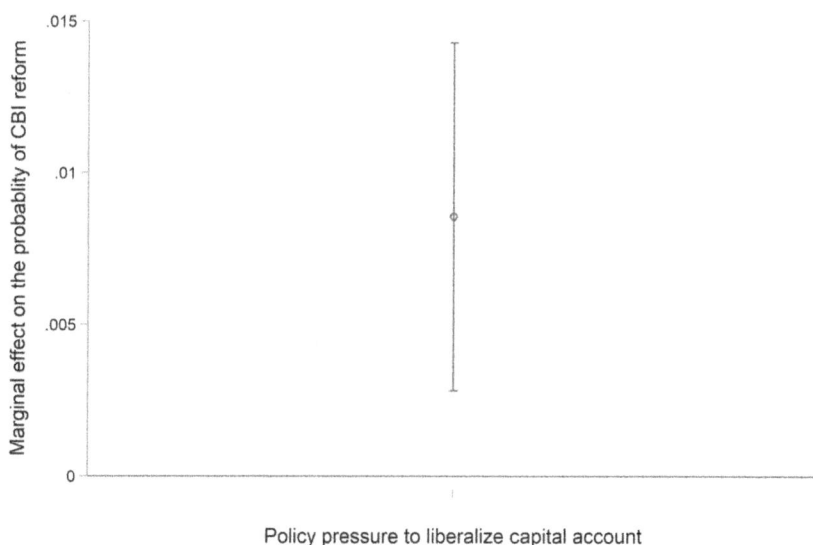

Figure 5.4. The Marginal Effect of Policy Pressure on the Likelihood of CBI Reform. *Source*: Author-created image.

More democratic regimes are more likely to adopt CBI, consistent with Broz (2003). Neither GDP nor economic growth affects much the likelihood of reforming central banks, in line with what Bodea and Hicks (2015a) find. FDI inflows assume a positive sign but achieve no statistical significance at the conventional levels, which is puzzling. But two things may explain why this might be the case. First, the data quality on FDI inflows is not high. Accurate and reliable statistics are universally lacking. This issue is especially severe for developing countries. Second, heterogeneity in FDI entry mode may dilute the effect of FDI on the adoption of CBI. FDI-thirsty states may use other policy means to compensate for their weak institutions including the absence of CBI, such as joint ventures (Betz & Pond, 2019; Lee et al., 2014a). However, greater FDI outflows impede the tendency of CBI reforms. Greater trade dependence is also positively signed but not statistically significant, partly consistent with Bernhard (1998). Both findings echo those made by Polillo and Guillén (2005). The appreciation of home currencies against the US dollar plays no role in inducing CBI reforms.

Employing the results reported in Table 5.1, Figure 5.5 plots the out-of-sample prediction of probabilities of CBI reforms as policy pressure to liberalize the capital account increases, while holding all other independent variables at their means. Again, this visualization provides clear evidence to the hypothesis: when a state faces increasing pressure to remove capital control, it will be prone to adopting CBI reform instead.

Furthermore, I split the sample into democracies and non-democracies and rerun the main model on these two sub-samples respectively. The results are reported in Table 5.2. It is easy to see that the findings from the main analysis are driven by the strategic considerations in non-democracies but less so in democracies. This finding qualifies Broz's (2003) argument that non-democracies have a penchant for the fixed exchange rate system as it provides more visible monetary policy commitment. Non-democracies will also pursue CBI reforms when the condition is right, which is when they are pressured to liberalize the capital account. Compared to CBI, liberalized financial flows will cause higher risks to autocratic governments. Free flows of capital weaken the economic advantages enjoyed by economic elites under the protection of the closed capital account. These elites constitute a large part of the winning coalition that sustains autocratic governments. They will reduce their political support if they find autocratic governments betray them. Therefore, to seek political survival, autocracies have lesser incentives to liberalize the capital account, which may significantly shorten their rule.

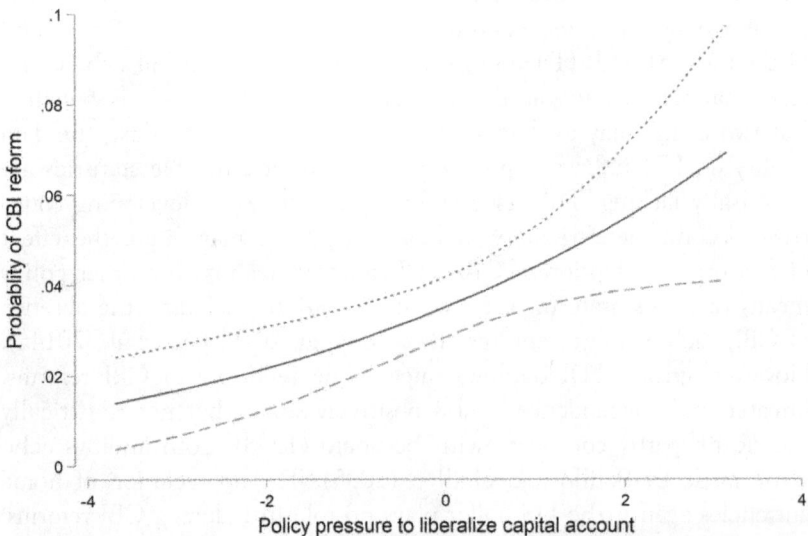

Figure 5.5. Probabilities of CBI Reform as Policy Pressure Varies. *Source:* Author-created image.

Table 5.2. Policy Pressure to Liberalize Capital Account and
CBI Reform by Political Regime

DV = CBI reform	(1) Democracies	(2) Non-democracies
Policy pressure	0.036	0.174***
	(0.042)	(0.054)
Level of emocracy	–0.005	0.010
	(0.030)	(0.013)
GDP	–0.012	0.008
	(0.052)	(0.069)
Economic growth	–0.023	0.001
	(0.016)	(0.006)
FDI inflows	–0.006	0.004
	(0.014)	(0.008)
FDI outflows	–0.003	–0.012**
	(0.008)	(0.005)
Trade	0.001	0.002
	(0.002)	(0.001)
Exchange rate	–0.000	–0.000
	(0.000)	(0.000)
Constant	–1.478***	–2.091***
	(0.412)	(0.465)
Observations	1,128	1,332
Number of countries	71	86
Log-likelihood	–205.9	–182.4
χ^2	3.962	19.21

Robust standard errors in parentheses

***p < 0.01, **p < 0.05, *p < 0.1

Source: Author-created image.

The relatively high independence enjoyed by the central bank in China
while keeping capital flows under tight control demonstrates this logic.

Robustness Checks

To ensure the corroborating findings are not artificial results of specific
model specifications or estimator choices, I conduct a series of robustness
checks. First, I add the average CBI in a region. The resulting findings are
entirely consistent with those obtained from the main analysis (Table 5.3).

Table 5.3. Policy Pressure to Liberalize Capital Account and CBI Reform: Extra Controls

DV = CBI reform	(1) Regional diffusion	(2) Public financial and macroeconomic condition
Policy pressure	0.106***	0.075*
	(0.036)	(0.043)
Level of democracy	0.015*	0.007
	(0.008)	(0.009)
GDP	0.034	–0.031
	(0.040)	(0.058)
Economic growth	–0.009	–0.030**
	(0.009)	(0.014)
FDI inflows	0.006	0.005
	(0.006)	(0.007)
FDI outflows	0.001	0.005
	(0.005)	(0.006)
Trade	0.001	0.002
	(0.001)	(0.001)
Exchange rate	–0.000	–0.000
	(0.000)	(0.000)
Government debt (% of GDP)		–0.002*
		(0.001)
Government revenue		–0.002
		(0.006)
Inflation		–0.001
		(0.001)
Regional diffusion of CBI	0.367	
	(0.250)	
Constant	–2.361***	–1.426***
	(0.304)	(0.393)
Observations	2,256	1,404
Number of countries	112	109
Log-likelihood	–318.4	–226.9
χ^2	24.33	11.32

Robust standard errors in parentheses

***$p < 0.01$, **$p < 0.05$, *$p < 0.1$

Source: Author-created image.

The policy pressure remains positive and highly statistically significant. Higher levels of democracy are associated with greater CBI. Large FDI outflows prevent governments from pursuing CBI. Other variables exert no significant impact on CBI, just like what main findings show. Interestingly, CBI's regional diffusion is weak, confirming Bodea and Hicks's (2015a) relevant findings.

Second, I add government debt and revenue (Table 5.3). Heavily indebted governments do not want to grant much independence to central banks, as doing so will limit their ability to finance their spending (Bodea & Higashijima, 2015). Therefore, when a government relies on public debt for its functioning, it rarely allows its central bank to operate independently or even to work against its will. Similarly, when a government receives high revenues, it should not care much about the possibility that an independent central bank's operation that orients toward keeping price stability will restrict its financial largess. As expected, heavy public debt reduces the probability of CBI reform. Puzzlingly, greater revenues fail to increase the likelihood of CBI reform. Rather, the coefficient is negative and statistically insignificant.

Third, instead of using a binary dependent variable, I focus on the continuous measurement of CBI, and then run a fixed effects model. Again, the results substantiate the hypothesis (Table 5.4). When policy pressure grows to liberalize the capital account, a state will increase the independence of its central bank. Democracy is correlated with high CBI. However, both FDI inflows and trade openness now attain statistical significance. This discrepancy with those from the main analysis is largely due to the difference in the two approaches to comprehending CBI reform. Looking into CBI reforms as a binary matter is more accurate as it captures the incurrence of a specific event, which does not occur in a temporally continuous way. Therefore, when we examine the conditions that are conducive to such reform, we can do so with high accuracy. If we turn to continuous degrees of CBI, we do not really investigate the conditions that lead to a reform. Rather, we explore those that sustain certain levels of CBI.

Fourth, I reconstruct the key independent variable in two ways. First, I calculate consecutive temporal differences in the average level of capital account openness in a region to capture yearly changes in this variable. I then dichotomize these differences by generating a new variable that equals 1 when a regional change in the average level of capital account openness is larger than the mean and 0 otherwise. Second,

Table 5.4. Policy Pressure to Liberalize Capital Account and CBI Reform: Continuous CBI

DV = Level of CBI	(1)
Policy pressure	0.012*
	(0.006)
Level of democracy	0.007***
	(0.001)
GDP	0.120***
	(0.033)
Economic growth	–0.000
	(0.000)
FDI inflows	0.001*
	(0.001)
FDI outflows	0.000
	(0.000)
Trade	0.001***
	(0.000)
Exchange rate	0.000
	(0.000)
Constant	–0.531*
	(0.271)
Observations	2,271
Number of countries	112
R-squared	0.224
Country FE	Yes

Robust standard errors in parentheses

***p < 0.01, **p < 0.05, *p < 0.1

Source: Author-created image.

I directly use the average level of capital account openness in a region to approximate the policy pressure facing a state to liberalize its own capital account. I then run a probit model and a fixed effects model on the data, respectively. For one more time, the results are in agreement with those produced in the main analysis (Table 5.5).

Finally, I control for the possible impact of participation in the IMF/World Bank's structural adjustment programs (SAPs). These programs are

Table 5.5. Policy Pressure to Liberalize Capital Account and CBI Reform: Alternative Key Independent Variables

DV = CBI reform	(1)	(2)
Increase in the regional average of capital account openness	0.331** (0.158)	
Regional average of capital account openness		0.070*** (0.021)
Level of democracy	0.011 (0.008)	0.003 (0.002)
GDP	–0.006 (0.044)	0.038 (0.027)
Economic growth	–0.002 (0.007)	–0.000 (0.000)
FDI inflows	0.005 (0.007)	0.000 (0.001)
FDI outflows	–0.012** (0.005)	0.000 (0.000)
Trade	0.000 (0.001)	0.000*** (0.000)
Exchange rate	–0.000 (0.000)	0.000 (0.000)
Constant	–2.185*** (0.432)	0.063 (0.216)
Observations	2,434	2,271
R-squared		0.365
Number of countries	114	112
Log-likelihood	–388.2	
χ^2	26.17	
Country FE		Yes

Robust standard errors in parentheses

***p < 0.01, **p < 0.05, *p < 0.1

Source: Author-created image.

designed to ensure that participating countries' policy and institutional environments are conducive to the operation of a free market. Reducing inflation is one goal of these programs (Stiglitz, 2003). It is likely that SAPs may contain elements of granting more independence to central banks for some participators as CBI contributes to lower inflation.

Table 5.6. Policy Pressure to Liberalize Capital Account and CBI Reform: Controlling for Participation in SAPs

DV = CBI reform	(1)
Policy pressure	0.115***
	(0.039)
Level of democracy	0.016**
	(0.008)
GDP	0.014
	(0.046)
Economic growth	−0.003
	(0.007)
FDI inflows	0.005
	(0.007)
FDI outflows	−0.013**
	(0.005)
Trade	0.001
	(0.001)
Exchange rate	−0.000
	(0.000)
Participation in SAPs	0.057
	(0.143)
Constant	−2.444***
	(0.427)
Observations	2,460
Number of countries	114
Log-likelihood	−386.9
χ^2	28.45

Robust standard errors in parentheses

***p < 0.01, **p < 0.05, *p < 0.1

Source: Author-created image.

However, with the inclusion of participation in SAPs, the results of interest remain almost identical to those from the main analysis (Table 5.6). The coefficient of participation in SAPs is positive but statistically insignificant at conventional levels.

The Case of the Philippines

Unlike its neighbors, such as Indonesia, Malaysia, and Thailand, which had completed major financial reforms during the 1970s and 1980s (Ariff, 1996), the Philippines was less welcoming to foreign investors until the mid-1990s (Thomsen, 1999). Due to the persistent tight control over the financial market in the Philippines, capital inflows to the country remained low and they experienced virtually no growth before the 1990s. For example, "the FDI inflows per capita were stagnant and often negative between 1970 and 1985" (Jamshid & Akbar, 2006, p. 87).

Refusing to imitate its neighbors and liberalize its financial market, the Philippine government instead granted more independence to its central bank. The central bank reform took place in June 1993 when the New Central Bank Act was passed. It had been 21 years since the last substantial amendment was made to the original law of the bank. The new law created a new central bank called Bangko Sentral ng Pilipinas (BSP), and it also transformed the old Central Bank into the Central Bank Board of Liquidators (CB-BoL) (Lamberte, 2002, p. 6). Differing from its predecessor, the BSP is "conceived [of] as a truly independent central bank" (Lamberte, 2002, p. 6). The reform redefined the bank's mandate: "a central bank must at all times maintain monetary policy credibility to enhance the effectiveness of its monetary policy instruments" (Lamberte, 2002, p. 6). In other words, after the reform, a new policy consensus emerged that "an independent central bank is key to a credible monetary policy" (Lamberte, 2002, 6). The bank's new institutional image contrasts starkly with the old one. They differ in both operation and policy goals. For instance, the old central bank was "dominated by cabinet secretaries, who had an interest in the central bank accommodating fiscal deficits and a bias towards a strong peso" (Hill, 2013, p. 122). The new one not only acquired independence but also removed the exchange rate from its policy focuses. Moreover, the BSP has gradually made targeted inflation its main policy approach (Hill, 2013, p. 122).

Economists widely believe that the central bank reform "was one of the most important and successful reforms in Philippine economic history" (Hill, 2013, p. 122). The newly independent BSP has kept inflation low over the post-reform years. Considering the political turmoil and external economic shocks since the reform year, this is a truly remarkable achievement. The presence of an effective central bank has also helped to stabilize the country's financial sector (Hill, 2013, p. 122). More importantly, an autonomous central bank sends a strong signal to investors. This signal has been complemented by incremental liberalization in "such strategic industries as oil, power generation, banking, financial services and capital markets, telecommunications, airlines, port and shipping industries" (Araral, 2006, p. 268). These reforms have created their own beneficiaries, who become constituencies that have further facilitated more difficult reforms, such as the abolition of subsidies and the reform of labor markets (Araral, 2006, p. 269). In this sense, central bank reform is a robust strategy that has paved the way for subsequent economic liberalization in a country that only achieves limited financial integration and yet faces great pressure from its economic competitors to liberalize its capital account. The effect of the bank reform is noteworthy. Despite fluctuations since the reform year, capital inflows have registered a faster growth "at an annual rate of 25 percent," which is more than impressive. Admittedly, its adjacent competitors were more economically successful. For example, Thailand, was placed among "the top twelve developing economy recipients of FDI" during the 1990s, while the size of foreign capital that the Philippines received was much smaller: the annual average value of FDI was merely $580 million for the same period of time (Jamshid & Akbar, 2006, pp. 87–88). Nevertheless, the immediately positive economic change triggered by the central bank reform attests to its undeniable effectiveness.

Restrictions on foreign capital were relaxed somewhat in the wake of the Asian financial crisis in 1997. Important restrictions, however, were left intact. For example, the Philippine government allowed foreign investors to buy business entities experiencing economic hardships, but they did not eliminate the equity limits, which remained "part of the 'Filipino First' clause of the Constitution" (Thomsen, 1999, p. 21). In contrast, the Philippines' neighbors—such as Indonesia, Malaysia, and Thailand—continued to deepen their financial reforms after the onset of the crisis (Thomsen, 1999, p. 21). Therefore, the minor improvements that the Philippines made in financial liberalization failed to earn the country substantial comparative advantages. In light of this situation, the BSP's independence was preserved in order to maintain the country's attractiveness to investors. A notable change was merely that BSP shifted its policy focus from monetary targeting to inflation targeting in 2002 (Lim, 2008).

Conclusion

Independent central banks and liberalized capital accounts both promote capital flows. Investors care about price stability, the government's financial restraint, and the promise of a stable macroeconomic environment. They also consider it highly desirable to have a greater degree of freedom when entering or leaving a country's financial market. For host governments, however, CBI and a liberalized capital account incur very different implementation costs despite their similar functions. Host governments prefer policies that attract investors, but cost less.

Relative to the liberalization of a capital account, pursuing CBI entails much lower costs. Financial openness destabilizes capital flows, introduces high market volatility, and increases overall economic risks. In contrast, CBI does not cause such dangers. Therefore, when a state faces increasing pressure to liberalize its capital account, it is likely to adopt CBI, which is a more cost-efficient policy choice. In other words, states tend to substitute CBI for capital account openness when they face pressure to pursue the latter.

Using data from 1970 to 2012, this chapter finds that a developing country exhibits a higher propensity to adopt CBI reform when, all other things being equal, the gap between its own capital account openness and neighbors' openness widens. This finding validates that strategic consideration motivates convergence on CBI across states.

This chapter contributes to the literature on CBI, financial liberalization, and policy diffusion. Current studies rarely examine CBI from a perspective of cross-issue policy diffusion, nor do they pay due attention to the substitution that occurs between CBI and the liberalization of capital accounts. Quinn (2003) fails to consider the variations in financial liberalization among neighboring states. It is important to acknowledge that states may employ other means to avoid harmful reforms. As Brooks and Kurtz (2012) have uncovered, variations in policy diffusion shed light on the possibility that states are capable of using policy substitutes to mitigate the pressure to adopt similar, liberal economic reforms. This chapter demonstrates that policy diffusion in one issue area can lead to policy convergence in another via the mechanism of substitution.

To reiterate, by focusing on the cross-issue policy substitution that occurs at the same analytical level, this chapter affirms that policymakers should not limit themselves to the policy that they are compelled to adopt or alter. Instead, they can search for more viable policies that produce similar results with smaller costs.

This chapter, along with the previous three, empirically demonstrates that strategic substitution leads to policy convergence. Each does so focusing on a specific type of substitution and therefore a particular type of convergence. To recap, chapter 2 argues and finds that states actively make BITs to avoid costly domestic judicial reforms to improve judicial independence, illustrating convergence through within-issue policy substitution. Chapter 3 shows that facing the pressure to diminish the legal protection of labor rights, states turn to PTAs for alternative policy remedy. It depicts how convergence occurs via cross-issue policy substitution. Chapter 4 reveals that leftist governments substitute lower corporate taxation for loose labor regulations, leading to a global decline in corporate tax rates, a policy convergence compatible with globalization. Taken together, these empirical exercises strongly bear out the main argument of the book: policy convergence that aids globalization can result from the strategic choice of states and therefore exhibits their adaptivity in order to maintain autonomy and fulfill accountability in an age of policy conformity.

Conclusion

Outwitting Globalization

Has globalization caused the slow demise of the nation-state? At the very least, is the nation-state in decline as globalization intensifies? There seems to be no consensus on the answers. Some contend that globalization will end the nation-state. Some merely acknowledge that globalization alters the environment in which states operate and survive. Others stand in the middle of these two positions and hold that globalization constrains states, but not to the extent that forfeits their control over sovereign affairs.

Regardless of the answers, we cannot deny that the political impact of globalization concerns not only the fate of the nation-state but also the future of human beings. If we foresee that globalization will eventually abolish the nation-state, then now is probably the time for us to envision a new form of governance on a broader scale—that is, a world-state. Alternatively, we might counter globalization's spread and its intruding power before it is too late. In other words, we must retreat from previous policies that promote globalization. If we insist that globalization does nothing but reshape the policy environment facing states, then we will continue to deepen it. If, however, we believe that globalization ties the hands of nation-states to various degrees and that states in general can still develop strategies to cope with it and even to thrive, then the issue becomes how we can better govern globalization to make it serve state-specific interests. If this is the case, then we should be optimistic about the future. We should thus be confident that the downside of globalization can be mitigated and managed to ensure both prosperity and policy autonomy.

To assess the relationship between globalization and the nation-state is a twofold task. First, we must understand the constraining power of globalization. Second, we need to explore how states deal with various challenges in creative ways. The latter task often proves more challenging than the former because the policy ingenuity that states exhibit frequently disguises itself as conceding authority and power.

Furthermore, our normative evaluations must be based on rigorous analyses of specific policy areas. No matter what standard we use to evaluate the relationship between globalization and the nation-state, we should refrain from making sweeping evaluations without investigating a sufficient number of cases.

Globalization Prevails?

Globalization profoundly alters the policy environment in which states live. Broad and intensive economic flows integrate states into a condition of strong interdependence (Bordo et al., 1999; Garrett, 2000; Goldstein et al., 2007; UNCTAD, 2016; WTO, 2014). National prosperity is now more contingent on a state's performance in promoting cross-border economic transactions. To achieve success in international economic competition hence becomes paramount. For policymakers, this often means enacting policies that maximize the chances of beating one's competitors in accumulating capital and gaining markets at the global level. International economic competition externalizes the impacts of national policies, and it increases the costs of refusing to adopt policies similar to those of one's competitors (Simmons & Elkins, 2004). Scholars consider these globalization-induced policy externalities to be the primary cause behind convergence, or the ever-growing similarity in policies across countries (Cao & Prakash, 2010; Davies & Vadlamannati, 2013; Elkins et al., 2006a; Garrett, 1995; Wang, 2018).

Under globalization, national policies are believed to exclusively converge on neoliberal economic dogmas (Davies & Vadlamannati, 2013; Jensen, 2013; Simmons & Elkins, 2004; Smith et al., 1999). Empirical evidence seemingly spans a wide range of issue areas, such as central bank independence (Bodea & Hicks, 2015a), corporate tax rates (Cao, 2010), economic liberalization (Simmons & Elkins, 2004), environmental protection (Cao & Prakash, 2010; Holzinger et al., 2008; Lee & Strang, 2006), investment protection (Elkins et al., 2006a), and social welfare spending (Brooks, 2005). All these findings appear to suggest that policy convergence has dominated policy autonomy and that policymakers have less and less room to maneuver in doing their job.

Scholars often charge that policy convergence materializes at the peril of public welfare—that is to say, it fosters a race to the bottom in governmental regulations (Olney, 2013; Razin & Sadka, 2018). Globalization not only appropriates the decision-making power that was previously monopolized by sovereign states but also fundamentally undermines states' political nature by forcing them to deviate further and further from their function of providing public goods (Bloom, 2016; Hellwig, 2008; Wu, 2017). Resistance is inconceivable because there is no escape from it (Garrett, 2000). The "golden straitjacket" that globalization puts on sovereign nations will kill the wearer (Friedman, 1999). Pessimistic scholars prophesize that the fate of the nation-state is sealed by the juggernaut of globalization (Albrow, 1996; Beeson, 2003; Ohmae, 1996).

Given the findings obtained throughout this book, however, there is reason to be optimistic that globalization does not completely subdue the nation-state. Globalization undeniably makes policy convergence more likely because economies are now utterly internationalized rather than confined within national borders. Nonetheless, this is merely a change in policy environment. States still find ways to cope and survive. Strategic substitution is one tactic that they employ. States adopt policies that are less politically costly but of equal economic efficiency to replace those that are politically prohibitive, although both are compatible with globalization. More importantly, strategic substitution leads to convergence as well. However, such convergence is distinctively different from the one that scholars have conventionally identified and worried about, as it reflects a diametrically opposing rationale. It is the states' shrewd political calculation rather than the coercion by globalization that drives the policy convergence unveiled in this book.

Rediscovering Policy Autonomy

Not all scholars share the pessimistic belief that globalization will end the nation-state through the proliferation of policy convergence. There is no shortage of studies that uncover the diversity in policy outcomes and portray states' resistance to the repressive force of globalization (i.e., Clark, 2009; Datz, 2019; Gritsch, 2005; Jordana et al., 2018; Mosley,

2005; Naoi, 2020; Nooruddin & Rudra, 2014; Shin, 2017; Swank, 2002; Wang, 2017a, 2017b). These studies often assume that policy differentiation represents the sole embodiment of policy autonomy under globalization. This is an understandable assumption because convergence is categorically considered to be a problem threatening states that they therefore need to overcome.

States, however, can exercise their policy autonomy in a variety of ways. Enacting different polices is only one of them. Pursuing similar policies is another. Policy convergence, hence, can also be interpreted as evidence of policy autonomy whenever its underlying strategic calculations are constructed to preserve sovereign policy space. Put differently, when states adapt to a policy environment that globalization has remade, convergence can emerge. Specifically, policy convergence can arise from a state's decision to substitute practical policies for the costlier ones that globalization pressures them to adopt. There is little work that explores convergence from the perspective of strategic substitution; only a few studies point in this direction (i.e., Genovese et al., 2017; Hays, 2003; Rickard, 2012; Shin, 2017). This book effectively develops the logic of convergence through policy substitution. By means of this convergence, states continue to survive and thrive in the constrained policy environment under globalization.

Furthermore, I posit that this convergence can occur either within or across issue areas and at the same analytical level or across analytical levels. I use the theoretical framework that I have constructed to comprehend policy changes in four areas that are impactful on globalization: bilateral investment treaties (chapter 2), preferential trade agreements (chapter 3), corporate taxation (chapter 4), and central bank independence (chapter 5). Evidence from rigorous statistical analysis and detailed case studies provides strong support for the claim that strategic substitution motivates policy convergence in these areas.

First, states utilize bilateral investment treaties to substitute for difficult domestic judicial reforms. When more of these treaties are made, the institutional benefits that they generate allow participating states to halt or even reverse judicial reforms that are intended to protect foreign investment. This causes judicial independence to deteriorate. Second, concluding preferential trade agreements makes it possible for states to sustain a high degree of legal protection for labor rights. Concluding trade agreements incurs lower political costs than reducing labor protection, but it generates similar economic advantages. Also, the pressure to deregulate the labor market practically motivates states to design PTAs with stronger labor clauses. However, when the costs of repressing labor are low, the incentive to employ PTAs will be weaker.

Third, leftist governments cut corporate tax rates in order to prevent labor rights laws from diminution. In other words, lightening the tax burden on firms enables leftist governments to retain policies that their core constituencies hold dear. Fourth, states grant more independence to their central banks to secure their control of capital flows. Maintaining politically independent central banks sends a credible signal to investors that the value of their foreign assets will not be subject to inflationary policy alterations. Therefore, when a state's neighboring competitors relax capital controls in order to attract investment, the state is inclined to heighten its central bank's level of independence. This serves the same goal as the relaxation of capital controls, but it also preserves the state's control over its own financial market.

Investigating these specific and important policy areas illustrates the logic of policy convergence that occurs via substitution in respective contexts. Policy convergence in these areas demonstrates not only that states are dexterously adaptive but also that the negative consequences of globalization can be ameliorated or avoided. In a number of circumstances, the worrisome downward policy convergence unleashed by globalization is somewhat prevented. Given these findings, the optimism is not unwarranted that globalization can be harnessed to serve the best interests of its individual participants.

Through the investigation of the four policies, this book hopes to contribute new perspectives to extant scholarship on each. At a higher and more ambitious level, the theoretical and empirical efforts made in this book allow it to engage in conversations with some significant strands of literature that share its broad concerns.

Globalizing International Political Economy

In international political economy scholarship, as a dominant rigorous theoretical framework, the open economy politics approach does not give sufficient credit to system-level factors. Its reductionist perspective neglects the shaping power of factors at the system level that are beyond the control of individual states (Lake, 2009). The findings in this book suggest that internationalized policy pressure can be an important source of policy changes at both domestic and international levels. Therefore, scholars of international political economy may find it helpful to model the role of the system-level factors that are not manifest in international regimes (Chaudoin et al., 2015; Oatley, 2011). This theoretical contribution adds to the classical literature that investigates other system-level factors, such as position in a global economy (Gourevitch, 1978), power distribution (Krasner, 1976), and international regimes (Keohane, 1984).

Globalization and Varieties of Capitalism

The theory of varieties of capitalism maintains that globalization does not alter the basic organization of production in individual states (Hall & Soskice, 2001). In other words, fundamental economic institutions do not converge. The research in this book provides further evidence for this theory. For example, labor rights are not sacrificed for economic efficiency. Financial liberalization fails to prevail as expected. Nevertheless, the policy tools that allow states to maintain their economic distinctiveness paradoxically lead to regulatory convergence, including the diffusion of preferential trade agreements, the reduction of corporate tax rates, and the spread of independent central banks. In other words, policy convergence in one issue area embodies the costs of maintaining policy distinctiveness in another. These findings echo recent research that demonstrates that a coordinated market economy does not necessarily pursue lower levels of deregulation (Pierre, 2015). Varieties of capitalism do coexist with policy uniformity. In this sense, by unifying explanations for policy differentiation and policy convergence under the single framework of policy substitution, this book enriches the theory of varieties of capitalism.

Neoliberal Economics and Policy Adaptivity

Scholars frequently blame neoliberal economics for the adverse effects of globalization (i.e., Stiglitz, 2003). The logic of policy substitution proposed in this book suggests that states are able to avoid at least some of these effects. States do not need to repress labor rights. They also do not need to capitulate when pressured to liberalize their capital account. Policy adaptivity frustrates the intrusiveness of economic neoliberalism, as is foreshadowed by the compensation literature (Adserà & Boix, 2002; Avelino et al., 2005; Nooruddin & Rudra, 2014; Rodrik, 1998). Additionally, neoliberal economics has made many policy suggestions, not all of which aim to achieve economic development at the expense of general societal welfare (de Soysa & Vadlamannati, 2011; Hall & Lawson, 2014; Rodrik & World Bank, 2006). Restraining executive power through judicial means, reducing trade barriers, and taming inflation all improve overall public well-being in states where these policies are administered appropriately. More importantly, as demonstrated in this book, these policies are employed not only to fulfill specific functions of economic efficiency but also to minimize political risks by substituting for the costly policy changes that globalization demands.

A Recipe for Survival and Prosperity

The policy implication of this study is evident. There are always ways to protect policy autonomy. Under globalization, it is possible to seek prosperity without surrendering sovereignty. States can be better off seeking out a wide range of policy tools; this will enable them to locate a cost-efficient but also welfare-improving policy instrument that can be as effective as an unpopular policy dictated by intensifying globalization. In other words, policymakers should not limit themselves to the policies that they are compelled to adopt or alter. Instead, they can seek those that serve similar functions but incur lower costs. Ultimately, policymakers who wish to enact politically feasible and economically efficient policies must continue to deepen their understanding of policy tools' functionality, efficiency, and consequences.

The Next Step?

The studies performed in this book open several fruitful avenues for future research. Given the findings of Hellwig (2008) that noneconomic issues assume growing importance in public assessments of political accountability, if policy autonomy can be exercised through active policy convergence, will the public's awareness of this strategic move paradoxically increase the weight that they assign to economic issues when it evaluates governmental performance? Furthermore, if policy convergence grows more extensive regardless of the causes behind it, how will this trend affect nationalism in general? Will it stimulate more populist sentiment (Rodrik, 2018)? If so, then we may expect that policy convergence will practically contribute to ongoing support for the nation-state as a way to organize legitimation; this is because the existence of uniform policies across states can inspire people to explore the cultural and ethnic uniqueness that culminates in their national identities. To that end, in line with some current views, globalization will eventually strengthen the nation-state (Thomson, 1995; Weiss, 1998; Zurn & Deitelhoff, 2015), albeit in a tortuous fashion. All of these questions can be answered empirically.

Scholars may also wish to consider the relationship between divergence and convergence. Is there an optimal configuration between the two? Because convergence only makes states similar or identical within certain relevant issue areas, this issue-confined policy identity may lead them to believe that convergence merely provides insufficient economic traction. Therefore, in a dynamic world, convergence will in turn contribute to more divergence at some point or in some other issue areas. A few studies have already noticed a possible correlation between trade agreements and tax rates (Hafner, 2015; Redoano, 2014). Is there a limit to the policy substitution that is carried across issue areas? If so, what will be the scope conditions for this substitution to occur?

It is also worth exploring how policy convergence affects international regimes. If states can automatically choose policies that are similar to those of their peers, then this will reduce the need for international coordination. In this sense, international regimes that are designed to serve such purpose will become less useful (Martin, 1992). This possibility echoes Rodrik's (2018) call for a reduction in the interference by global governance agencies: "We must understand that the best contribution global arrangements can make is to make the nation state [sic] work better, not to weaken or constrain it. Correspondingly, the appropriate role for global institutions is to enhance key democratic norms of representation, participation, deliberation, rule of law, and transparency—without prejudging policy outcomes or requiring harmonization" (p. 17).

Finally, how does policy convergence in issue areas of significant economic impact affect the durability of peace among nation-states? Will enacting similar policies help to avoid conflict by drawing countries closer together, as democracy has done (Russett & Oneal, 2001)? Alternatively, will the rising nationalism induced by convergence make war more likely? Exploring this nexus will contribute to a better understanding of the political economy of conflict.

Notes

Introduction

1. Friedman's (2005) original words are: "In Globalization 1.0, which began around 1492, the world went from size large to size medium. In Globalization 2.0, the era that introduced us to multinational companies, it went from size medium to size small. And then around 2000 came Globalization 3.0, in which the world went from being small to tiny."

2. Globalization has different aspects. As an operationalized concept, it is defined as follows: "Globalization describes the process of creating networks of connections among actors at intra- or multi-continental distances, mediated through a variety of flows including people, information and ideas, capital, and goods. Globalization is a process that erodes national boundaries, integrates national economies, cultures, technologies and governance, and produces complex relations of mutual interdependence" (Dreher, 2006). Globalization assumes at least three distinct faces: economic, social, and political (Dreher, 2006; Gygli et al., 2019). In this book, I focus on its economic dimension (trade and capital flows), treating it as a more fundamental cause that motivates changes in other areas, even if some of these changes can also be considered as indications of globalization.

3. Even the most advanced responsibility to protect (R2P) theory has no intention of replacing sovereignty with something else. In fact, R2P is not theoretically innovative because no sovereignty theorists have ever conceived a concept of absolute sovereignty, at least not in words (Glanville, 2013). Instead, R2P constitutes an endeavor to reconceptualize sovereignty to clarify sovereignty's telos, which is ensuring faithful services to society and constituencies.

4. As an analytical concept, policy convergence overlaps with isomorphism, policy diffusion, and transfer to various degrees and in different ways (Knill, 2005).

5. The concept of policy externalities is an improvement on early spatial externalities (see Anselin, 2003).

6. This reality is also reflected in the rapidly growing number of studies concerning policy diffusion. According to Graham et al. (2013), from 1958 to 2008, 781 articles about policy interdependence were published in leading political science journals. For the first 10 years of the 21st century, the literature increased dramatically across all the major subfields in political science and had grown twice as fast as in the 1990s (Graham et al., 2013). This tendency suggests that convergence is one of the major concerns and academic foci of scholars.

Chapter 1. Measured Adaptivity

1. Scholars debate how influential globalization is when it comes to directing national policies. There are at least three perspectives: globalists, transformationalists, and skeptics (Held et al., 1999). Globalists believe that globalization will end the nation-state (Albrow, 1996; Ohmae, 1996), while skeptics cast doubt on this belief by arguing that globalization is merely a result of states' choices (Hirst & Thompson, 1995; Krasner, 1999a). Transformationalists sit somewhere in between these two positions; they maintain that globalization involves both integration and differentiation (Held et al., 1999).

2. In contrast to Hay's typology, Knill's (2005) is based on the operationalization and measurement of convergence. This is an important contribution insofar as it facilitates the collating of empirical evidence. Nonetheless, this research design–oriented classification makes no distinction among various types of convergences that possess substantive differences from one another.

3. This constraint varies according to each state's economic power and status (Weiss, 2005).

4. The current scholarship on policy autonomy under globalization bears on historical institutionalism. It emphasizes the inertia of existing institutions by evaluating how they shape the resources, opportunities, and preferences of policy actors in a way that generates path dependence (Pierson, 2004; Thelen & Steinmo, 1992). Because of institutional stickiness, policy distinctiveness spreads widely across issue areas. These differences are ascribed, among other factors, to political parties (Bremer, 2018; Garrett, 1995; Garrett & Lange, 1991, 1995; Grieco et al., 2009; Hwang & Lee, 2014; Milner & Judkins, 2004; Mukherjee et al., 2009; Pinto & Pinto, 2008); state structures (Lütz, 2004), regimes (Bearce & Hallerberg, 2011; Milner & Kubota, 2005), social cleavages (Morrison, 2011), median voter matters (Ward et al., 2011), and the legacy of the economic development model (Brooks & Kurtz, 2012).

5. I consider policies that are intended to address the subject matter of similar or identical nature as within–issue area policies, and otherwise across–issue area ones.

6. This is not saying that substitution as a convergence-producing mechanism is uniformly present across all states. Depending on issue areas, such substitution may be lacking in some. For example, using BITs to avoid judicial reform does not apply to developed nations.

7. Whether this policy convergence also leads to outcome or process convergence is beyond the scope of this book.

8. Recent scholarship has examined the Type 1 convergence (Shin, 2017). Kono (2006) finds that democracies are likely to substitute non-tariff trade barriers for tariffs due to the greater obscurity of the former that allows this obfuscation to evade the public eye. This is apparently a type of convergence caused by substitution within the same issue area. However, this substitution occurs between two policies that impede globalization. Therefore, the resulting convergence is not a Type 1 convergence identified here.

Chapter 2. The Proliferation of [Bilateral Investment Treaties and Judicial Independence

1. An increasing number of carefully designed empirical studies reveal that BITs do indeed promote FDI to host states (Busse et al., 2010; Haftel, 2010; Kerner, 2009; Neumayer & Spess, 2005; Salacuse & Sullivan, 2005; Wang & Youn, 2018).

2. Also see Ranjan and Anand (2020) for a case study of India.

3. For detailed information on the indicators they have used, please see Linzer and Staton (2015).

Chapter 3. Labor Rights and the Making of Preferential Trade Agreements

1. Recent studies seem to demonstrate the possibility that improving compliance with labor rights laws can occur at a firm level via the global supply chain (Distelhorst & Locke, 2018; Malesky & Mosley, 2018). As these studies have also shown, however, such firm-level upgrades are limited (Distelhorst & Locke, 2018) and highly contingent (Malesky & Mosley, 2018). In most industries, firms do not get rewarded for enforcing high labor standards—in other words, they do not receive more orders from abroad (Amengual & Distelhorst, 2019; Distelhorst & Locke, 2018). The lack of a reward will discourage firms from protecting workers more consistently in the first place. Markups, which represent another factor that might induce firms to upgrade protections for labor (Malesky & Mosley, 2018), vary greatly in themselves, across sectors, and

across time. Therefore, they cannot be a reliable mechanism to sustain broad improvements in the field of labor protection. Although it is laudable when upgrades occur at the firm level, the reasons mentioned earlier make it difficult to expect that these upgrades will make a difference at the larger scale of the state level. The constant race to the bottom that has occurred over the past decades confirms this.

2. This does not mean, however, that there are no concerns about or opposition to the making of PTAs from other interest groups. These might include environmental groups or workers who lack an appropriate understanding of the agreement's benefits (Naoi & Urata, 2013). Just as previously discussed, these concerns can be mitigated somewhat either by including nontrade issue clauses in the agreements (Milewicz et al., 2018), or by excluding important sectors from them (Naoi & Urata, 2013).

3. It should, however, be remembered that this probabilistic prediction by no means suggests that states include labor provisions in PTAs only when they are pressured to lower legal protections for labor. Some states—such as the US—can insist on the inclusion of labor provisions even when they do not face such pressure (DOL & USTR, 2015). To ensure that the results are not driven by US trade agreements, I drop all of these agreements in robustness checks. Once again, the expectation is borne out.

4. In this chapter, I focus on general behavioral patterns of states. Although there might be interesting variations attributable to disparity in the level of economic development within a dyad, it is beyond the scope of this chapter to explore them. However, to demonstrate robustness of the generality of these theoretical predictions, I perform a set of tests using split samples. I divide the sample into three subgroups: North-North, North-South, and South-South dyads. The results do lend broad support to the hypotheses advanced here. Please see Tables A24–A26 in the appendix.

5. Treaty ratification is governed by a different dynamic than treaty formation (Haftel & Thompson, 2013; Kelley, & Pevehouse, 2015) and therefore is not fit for the test of the proposed hypotheses. This also explains why existing literature predominately focuses on PTA formation rather than ratification.

6. Policy pressure describes a situation in which *each* state in a dyad faces pressure directed on it, which means a monadic design should yield similar results to those using a dyadic approach. In the section on robustness checks later in this chapter I perform a monadic analysis.

7. Forty-two percent of PTAs in the sample include some labor provisions. However, meaningful and enforceable ones only account for less than 25 percent of the PTAs covered.

8. The United Nations Comtrade dataset group tradable commodities into 10 categories: food and live animals; beverages and tobacco; crude materials, inedible, except fuels; and so on. To more accurately capture competitiveness in

exports between states, I employ the average similarity scores for states' export profiles across these ten categories. As a robustness check, using FDI to produce the weighting matrix does not alter the results.

9. In the published version, Barry et al. only include observations until 2010. I have the privilege to use data beyond that year with their approval.

10. This is also a standard practice in current literature (Greenhill et al., 2009; Lim et al., 2015; Mosley, 2011; Wang, 2017a).

11. Longer lags are tried in robustness checks, which do not affect the statistical inference.

12. The model is estimated using a sample in which dyads have already signed a PTA. However, considering the selection effect does not affect the statistical inference.

13. Due to space limitations, the results of the robustness checks in this section are stored in an online appendix (https://www.zhiyuanwang.org/research).

Chapter 4. Partisanship, Labor, and Corporate Taxation

1. Labor rights here refer to collective labor rights, that is, rights to the freedom of association and collective bargaining. These rights are by nature procedural and determine individual or substantive rights (Langille, 1997), such as the rights to maximum work hours, minimum wage, occupational health and safety, and so forth. More details will be presented in the research design section.

2. This, however, does not imply that rightist parties incur no costs in restricting labor rights. Their ideological opponents surely make it difficult to pass such policies, especially when labor unions are powerful (Alvarez et al., 1991). However, fearing possible political penalties from their own constituencies, rightist parties may not yield to strong unions. More importantly, even if they propose to do so, unions will not perceive such a defection as credible (Alvarez et al., 1991). Furthermore, the presence of strong unions only obscures the ideological differences between leftist and rightist parties under very restricted conditions (Otjes & Green-Pedersen, 2019). In other words, unions do not expect that rightist parties will represent their interests anyway. Therefore, rightist parties do not face political costs when lowering labor rights protection in the way their leftist opponents do in the same circumstances, explaining why labor market deregulation often occurs under rightist governments (Lodovici, 2000).

3. This does not mean there are no other alternatives. However, in terms of economic impact and efficiency, few often-considered policies are comparable to cutting tax rates. For example, environmental deregulation is not as economically efficient as we have normally assumed; environmental regulation imposes on average small costs on firms (Wheeler, 2001). Moreover, environmental deregulation may prove more difficult in many states, as it negatively affects

larger constituencies (Bernauer & Caduff, 2004; Cao & Prakash, 2012). Empirically, there environmental protection does not involve a race to the bottom (Drezner, 2001; Konisky, 2007; Konisky & Woods, 2010). Rather, a climb to the top mostly occurs (Holzinger & Sommerer, 2011; Vogel, 1995). Therefore, environmental deregulation is not a viable alternative for governments to attract foreign capital. Tax incentives, on the other hand, seem to be feasible. In the robustness checks, I use effective tax rates (actual tax rates after tax incentives) to address the possibility that governments may employ tax incentives to deflect the pressure to lower labor rights protection. The results support the proposed hypothesis. In addition, governments can also use other means to achieve the same purpose, such as investing in infrastructure and improving public services. In the robustness checks, I use government expenses (excluding military spending) as a proxy to examine this possibility. The results are in strong agreement with those in the main analysis.

4. Nevertheless, the evidence is not fully supported or conclusive. A few studies have revealed no such positive association between tax incentives and higher capital flows (Cleeve, 2008).

5. However, developing nations still face the risk of potential revenue loss in the short run if they reduce tax rates, which is why they receive foreign aid for implementing economic reform (Baccini & Urpelainen, 2012).

6. This survey does not cover all states in the world. The number of surveyed states varies from 86 to 145 across time.

7. I am aware of some recent criticism that questions assuming a unified left-right divide on the global level (Rudra & Tobin, 2017). As acute as this criticism is, there is no wide consensus emerging to address this issue in a more effective way. So, I will adhere to the conventional use and operationalization of the partisanship in this chapter.

8. It should be noted that the leftist governments in the dataset include those in both democracies and non-democracies, such as communist countries. Despite the obvious ideological similarity between the leftist parties under two opposite regimes, such as representing the working class and fighting for equality, the difference is also evident: one accepts and respects democratic rule and thus participates in regularized political competition while the other categorically rejects such political institutions and embraces the autocratic rule instead (Ware, 1996). In robustness checks, I drop these leftist governments in non-democracies from the sample.

9. It is possible that a reverse causality exists between corporate tax rates and leftist governments, that is, existing lower corporate tax rates may increase the likelihood of a subsequent leftist government. To address this issue, I run a two-stage least square model that instrumentalizes leftist governments using the number of leftist governments in the region a state belongs to. The results are even stronger. Please see Table A.10 in the online appendix (https://www.zhiyuanwang.org/research).

10. As mentioned earlier, the KPMG Corporate Tax Rate Surveys do not encompass all states in the world. The highest number of states covered until 2012, the last year in the labor rights data used here, is 110. Furthermore, the included variables are cross-missing. Therefore, the total number of states in the sample reduces to 101. A list of states in the sample is provided in the online appendix (https://www.zhiyuanwang.org/research).

11. I also run random effect analyses. The results are reported in the section on robustness checks, which are mostly consistent with those from the fixed effect estimations, only weaker.

12. I use a Party Government dataset (Seki & Williams, 2014) to identify coalition governments.

Chapter 5. Diffused Capital Account Openness and Central Bank Independence

1. As Fernández-Albertos (2015) has correctly described, "the magnitude of the general trend is striking: the mean degree of independence increased by about two standard deviations in only two decades" (p. 219). See also Crowe and Meade (2007, 2008) and Cukierman (2008).

2. There exists an impossible trinity: free flows of capital, monetary policy autonomy, and fixed exchange rate cannot be all in place at the same time (Obstfeld et al., 2005).

3. Admittedly, capital account openness may also create financial constraint. It can only do so, however, when CBI is low or when a fixed exchange-rate system is present (Kim, 2003).

References

Acemoglu, D., & Robinson, J. A. (2008). Persistence of power, elites, and institutions. *American Economic Review*, 98(1), 267–293. https://doi.org/ doi: 10.1257/aer.98.1.267

Adserà, A., & Boix, C. (2002). Trade, democracy, and the size of the public sector: The political underpinnings of openness. *International Organization*, 56(2), 229–262. https://doi.org/10.2307/3078605

Agnew, J. (2017). *Globalization and sovereignty: Beyond the territorial trap*. Rowman & Littlefield.

Albrow, M. (1996). *The global age: State and society beyond modernity*. Polity.

Alesina, A., & Summers, L. H. (1993). Central bank independence and macroeconomic performance: Some comparative evidence. *Journal of Money, Credit and Banking*, 25(2), 151–162. https://doi.org/10.2307/2077833

Alfaro, L., Chanda, A., Kalemli-Ozcan, S., & Sayek, S. (2010). Does foreign direct investment promote growth? Exploring the role of financial markets on linkages. *Journal of Development Economics*, 91(2), 242–256. https://doi. org/https://doi.org/10.1016/j.jdeveco.2009.09.004

Allee, T., & Peinhardt, C. (2010). Delegating differences: Bilateral investment treaties and bargaining over dispute resolution provisions. *International Studies Quarterly*, 54, 1–26.

Alvarez, R. M., Garrett, G., & Lange, P. (1991). Government partisanship, labor organization, and macroeconomic performance. *American Political Science Review*, 85(2), 539–556. https://doi.org/10.2307/1963174

Amengual, M., & Distelhorst, G. Global purchasing as labor regulation: The missing middle. *Industrial and Labor Relations Review*. http://eureka.sbs. ox.ac.uk/7306/

Andrews, D. M. (1994). Capital mobility and state autonomy: Toward a structural theory of international monetary relations. *International Studies Quarterly*, 38(2), 193–218. https://doi.org/10.2307/2600975

Angelopoulos, K., Economides, G., & Kammas, P. (2009). *Do political incentives matter for tax policies? Ideology, opportunism and the tax structure.* Scottish Institute for Research in Economics (SIRE).

Anselin, L. (2003). Spatial externalities, spatial multipliers, and spatial econometrics. *International Regional Science Review, 26*(2), 153–166. https://doi.org/10.1177/0160017602250972

Araral, E. K. (2006). The political economy of policy reform in the Philippines: 1992–1998. *Journal of Policy Reform, 9*(4), 261–274. https://doi.org/10.1080/13841280601101599

Ariff, M. (1996). Effects of financial liberalization on four Southeast Asian financial markets, 1973–94. *ASEAN Economic Bulletin, 12*(3), 325–338. http://www.jstor.org/stable/25770605

Armour, J., Deakin, S., & Siems, M. (2016). *CBR Leximetric datasets* [dataset]. https://doi.org/10.17863/CAM.506

Arteta, C., Eichengreen, B., & Wyplosz, C. (2001). When does capital account liberalization help more than it hurts? *National Bureau of Economic Research Working Paper Series, No. 8414.* https://doi.org/10.3386/w8414

Auerbach, A. J. (2006). Why have corporate tax revenues declined? Another look. *National Bureau of Economic Research Working Paper Series, No. 12463.* https://doi.org/10.3386/w12463

Avelino, G., Brown, D. S., & Hunter, W. (2005). The effects of capital mobility, trade openness, and democracy on social spending in Latin America, 1980–1999. *American Journal of Political Science, 49*(3), 625–641. https://doi.org/10.2307/3647736

Aylin, A. (2013). Judicial independence across democratic regimes: Understanding the varying impact of political competition. *Law & Society Review, 47*(1), 105–134. https://doi.org/doi:10.1111/lasr.12003

Azman-Saini, W. N. W., Baharumshah, A. Z., & Law, S. H. (2010). Foreign direct investment, economic freedom and economic growth: International evidence. *Economic Modelling, 27*(5), 1079–1089. https://doi.org/https://doi.org/10.1016/j.econmod.2010.04.001

Baccini, L., & Dür, A. (2011). The new regionalism and policy interdependence. *British Journal of Political Science, 42*(1), 57–79. https://doi.org/10.1017/S0007123411000238

Baccini, L., & Dür, A. (2015). Investment discrimination and the proliferation of preferential trade agreements. *Journal of Conflict Resolution, 59*(4), 617–644. https://doi.org/10.1177/0022002713516844

Baccini, L., & Koenig-Archibugi, M. (2014). Why do states commit to international labour standards? The importance of "rivalry" and "friendship" *World Politics, 66*(3), 446–490.

Baccini, L., & Urpelainen, J. (2012). Strategic side payments: Preferential trading agreements, economic reform, and foreign aid. *Journal of Politics, 74*(4), 932–949. https://doi.org/10.1017/s0022381612000485

Baccini, L., & Urpelainen, J. (2014). International institutions and domestic politics: Can preferential trading agreements help leaders promote economic reform? *Journal of Politics*, 76(01), 195–214. https://doi.org/doi:10.1017/S0022381613001278

Bach, D. (2010). Varieties of cooperation: The domestic institutional roots of global governance. *Review of International Studies*, 36(3), 561–589. www.jstor.org/stable/40783286

Baier, S. L., & Bergstrand, J. H. (2007). Do free trade agreements actually increase members' international trade? *Journal of International Economics*, 71(1), 72–95. https://doi.org/https://doi.org/10.1016/j.jinteco.2006.02.005

Baker, A. (2009). *The market and the masses in Latin America*. Cambridge University Press.

Ballard-Rosa, C., Mosley, L., & Wellhausen, R. L. (2019). Contingent advantage? Sovereign borrowing, democratic institutions and global capital cycles. *British Journal of Political Science*, 51(1), 353–373. https://doi.org/10.1017/S0007123418000455

Barro, R. J., & Gordon, D. B. (1983). Rules, discretion and reputation in a model of monetary policy. *Journal of Monetary Economics*, 12(1), 101–121. https://doi.org/http://dx.doi.org/10.1016/0304-3932(83)90051-X

Barry, C. M., Cingranelli, D. L., & Clay, K. C. (2022). Labor rights in comparative perspective: The WorkR dataset. *International Interactions*, 48(2), 327–344. https://doi.org/10.1080/03050629.2022.2040495

Barry, C. M., Clay, K. C., & Flynn, M. E. (2013). Avoiding the spotlight: Human rights shaming and foreign direct investment. *International Studies Quarterly*, 57, 532–544.

Barthel, F., Busse, M., & Neumayer, E. (2009). The impact of double taxation treaties on foreign direct investment: Evidence from large dyadic panel data. *Contemporary Economic Policy*, 28(3), 366–377. https://doi.org/10.1111/j.1465-7287.2009.00185.x

Bartolini, L., & Drazen, A. (1997). Capital-account liberalization as a signal. *American Economic Review*, 87(1), 138–154. http://www.jstor.org/stable/2950858

Basinger, S. J., & Hallerberg, M. (2004). Remodeling the competition for capital: How domestic politics erases the race to the bottom. *American Political Science Review*, 98(02), 261–276. https://doi.org/doi:10.1017/S0003055404001133

Bates, R. (2010). *Prosperity and violence: The political economy of development*. W. W. Norton.

Bearce, D. H., & Hallerberg, M. (2011). Democracy and de facto exchange rate regimes. *Economics & Politics*, 23(2), 172–194. https://doi.org/10.1111/j.1468-0343.2011.00381.x

Beazer, Q. H., & Blake, D. J. (2018). The conditional nature of political risk: How home institutions influence the location of foreign direct investment.

American Journal of Political Science, 62(2), 470–485. https://doi.org/https://doi.org/10.1111/ajps.12344

Beazer, Q. H., & Woo, B. (2016). IMF conditionality, government partisanship, and the progress of economic reforms. *American Journal of Political Science, 60*(2), 304–321. https://doi.org/doi:10.1111/ajps.12200

Beck, N., Katz, J. N., & Tucker, R. (1998). Taking time seriously: Time-series-cross-section analysis with a binary dependent variable. *American Journal of Political Science, 42*(4), 1260–1288. http://www.jstor.org/stable/2991857

Beeson, M. (2003). Sovereignty under siege: Globalisation and the state in Southeast Asia. *Third World Quarterly, 24*(2), 357–374. https://doi.org/10.1080/014365903 | 2000074637

Behar, A., & Cirera-i-Crivillé, L. (2013). Does it matter who you sign with? Comparing the impacts of north–south and south–south trade agreements on bilateral trade. *Review of International Economics, 21*(4), 765–782. https://doi.org/10.1111/roie.12069

Belderbos, R., & Zou, J. (2006). Foreign investment, divestment and relocation by Japanese electronics firms in East Asia. *Asian Economic Journal, 20*(1), 1–27. https://doi.org/10.1111/j.1467-8381.2006.00222.x

Bennett, C. J. (1991). What is policy convergence and what causes it? *British Journal of Political Science, 21*(2), 215–233. www.jstor.org/stable/193876

Bernanke, B. S. (2010). *Central bank independence, transparency, and accountability.* A speech at the Institute for Monetary and Economic Studies International Conference, Bank of Japan, Tokyo, Japan.

Bernauer, T., & Caduff, L. (2004). In whose interest? Pressure group politics, economic competition and environmental regulation. *Journal of Public Policy, 24*(1), 99–126. https://doi.org/10.1017/S0143814X04000054

Bernhard, W. (1998). A political explanation of variations in central bank independence. *American Political Science Review, 92*(2), 311–327. https://doi.org/10.2307/2585666

Bernhard, W. (2002). *Banking on reform: Political parties and central bank independence in the industrial democracies.* University of Michigan Press. https://doi.org/10.3998/mpub.17115

Bernhard, W., Broz, J. L., & Clark, W. R. (2002). The political economy of monetary institutions. *International Organization, 56*(4), 693–723. http://www.jstor.org/stable/3078645

Besley, T., & Burgess, R. (2004). Can labor regulation hinder economic performance? Evidence from India. *Quarterly Journal of Economics, 119*(1), 91–134.

Betz, T., & Pond, A. (2019). Foreign financing and the international sources of property rights. *World Politics, 71*(3), 503–541.

Bhagwati, J. (2004). *In defense of globalization.* Oxford University Press.

Bia, M., & Mattei, A. (2008). A Stata package for the estimation of the dose-response function through adjustment for the generalized propensity score. *Stata Journal, 8*(3), 354–373. https://doi.org/10.1177/1536867x0800800303

Biglaiser, G., & Staats, J. L. (2012). Finding the "democratic advantage" in sovereign bond ratings: The importance of strong courts, property rights protection, and the rule of law. *International Organization*, 66(3), 515–535. https://doi.org/10.1017/S0020818312000185

Blanton, R. G., Blanton, S. L., & Peksen, D. (2015). The impact of IMF and World Bank programs on labor rights. *Political Research Quarterly*. https://doi.org/10.1177/1065912915578462

Blanton, S., & Blanton, R. (2007). What attracts foreign investors? An examination of human rights and foreign direct investment. *Journal of Politics*, 69(1), 143–155.

Blanton, S. L., & Blanton, R. G. (2009). A sectoral analysis of human rights and FDI: Does industry type matter? *International Studies Quarterly*, 53(2), 473–493.

Blonigen, B. A., & Piger, J. (2014). Determinants of foreign direct investment. *Canadian Journal of Economics/Revue canadienne d'économique*, 47(3), 775–812. https://doi.org/https://doi.org/10.1111/caje.12091

Bloom, P. (2016). *Authoritarian capitalism in the age of globalization*. Edward Elgar.

Bodea, C. (2010). Exchange rate regimes and independent central banks: A correlated choice of imperfectly credible institutions. *International Organization*, 64(03), 411–442. https://doi.org/doi:10.1017/S0020818310000111

Bodea, C. (2013). Independent central banks, regime type, and fiscal performance: The case of post-communist countries. *Public Choice*, 155(1), 81–107. https://doi.org/10.1007/s11127-011-9843-6

Bodea, C. (2014). Fixed exchange rates, independent central banks and price stability in postcommunist countries: Conservatism and credibility. *Economics & Politics*, 26(2), 185–211. https://doi.org/https://doi.org/10.1111/ecpo.12030

Bodea, C., & Hicks, R. (2015a). International finance and central bank independence: Institutional diffusion and the flow and cost of capital. *Journal of Politics*, 77(1), 268–284. https://doi.org/10.1086/678987

Bodea, C., & Hicks, R. (2015b). Price stability and central bank independence: Discipline, credibility, and democratic institutions. *International Organization*, 69(01), 35–61. https://doi.org/doi:10.1017/S0020818314000277

Bodea, C., & Hicks, R. (2018). Sovereign credit ratings and central banks: Why do analysts pay attention to institutions? *Economics & Politics*, 30(3), 340–365. https://doi.org/https://doi.org/10.1111/ecpo.12113

Bodea, C., & Higashijima, M. (2015). Central bank independence and fiscal policy: Can the central bank restrain deficit spending? *British Journal of Political Science*, 47(1), 47–70. https://doi.org/10.1017/S0007123415000058

Boix, C. (1997). Political parties and the supply side of the economy: The provision of physical and human capital in advanced economies, 1960–90. *American Journal of Political Science*, 41(3), 814–845. https://doi.org/10.2307/2111676

Bordo, M. D., Eichengreen, B., Irwin, D. A., Frankel, J., & Taylor, A. M. (1999). Is globalization today really different from globalization a hundred years ago? [with comments and discussion]. *Brookings Trade Forum*, 1–72. www.jstor.org/stable/25063137

Botero, J. C., Djankov, S., Porta, R. L., Lopez-de-Silanes, F., & Shleifer, A. (2004). The regulation of labor. *Quarterly Journal of Economics*, 119(4), 1339–1382.

Bradley, D., Huber, E., Moller, S., Nielsen, F., & Stephens, J. D. (2003). Distribution and redistribution in postindustrial democracies. *World Politics*, 55(2), 193–228. http://www.jstor.org/stable/25054218

Brambor, T., Clark, W. R., & Golder, M. (2006). Understanding interaction models: Improving empirical analyses. *Political Analysis*, 14(1), 63–82. https://doi.org/10.1093/pan/mpi014

Bremer, B. (2018). The missing left? Economic crisis and the programmatic response of social democratic parties in Europe. *Party Politics*, 24(1), 23–38. https://doi.org/10.1177/1354068817740745

Brooks, S. M. (2002). Social protection and economic integration: The politics of pension reform in an era of capital mobility. *Comparative Political Studies*, 35(5), 491–523. https://doi.org/10.1177/0010414002035005001

Brooks, S. M. (2004). Explaining capital account liberalization in Latin America: A transitional cost approach. *World Politics*, 56(3), 389–430. http://www.jstor.org/stable/25054265

Brooks, S. M. (2005). Interdependent and domestic foundations of policy change: The diffusion of pension privatization around the world. *International Studies Quarterly*, 49(2), 273–294. https://doi.org/10.2307/3693515

Brooks, S. M., & Kurtz, M. J. (2012). Paths to financial policy diffusion: Statist legacies in Latin America's globalization. *International Organization*, 66(1), 95–128. https://doi.org/10.1017/S0020818311000385

Brown, N. J. (2002). *Constitutions in a nonconstitutional world: Arab basic laws and the prospects for accountable government*. State University of New York Press.

Broz, J. L. (2003). Political system transparency and monetary commitment regimes. *International Organization*, 56(4), 861–887. https://doi.org/10.1162/002081802760403801

Bueno de Mesquita, B., Smith, A., M. Siverson, R., & Morrow, J. D. (2003). *The logic of political survival*. MIT Press.

Buller, J., & Whisker, B. (2020). Inter-organisational distrust and the political economy of central bank independence in the UK. *New Political Economy*, 1–17. https://doi.org/10.1080/13563467.2020.1766429

Burkovskaya, A. (2019). Political economy behind central bank independence. *Journal of Macroeconomics*, 61, 103121. https://doi.org/https://doi.org/10.1016/j.jmacro.2019.103121

Busse, M., Königer, J., & Nunnenkamp, P. (2010). FDI promotion through bilateral investment treaties: More than a bit? *Review of World Economics*, 146(1), 147–177. https://doi.org/10.1007/s10290-009-0046-x

Bussière, M., & Fratzscher, M. (2008). Financial openness and growth: Short-run gain, long-run pain? *Review of International Economics*, 16(1), 69–95. https://doi.org/https://doi.org/10.1111/j.1467-9396.2007.00727.x

Büthe, T., & Milner, H. V. (2008). The politics of foreign direct investment into developing countries: Increasing FDI through international trade agreements? *American Journal of Political Science*, 52(4), 741–762.

Cammett, M., & Posusney, M. P. (2010). Labor standards and labor market flexibility in the Middle East: Free trade and freer unions? *Studies in Comparative International Development*, 45(2), 250–279. https://doi.org/10.1007/s12116-010-9062-z

Cao, X. (2010). Networks as channels of policy diffusion: Explaining worldwide changes in capital taxation, 1998–2006. *International Studies Quarterly*, 54(3), 823–854. https://doi.org/10.1111/j.1468-2478.2010.00611.x

Cao, X., & Prakash, A. (2010). Trade competition and domestic pollution: A panel study, 1980–2003. *International Organization*, 64(03), 481–503. https://doi.org/doi:10.1017/S0020818310000123

Cao, X., & Prakash, A. (2012). Trade competition and environmental regulations: Domestic political constraints and issue visibility. *Journal of Politics*, 74(1), 66–82. https://doi.org/10.1017/s0022381611001228

Caraway, T. L. (2009). Labor rights in East Asia: Progress or regress? *Journal of East Asian Studies*, 9(2), 153–186. https://doi.org/10.1017/S1598240800002976

Caraway, T. L., Rickard, S. J., & Anner, M. S. (2012). International negotiations and domestic politics: The case of IMF labor market conditionality. *International Organization*, 66(01), 27–61. https://doi.org/doi:10.1017/S0020818311000348

Carnegie, A. (2015). *Power plays: How international institutions reshape coercive diplomacy*. Cambridge University Press.

Carter, D. B., & Signorino, C. S. (2010). Back to the future: Modeling time dependence in binary data. *Political Analysis*, 18(3), 271–292. https://doi.org/10.1093/pan/mpq013

Chaudoin, S., Milner, H. V., & Pang, X. (2015). International systems and domestic politics: Linking complex interactions with empirical models in international relations. *International Organization*, 69(2), 275–309. https://doi.org/10.1017/S0020818314000356

Cheibub, J. A. (1998). Political regimes and the extractive capacity of governments: Taxation in democracies and dictatorships. *World Politics*, 50(3), 349–376. https://doi.org/10.2307/25054045

Chen, F. (2016). China's road to the construction of labor rights. *Journal of Sociology*, 52(1), 24–38. https://doi.org/doi:10.1177/1440783315587414

Chen, Y.-F., & Funke, M. (2009). China's new labour contract law: No harm to employment? *China Economic Review*, 20(3), 558–572. https://doi.org/https://doi.org/10.1016/j.chieco.2009.03.008

Chinn, M. D., & Ito, H. (2006). What matters for financial development? Capital controls, institutions, and interactions. *Journal of Development Economics*, 81(1), 163–192. https://doi.org/https://doi.org/10.1016/j.jdeveco.2005.05.010

Chinn, M. D., & Ito, H. (2008). A new measure of financial openness. *Journal of Comparative Policy Analysis: Research and Practice*, 10(3), 309–322. https://doi.org/10.1080/13876980802231123

Clark, D. H. (2001). Trading butter for guns: Domestic Imperatives for foreign policy substitution. *Journal of Conflict Resolution*, 45(5), 636–660. https://doi.org/10.1177/0022002701045005005

Clark, D. H., & Reed, W. (2005). The strategic sources of foreign policy substitution. *American Journal of Political Science*, 49(3), 609–624. https://doi.org/10.2307/3647735

Clark, W. R. (2009). *Capitalism, not globalism: Capital mobility, central bank independence, and the political control of the economy.* University of Michigan Press.

Cleeve, E. (2008). How effective are fiscal incentives to attract FDI to sub-Saharan Africa? *Journal of Developing Areas*, 42(1), 135–153. http://www.jstor.org/stable/40376198

Cohen, B. J. (1996). Phoenix risen: The resurrection of global finance [Reviewed works: *Monetary Sovereignty: The Politics of Central Banking in Western Europe*, John B. Goodman; *States and the Reemergence of Global Finance: From Bretton Woods to the 1990s*, Eric Helleiner; *Governing the Global Economy: International Finance and the State*, Ethan B. Kapstein; *Business and Banking: Political Change and Economic Integration in Western Europe*, Paulette Kurzer; *Domestic Choices, International Markets: Dismantling National Barriers and Liberalizing Securities Markets*, Andrew C. Sobel]. *World Politics*, 48(2), 268–296. www.jstor.org/stable/25053963

Cohen, M. D., March, J. G., & Olsen, J. P. (1972). A garbage can model of organizational choice. *Administrative Science Quarterly*, 17(1), 1–25. https://doi.org/10.2307/2392088

Cohen, M. D., March, J. G., & Olsen, J. P. (2012). "A garbage can model" at forty: A solution that still attracts problems. In L. Alessandro & J. R. Harrison (Eds.), *The garbage can model of organizational choice: Looking forward at forty* (vol. 36, pp. 19–30). Emerald Group. https://doi.org/10.1108/S0733-558X(2012)0000036005

Compa, L. A. (1993). Labor rights and labor standards in international trade. *Law & Policy in International Business*, 25, 165–191.

Cook, L. (1993). *The Soviet social contract and why it failed: Welfare policy and workers' politics from Brezhnev to Yeltsin.* Harvard University Press.

Cook, M. L. (2002). Labor reform and dual transitions in Brazil and the Southern Cone. *Latin American Politics and Society, 44*(1), 1–34. https://doi.org/10.1111/j.1548-2456.2002.tb00195.x

Crabtree, C., & Nelson, M. J. (2017). New evidence for a positive relationship between de facto judicial independence and state respect for empowerment rights. *International Studies Quarterly, 61*(1), 210–224. https://doi.org/10.1093/isq/sqw056

Crowe, C., & Meade, E. E. (2007). The evolution of central bank governance around the world. *Journal of Economic Perspectives, 21*(4), 69–90. https://doi.org/10.1257/jep.21.4.69

Crowe, C., & Meade, E. E. (2008). Central bank independence and transparency: Evolution and effectiveness. *European Journal of Political Economy, 24*(4), 763–777. https://doi.org/http://dx.doi.org/10.1016/j.ejpoleco.2008.06.004

Cruz, C., Keefer, P., & Scartascini, C. (2016). *The database of political institutions 2015 (DPI2015)*. https://publications.iadb.org/handle/11319/7408

Cukierman, A. (1992). *Central bank strategy, credibility and independence: Theory and evidence*. MIT Press.

Cukierman, A. (2008). Central bank independence and monetary policy-making institutions—past, present and future. *European Journal of Political Economy, 24*(4), 722–736. https://doi.org/https://doi.org/10.1016/j.ejpoleco.2008.07.007

Cukierman, A., Miller, G. P., & Neyapti, B. (2002). Central bank reform, liberalization and inflation in transition economies—An international perspective. *Journal of Monetary Economics, 49*(2), 237–264. https://doi.org/http://dx.doi.org/10.1016/S0304-3932(01)00107-6

Cukierman, A., Webb, S. B., & Neyapti, B. (1992). Measuring the independence of central banks and its effect on policy outcomes. *World Bank Economic Review, 6*(3), 353–398. http://www.jstor.org/stable/3989977

Datz, G. (2019). Financial globalization and domestic policy autonomy in Latin America. In *Oxford research encyclopedia, politics*. Oxford University Press.

Davies, G. A. M. (2016). Policy selection in the face of political instability: Do states divert, repress, or make concessions? *Journal of Conflict Resolution, 60*(1), 118–142. https://doi.org/10.1177/0022002714541842

Davies, R. B., & Vadlamannati, K. C. (2013). A race to the bottom in labor standards? An empirical investigation. *Journal of Development Economics, 103*, 1–14. https://doi.org/https://doi.org/10.1016/j.jdeveco.2013.01.003

de Haan, J., & Eijffinger, S. C. W. (2016). *The politics of central bank independence*. https://ssrn.com/abstract=2887931

de Soysa, I., & Vadlamannati, K. C. (2011). Does being bound together suffocate, or liberate? The effects of economic, social, and political globalization on human rights, 1981–2005. *Kyklos, 64*(1), 20–53. https://doi.org/10.1111/j.1467-6435.2010.00493.x

Dean, A. (2015). Power over profits. *Politics & Society, 43*(3), 333–360. https://doi.org/10.1177/0032329215584788

Dellepiane-Avellaneda, S. (2012). Gordon unbound: The heresthetic of central bank independence in Britain. *British Journal of Political Science, 43*(2), 263–293. https://doi.org/10.1017/S0007123412000221

Devereux, M. P. (2007). *Developments in the taxation of corporate profit in the OECD since 1965: Rates, bases and revenues.* Oxford University Centre for Business Taxation.

Devereux, M. P., Griffith, R., & Klemm, A. (2002). Corporate income tax reforms and international tax competition. *Economic Policy, 17*(35), 449–495. https://doi.org/10.1111/1468-0327.00094

Devereux, M. P., & Keuschnigg, C. (2008). *The distorting arm's length principle in international transfer pricing.* Oxford University Centre for Business Taxation.

Devereux, M. P., Lockwood, B., & Redoano, M. (2008). Do countries compete over corporate tax rates? *Journal of Public Economics, 92*(5), 1210–1235. https://doi.org/https://doi.org/10.1016/j.jpubeco.2007.09.005

Dietrich, S., & Murdie, A. (2016). Human rights shaming through INGOs and foreign aid delivery. *Review of International Organizations,* 1–26. https://doi.org/10.1007/s11558-015-9242-8

Dincer, N., & Eichengreen, B. (2009). Central bank transparency: Causes, consequences and updates. *National Bureau of Economic Research Working Paper Series, No. 14791.* https://doi.org/10.3386/w14791

Dincer, N. N., & Eichengreen, B. (2014). Central bank transparency and independence: Updates and new measures. *International Journal of Central Banking, 10*(1), 189–259.

Distelhorst, G., & Locke, R. M. (2018). Does compliance pay? Social standards and firm-level trade. *American Journal of Political Science, 62*(3), 695–711. https://doi.org/10.1111/ajps.12372

Dobbin, F., Simmons, B., & Garrett, G. (2007). The global diffusion of public policies: Social construction, coercion, competition, or learning? *Annual Review of Sociology, 33*(1), 449–472. https://doi.org/10.1146/annurev.soc.33.090106.142507

DOL and USTR. (2015). *Standing up for workers: Promoting labor rights through trade.* Retrieved from https://ustr.gov/about-us/policy-offices/press-office/reports-and-publications/2015/standing-workers-promoting-labor

Dolzer, R. (2004). The impact of international investment treaties on domestic administrative law. *NYU Journal of International Law and Politics, 37,* 953–972.

Downs, G. W., Rocke, D. M., & Barsoom, P. N. (1996). Is the good news about compliance good news about cooperation? *International Organization, 50*(3), 379–406.

Dreher, A. (2006). Does globalization affect growth? Evidence from a new index of globalization. *Applied Economics*, *38*(10), 1091–1110. https://doi.org/10.1080/00036840500392078

Drezner, D. W. (2000). Bargaining, enforcement, and multilateral sanctions: When is cooperation counterproductive? *International Organization*, *54*(1), 73–102. http://www.jstor.org/stable/2601318

Drezner, D. W. (2001). Globalization and policy convergence. *International Studies Review*, *3*(1), 53–78. www.jstor.org/stable/3186512

Drezner, D. W. (2005). Globalization, harmonization, and competition: The different pathways to policy convergence. *Journal of European Public Policy*, *12*(5), 841–859. https://doi.org/10.1080/13501760500161472

Dür, A., Baccini, L., & Elsig, M. (2014). The design of international trade agreements: Introducing a new database. *Review of International Organizations*, *9*(3), 353–375.

Edwards, S. (2001). Capital mobility and economic performance: Are emerging economies different? *National Bureau of Economic Research Working Paper Series, No. 8076.* https://doi.org/10.3386/w8076

Eichengreen, B. (2001). Capital account liberalization: What do cross-country studies tell us? *World Bank Economic Review*, *15*(3), 341–365. http://www.jstor.org/stable/3990106

Eijffinger, S. C. W., & Geraats, P. M. (2006). How transparent are central banks? *European Journal of Political Economy*, *22*(1), 1–21. https://doi.org/https://doi.org/10.1016/j.ejpoleco.2005.09.013

El-Mikawy, N., & Handoussa, H. (Eds.). (2002). *Institutional reform & economic development in Egypt.* American University in Cairo Press.

Elfstrom, M., & Kuruvilla, S. (2014). The changing nature of labor unrest in China. *Industrial & Labor Relations Review*, *67*(2), 453–480. https://doi.org/10.1177/001979391406700207

Elkins, Z., Guzman, A. T., & Simmons, B. A. (2006a). Competing for capital: The diffusion of bilateral investment treaties, 1960–2000. *International Organization*, *60*(04), 811–846. https://doi.org/doi:10.1017/S0020818306060279

Elkins, Z., Guzman, A. T., & Simmons, B. A. (2006b). Competing for capital: The diffusion of bilateral investment treaties, 1960–2000. *International Organization*, *60*(04). https://doi.org/10.1017/s0020818306060279

Epperly, B. (2017). Political competition and de facto judicial independence in non-democracies. *European Journal of Political Research*, *56*(2), 279–300. https://doi.org/10.1111/1475-6765.12186

Ernesto López-Córdova, J., & Meissner, C. M. (2003). Exchange-rate regimes and international trade: Evidence from the classical gold standard era. *American Economic Review*, *93*(1), 344–353. https://doi.org/10.1257/000282803321455331

Esping-Andersen, G. (1985). *Politics against markets: The social democratic road to power*. Princeton University Press.

Feenstra, R. C., Inklaar, R., & Timmer, M. P. (2015). The next generation of the Penn World Table. *American Economic Review, 105*(10), 3150–3182. https://doi.org/10.1257/aer.20130954

Fernández-Albertos, J. (2015). The politics of central bank independence. *Annual Review of Political Science, 18*(1), 217–237. https://doi.org/10.1146/annurev-polisci-071112-221121

Fialová, K., & Schneider, O. (2009). Labor market institutions and their effect on labor market performance in the new EU member countries. *Eastern European Economics, 47*(3), 57–83. https://doi.org/10.2753/EEE0012-8775470303

Fleming, J. M. (1962). Domestic financial policies under fixed and under floating exchange rates (Politiques finacièrieures intérieures avec un système de taux de change fixe et avec un système de taux de change fluctuant) (Política financiera interna bajo sistemas de tipos de cambio fijos o de tipos de cambio fluctuantes). *Staff Papers (International Monetary Fund), 9*(3), 369–380. https://doi.org/10.2307/3866091

Franck, S. D. (2007). Foreign direct investment, investment treaty arbitration, and the rule of law. *Pacific McGeorge Global Business & Development Law Journal, 19*(2), 337–373.

Franzese, R. J., Jr. (1999). Partially independent central banks, politically responsive governments, and inflation. *American Journal of Political Science, 43*(3), 681–706. https://doi.org/10.2307/2991831

Franzese, R. J., & Hays, J. C. (2008). Contagion, common exposure, and selection: Empirical modeling of the theories and substance of interdependence in political science. *IPSA Concepts & Methods Newsletter, 4*(2), 2–8.

Friedman, T. (1999). *The Lexus and the olive tree: Understanding globalization*. Anchor Books.

Friedman, T. (2005). *Why the world is flat?* [interview]. www.wired.com

Fuest, C., Peichl, A., & Siegloch, S. (2018). Do higher corporate taxes reduce wages? Micro evidence from Germany. *American Economic Review, 108*(2), 393–418. https://doi.org/doi: 10.1257/aer.20130570

Furceri, D., & Loungani, P. (2018). The distributional effects of capital account liberalization. *Journal of Development Economics, 130*, 127–144. https://doi.org/https://doi.org/10.1016/j.jdeveco.2017.09.007

Gallagher, M. E. (2004). "Time is money, efficiency is life": The transformation of labor relations in China. *Studies in Comparative International Development, 39*(2), 11–44. https://doi.org/10.1007/bf02686276

Garretson, H., & Peeters, J. (2006). *Capital mobility, agglomeration and corporate tax rates: Is the race to the bottom for real?* De Nederlandsche Bank.

Garrett, G. (1995). Capital mobility, trade, and the domestic politics of economic policy. *International Organization, 49*(4), 657–687. www.jstor.org/stable/2706922

Garrett, G. (1998). *Partisan politics in the global economy*. Cambridge University Press.

Garrett, G. (2000). The causes of globalization. *Comparative Political Studies, 33*(6–7), 941–991. https://doi.org/10.1177/001041400003300610

Garrett, G., & Lange, P. (1991). Political responses to interdependence: What's "left" for the left? *International Organization, 45*(4), 539–564. https://doi.org/10.2307/2706947

Garrett, G., & Lange, P. (1995). Internationalization, institutions, and political change. *International Organization, 49*(4), 627–655. https://doi.org/10.1017/S0020818300028460

Garriga, A. C. (2016). Central bank independence in the world: A new data set. *International Interactions, 42*(5), 849–868. https://doi.org/10.1080/03050629.2016.1188813

Genovese, F., Kern, F. G., & Martin, C. (2017). Policy alteration: Rethinking diffusion processes when policies have alternatives. *International Studies Quarterly, 61*(2), 236–252. https://doi.org/10.1093/isq/sqx012

Genschel, P., Lierse, H., & Seelkopf, L. (2016). Dictators don't compete: Autocracy, democracy, and tax competition. *Review of International Political Economy, 23*(2), 290–315. https://doi.org/10.1080/09692290.2016.1152995

Ghias, S. A. (2010). Miscarriage of chief justice: Judicial power and the legal complex in Pakistan under Musharraf. *Law & Social Inquiry, 35*(4), 985–1022. http://www.jstor.org/stable/40926291

Gibler, D. M., & Sarkees, M. (2004). Measuring alliances: The correlates of war formal interstate alliance data set, 1816–2000. *Journal of Peace Research, 41*(2), 211–222.

Ginsburg, T. (2003). *Judicial review in new democracies: Constitutional courts in Asian cases*. Cambridge University Press.

Ginsburg, T. (2005). International substitutes for domestic institutions: Bilateral investment treaties and governance. *International Review of Law and Economics, 25*(1), 107–123. https://doi.org/https://doi.org/10.1016/j.irle.2004.06.002

Ginsburg, T., & Moustafa, T. (2008). Introduction: The functions of courts in authoritarian politics. In T. Ginsburg & T. Moustafa (Eds.), *Rule by law: The politics of courts in authoritarian regimes* (pp. 1–22). Cambridge University Press.

Ginsburg, T., & Versteeg, M. (2014). Why do countries adopt constitutional review? *Journal of Law, Economics, and Organization, 30*(3), 587–622. https://doi.org/10.1093/jleo/ewt008

Giordano, R., & Tommasino, P. (2011). What determines debt intolerance? The role of political and monetary institutions. *European Journal of Political Economy, 27*(3), 471–484. https://doi.org/https://doi.org/10.1016/j.ejpoleco.2011.02.001

Glanville, L. (2013). The myth of "traditional" sovereignty. *International Studies Quarterly, 57*(1), 79–90. https://doi.org/10.1111/isqu.12004

Gleditsch, N. P., Wallensteen, P., Eriksson, M., Sollenberg, M., & Strand, H. (2002). Armed conflict 1946–2001: A new dataset. *Journal of Peace Research, 39*(5), 615–637.

Glick, R., Guo, X., & Hutchison, M. (2006). Currency crises, capital-account liberalization, and selection bias. *Review of Economics and Statistics, 88*(4), 698–714. https://doi.org/10.1162/rest.88.4.698

Goldblatt, D., Held, D., McGrew, A., & Perraton, J. (1997). Economic globalization and the nation-state: Shifting balances of power. *Alternatives, 22*(3), 269–285. https://doi.org/10.1177/030437549702200301

Goldin, I. (2013). *Divided nations: Why global governance is failing, and what we can do about it.* Oxford University Press.

Goldstein, J. L., Rivers, D., & Tomz, M. (2007). Institutions in international relations: Understanding the effects of the GATT and the WTO on world trade. *International Organization, 61*(01), 37–67. https://doi.org/doi:10.1017/S0020818307070014

Goodman, J. B. (1991). The politics of central bank independence. *Comparative Politics, 23*(3), 329–349. https://doi.org/10.2307/422090

Goodman, J. B., & Pauly, L. W. (1993). The obsolescence of capital controls? Economic management in an age of global markets. *World Politics, 46*(1), 50–82. https://doi.org/10.2307/2950666

Gourevitch, P. A. (1978). The second image reversed: The international sources of domestic politics. *International Organization, 32*(4), 881–912.

Graham, E. R., Shipan, C. R., & Volden, C. (2013). The diffusion of policy diffusion research in political science. *British Journal of Political Science, 43*(03), 673–701. https://doi.org/doi:10.1017/S0007123412000415

Greene, W. (2004). The behaviour of the maximum likelihood estimator of limited dependent variable models in the presence of fixed effects. *Econometrics Journal, 7*(1), 98–119. https://doi.org/10.1111/j.1368-423X.2004.00123.x

Greenhill, B., Mosley, L., & Prakash, A. (2009). Trade-based diffusion of labor rights: A panel study, 1986–2002. *American Political Science Review, 103*(4), 669–690. https://doi.org/10.2307/27798531

Greffenius, S. (1986). Foreign policy substitution in the Arab–Israeli conflict. *International Interactions, 13*(1), 1–21. https://doi.org/10.1080/03050628608434666

Grieco, J. M., Gelpi, C. F., & Warren, T. C. (2009). When preferences and commitments collide: The effect of relative partisan shifts on international treaty compliance. *International Organization, 63*(2), 341–355. www.jstor.org/stable/40345937

Griffin, L. J., McCammon, H. J., & Botsko, C. (1990). The unmaking of a movement? The crisis of U.S. trade unions in comparative perspective. In M. T. Hallinan, D. M. Klein, & J. Glass (Eds.), *Changes in societal institutions* (pp. 169–194). Plenum.

Gritsch, M. (2005). The nation-state and economic globalization: Soft geo-politics and increased state autonomy? *Review of International Political Economy*, *12*(1), 1–25. https://doi.org/10.1080/09692290500049854

Grossman, G. M., & Helpman, E. (1995). The politics of free-trade agreements. *American Economic Review*, *85*(4), 667–690. http://www.jstor.org/stable/2118226

Grossman, G. M., & Helpman, E. (2015). Globalization and growth. *American Economic Review*, *105*(5), 100–104. https://doi.org/10.1257/aer.p20151068

Gruben, W. C., & McLeod, D. (2002). Capital account liberalization and inflation. *Economics Letters*, *77*(2), 221–225. https://doi.org/https://doi.org/10.1016/S0165-1765(02)00137-4

Grubert, H. (2001). Tax planning by companies and tax competition by governments: Is there evidence of changes in behavior? In J. R. Hines Jr. (Ed.), *International taxation and multinational activity* (pp. 113–139). University of Chicago Press.

Gupta, A. S. (2007). *Does capital account openness lower inflation?* Indian Council for Research on International Economic Relations.

Guthrie, B. K. (2013). Beyond investment protection: An examination of the potential influence of investment treaties on domestic rule of law. *New York University Journal of International Law and Politics*, *45*(4), 1151–1200.

Guzman, A. T. (1998). Why LDCs sign treaties that hurt them: Explaining the popularity of bilateral investment treaties. *Virginia Journal of International Law*, *38*, 639–688.

Gygli, S., Haelg, F., Potrafke, N., & Sturm, J.-E. (2019). The KOF globalisation index—revisited. *Review of International Organizations*, *14*(3), 543–574. https://doi.org/10.1007/s11558-019-09344-2

Hafner, K. A. (2015). Tax competition and economic integration. *Review of Development Economics*, *19*(1), 45–61. https://doi.org/https://doi.org/10.1111/rode.12124

Hafner-Burton, E. M., & Tsutsui, K. (2005). Human rights in a globalizing world: The paradox of empty promises. *American Journal of Sociology*, *110*(5), 1373–1411.

Haftel, Y. Z. (2010). Ratification counts: US investment treaties and FDI flows into developing countries. *Review of International Political Economy*, *17*(2), 348–377. https://doi.org/10.1080/09692290903333103

Haftel, Y. Z., & Thompson, A. (2013). Delayed ratification: The domestic fate of bilateral investment treaties. *International Organization*, *67*(2), 355–387.

Haggard, S. (1990). *Pathways from the periphery: The politics of growth in the newly industrializing countries*. Cornell University Press.

Hall, J. C., & Lawson, R. A. (2014). Economic freedom of the world: An accounting of the literature. *Contemporary Economic Policy, 32*(1), 1–19. https://doi.org/https://doi.org/10.1111/coep.12010

Hall, P. A., & Soskice, D. (2001). An introduction to varieties of capitalism. In P. A. Hall & D. Soskice (Eds.), *Varieties of capitalism: The institutional foundations of comparative advantage* (pp. 1–68). Oxford University Press.

Hallerberg, M. (2003). Veto players and the choice of monetary institutions. *International Organization, 56*(4), 775–802. https://doi.org/10.1162/002081802760403775

Hameiri, S., & Jones, L. (2016). Global governance as state transformation. *Political Studies, 64*(4), 793–810. https://doi.org/10.1111/1467-9248.12225

Hay, C. (2001). Contemporary capitalism, globalization, regionalization and the persistence of national variation. *Review of International Studies, 26*(4), 509–531. https://doi.org/10.1017/S026021050000509X

Hayo, B., & Voigt, S. (2003). *Explaining de facto judicial independence.* https://EconPapers.repec.org/RePEc:wpa:wuwple:0306001

Hays, J. C. (2003). Globalization and capital taxation in consensus and majoritarian democracies. *World Politics, 56*(01), 79–113. https://doi.org/doi:10.1353/wp.2004.0004

Hays, J. C., Ehrlich, S. D., & Peinhardt, C. (2005). Government spending and public support for trade in the OECD: An empirical test of the embedded liberalism thesis. *International Organization, 59*(02). https://doi.org/10.1017/s0020818305050150

Heckman, J. J., & Pages, C. (2000). The cost of job security regulation: Evidence from Latin American labor markets. *National Bureau of Economic Research Working Paper Series, No. 7773.* https://doi.org/10.3386/w7773

Held, D., McGrew, A., Goldblatt, D., & Perraton, J. (1999). *Global transformations: Politics, economics, and culture.* Stanford University Press.

Hellwig, T. (2008). Globalization, policy constraints, and vote choice. *Journal of Politics, 70*(4), 1128–1141. https://doi.org/10.1017/s0022381608081103

Helmke, G. (2002). The logic of strategic defection: Court-executive relations in Argentina under dictatorship and democracy. *American Political Science Review, 96*(2), 291–303. http://www.jstor.org/stable/3118026

Henisz, W. J., & Mansfield, E. D. (2019). The political economy of financial reform: De jure liberalization vs. de facto implementation. *International Studies Quarterly, 63*(3), 589–602. https://doi.org/10.1093/isq/sqz035

Henry, P. B. (2006). Capital account liberalization: Theory, evidence, and speculation. *National Bureau of Economic Research Working Paper Series, No. 12698.* https://doi.org/10.3386/w12698

Hensel, P. R. (2014). *ICOW colonial history data set, version 1.0.* http://www.paulhensel.org/icowcol.html

Hill, H. (2013). The political economy of policy reform: Insights from Southeast Asia. *Asian Development Review, 30*(1), 108–130. https://doi.org/10.1162/ADEV_a_00005

Hines, J. R. (1999). Lessons from behavioral responses to international taxation. *National Tax Journal, 52*(2), 305–322. http://www.jstor.org/stable/41789395

Hirst, P., & Thompson, G. (1995). Globalization and the future of the nation state. *Economy and Society, 24*(3), 408–442. https://doi.org/10.1080/03085149500000017

Hoberg, G. (2001). Globalization and policy convergence: Symposium overview. *Journal of Comparative Policy Analysis: Research and Practice, 3*(2), 127–132. https://doi.org/10.1080/13876980108412657

Hofmann, C., Osnago, A., & Ruta, M. (2017). *Horizontal depth a new database on the content of preferential trade agreements.* World Bank.

Hollyer, J. R., & Rosendorff, B. P. (2012). Leadership survival, regime type, policy uncertainty and PTA accession. *International Studies Quarterly, 56*(4), 748–764. https://doi.org/10.1111/j.1468-2478.2012.00750.x

Holzinger, K., & Knill, C. (2005). Causes and conditions of cross-national policy convergence. *Journal of European Public Policy, 12*(5), 775–796. https://doi.org/10.1080/13501760500161357

Holzinger, K., Knill, C., & Sommerer, T. (2008). Environmental policy convergence: The impact of international harmonization, transnational communication, and regulatory competition. *International Organization, 62*(04), 553–587. https://doi.org/doi:10.1017/S002081830808020X

Holzinger, K., & Sommerer, T. (2011). "Race to the bottom" or "Race to Brussels"? Environmental competition in Europe. *JCMS: Journal of Common Market Studies, 49*(2), 315–339. https://doi.org/10.1111/j.1468-5965.2010.02135.x

Hungin, H., & James, S. (2019). Central bank reform and the politics of blame avoidance in the UK. *New Political Economy, 24*(3), 334–349. https://doi.org/10.1080/13563467.2018.1446924

Hwang, W., & Lee, H. (2014). Globalization, factor mobility, partisanship, and compensation policies. *International Studies Quarterly, 58*(1), 92–105. https://doi.org/10.1111/isqu.12070

Ikenberry, G. J. (1986). The irony of state strength: Comparative responses to the oil shocks in the 1970s. *International Organization, 40*(1), 105–137. www.jstor.org/stable/2706744

Inclan, C., Quinn, D. P., & Shapiro, R. Y. (2001). Origins and consequences of changes in U.S. corporate taxation, 1981–1998. *American Journal of Political Science, 45*(1), 179–201. https://doi.org/10.2307/2669366

International Monetary Fund. (2000). *Globalization: Threat or opportunity?* https://www.imf.org/external/np/exr/ib/2000/041200to.htm

International Trade Union Confederation. (2014). *The world's worst countries for workers.* https://www.ituc-csi.org/IMG/pdf/survey_ra_2014_eng_v2.pdf

Iyer, K. (2010). The determinants of firm-level export intensity in New Zealand agriculture and forestry. *Economic Analysis and Policy, 40*(1), 75–86. https://doi.org/https://doi.org/10.1016/S0313-5926(10)50005-5

Jamshid, D., & Akbar, T. (2006). The effects of foreign direct investment and imports on economic growth: A comparative analysis of Thailand and the Philippines (1970–1998). *Journal of Developing Areas, 39*(2), 79–100. http://www.jstor.org/stable/4193005

Jandhyala, S., Henisz, W. J., & Mansfield, E. D. (2011). Three waves of BITs: The global diffusion of foreign investment policy. *Journal of Conflict Resolution, 55*(6), 1047–1073. https://doi.org/10.1177/0022002711414373

Jaumotte, F. (2004). Foreign direct investment and regional trade agreements: The market size effect revisited. *IMF Working Paper, No. 04/206.*

Jensen, N. M. (2013). Domestic institutions and the taxing of multinational corporations. *International Studies Quarterly, 57*(3), 440–448. https://doi.org/doi:10.1111/isqu.12015

Jensen, N. M., Malesky, E., Medina, M., & Ozdemir, U. (2014). Pass the bucks: Credit, blame, and the global competition for investment. *International Studies Quarterly, 58*(3), 433–447. https://doi.org/doi:10.1111/isqu.12106

Jodi, F. (2005). Judicial reform as insurance policy: Mexico in the 1990s. *Latin American Politics and Society, 47*(1), 87–113. https://doi.org/doi:10.1111/j.1548-2456.2005.tb00302.x

Jordana, J., Fernández-i-Marín, X., & Bianculli, A. C. (2018). Agency proliferation and the globalization of the regulatory state: Introducing a data set on the institutional features of regulatory agencies. *Regulation & Governance, 12*(4), 524–540. https://doi.org/https://doi.org/10.1111/rego.12189

Julio, R. F. (2007). Fragmentation of power and the emergence of an effective judiciary in Mexico, 1994–2002. *Latin American Politics and Society, 49*(1), 31–57. https://doi.org/doi:10.1111/j.1548-2456.2007.tb00373.x

Kambourov, G. (2009). Labour market regulations and the sectoral reallocation of workers: The case of trade reforms. *Review of Economic Studies, 76*(4), 1321–1358. https://doi.org/10.1111/j.1467-937X.2009.00552.x

Kang, Y. (2015). Trade, labour market rigidity, and aggregate productivity in OECD countries. *Applied Economics, 47*(6), 531–543. https://doi.org/10.1080/00036846.2014.975330

Keefer, P., & Stasavage, D. (2003). The limits of delegation: Veto players, central bank independence, and the credibility of monetary policy. *American Political Science Review, 97*(03), 407–423. https://doi.org/doi:10.1017.S0003055403000777

Keen, M., & Simone, A. (2004). Is tax competition harming developing countries more than developed? *Tax Notes International, 34*(13), 1317–1325.

Kelley, J. G., & Pevehouse, J. C. W. (2015). An opportunity cost theory of US treaty behavior. *International Studies Quarterly*, 59(3), 531–543. https://doi.org/10.1111/isqu.12185

Keohane, R. O. (1984). *After hegemony: Cooperation and discord in the world political economy*. Princeton University Press.

Kerner, A. (2009). Why should I believe you? The costs and consequences of bilateral investment treaties. *International Studies Quarterly*, 53(1), 73–102. https://doi.org/10.1111/j.1468-2478.2008.01524.x

Kerr, C. (1983). *The future of industrial societies: Convergence or continuing diversity?* Harvard University Press.

Kerrissey, J. (2015). Collective labor rights and income inequality. *American Sociological Review*. https://doi.org/10.1177/0003122415583649

Kim, M. (2012). Ex ante due diligence: Formation of PTAs and protection of labor rights. *International Studies Quarterly*, 56(4), 704–719. https://doi.org/10.2307/41804826

Kim, S. E., & Pelc, K. J. (2021). The politics of trade adjustment versus trade protection. *Comparative Political Studies*, 54(13), 2354–2381. https://doi.org/10.1177/0010414020957687

Kim, W. (2003). Does capital account liberalization discipline budget deficit? *Review of International Economics*, 11(5), 830–844. https://doi.org/https://doi.org/10.1046/j.1467-9396.2003.00420.x

Klein, M. W., & Olivei, G. P. (2008). Capital account liberalization, financial depth, and economic growth. *Journal of International Money and Finance*, 27(6), 861–875. https://doi.org/https://doi.org/10.1016/j.jimonfin.2008.05.002

Klein, M. W., & Shambaugh, J. C. (2006). Fixed exchange rates and trade. *Journal of International Economics*, 70(2), 359–383. https://doi.org/https://doi.org/10.1016/j.jinteco.2006.01.001

Klemm, A., & Van Parys, S. (2009). Empirical evidence on the effects of tax incentives. *IMF Working Paper, No. 09/136*.

Knill, C. (2005). Introduction: Cross-national policy convergence: Concepts, approaches and explanatory factors. *Journal of European Public Policy*, 12(5), 764–774. https://doi.org/10.1080/13501760500161332

Kobrin, S. J. (2017). Bricks and mortar in a borderless world: Globalization, the backlash, and the multinational enterprise. *Global Strategy Journal*, 7(2), 159–171. https://doi.org/https://doi.org/10.1002/gsj.1158

Konisky, D. M. (2007). Regulatory competition and environmental enforcement: Is there a race to the bottom? *American Journal of Political Science*, 51(4), 853–872. https://doi.org/10.2307/4620104

Konisky, D. M., & Woods, N. D. (2010). Exporting air pollution? Regulatory enforcement and environmental free riding in the United States. *Political Research Quarterly*, 63(4), 771–782. https://doi.org/10.1177/1065912909334429

Kono, D. Y. (2006). Optimal obfuscation: Democracy and trade policy transparency. *American Political Science Review, 100*(3), 369–384. http://www.jstor.org/stable/27644361

Kono, D. Y. (2008). Democracy and trade discrimination. *Journal of Politics, 70*(4), 942–955. https://doi.org/10.1017/s0022381608080985

Korpi, W. (1985). Power resources approach vs. action and conflict: On causal and intentional explanations in the study of power. *Sociological Theory, 3*(2), 31–45. https://doi.org/10.2307/202223

Korpi, W. (1989). Power, politics, and state autonomy in the development of social citizenship: Social rights during sickness in eighteen OECD countries since 1930. *American Sociological Review, 54*(3), 309–328. https://doi.org/10.2307/2095608

KPMG. (2006). *2006 global tax rate survey.* https://assets.kpmg.com/content/dam/kpmg/pdf/2015/11/global-tax-rate-survey-2015-v2-web.pdf

KPMG. (2015). *2015 global tax rate survey.* https://assets.kpmg.com/content/dam/kpmg/pdf/2015/11/global-tax-rate-survey-2015-v2-web.pdf

Krasner, S. (1976). State power and the structure of international trade. *World Politics, 28*(3), 317–347.

Krasner, S. D. (1999a). Globalization and sovereignty. In D. A. Smith, D. J. Solinger, & S. C. Topik (Eds.), *States and sovereignty in the global economy* (pp. 34–52). Routledge.

Krasner, S. D. (1999b). *Sovereignty: Organized hypocrisy.* Princeton University Press.

Kriesi, H., Grande, E., Lachat, R., Dolezal, M., Bornschier, S., & Frey, T. (2006). Globalization and the transformation of the national political space: Six European countries compared. *European Journal of Political Research, 45*(6), 921–956. https://doi.org/https://doi.org/10.1111/j.1475-6765.2006.00644.x

Kristal, T. (2010). Good times, bad times: Postwar labor's share of national income in capitalist democracies. *American Sociological Review, 75*(5), 729–763. https://doi.org/10.1177/0003122410382640

Kucera, D. (2002). Core labour standards and foreign direct investment. *International Labour Review, 141*(1–2), 31–69.

Kumar, M. S., & Quinn, D. P. (2012). *Globalization and corporate taxation.* International Monetary Fund.

Kurtz, M. J. (2002). Understanding the third world welfare state after neoliberalism: The politics of social provision in Chile and Mexico. *Comparative Politics, 34*(3), 293–313. https://doi.org/10.2307/4146955

Kwack, J.-s. (2017). Labor cost ratio rises at South Korean firms. *Hankyoreh.* http://english.hani.co.kr/arti/english_edition/e_business/807251.html

Kwon, H. Y., & Pontusson, J. (2005). *The rise and fall of government partisanship: Dynamics of social spending in OECD countries, 1962–2000.*

Kydland, F. E., & Prescott, E. C. (1977). Rules rather than discretion: The inconsistency of optimal plans. *Journal of Political Economy*, 85(3), 473–491. https://doi.org/10.2307/1830193

Lake, D. A. (2009). Open economy politics: A critical review. *Review of International Organizations*, 4(3), 219–244. https://doi.org/10.1007/s11558-009-9060-y

Lambert, D., & McKoy, S. (2009). Trade creation and diversion effects of preferential trade associations on agricultural and food trade. *Journal of Agricultural Economics*, 60(1), 17–39. https://doi.org/10.1111/j.1477-9552.2008.00184.x

Lamberte, M. B. (2002). *Central banking in the Philippines: Then, now and the future.* Philippine Institute for Development Studies.

Landes, W. M., & Posner, R. A. (1975). The independent judiciary in an interest-group perspective. *Journal of Law & Economics*, 18(3), 875–901. http://www.jstor.org/stable/725070

Lange, P., & Garrett, G. (1985). The politics of growth: Strategic interaction and economic performance in the advanced industrial democracies, 1974–1980. *Journal of Politics*, 47(3), 792–827. https://doi.org/10.2307/2131212

Langille, B. A. (1997). Eight ways to think about international labour standards. *Journal of World Trade*, 31, 27–35.

LaPorta, R., Lopez-de-Silane, F., Pop-Eleches, C., & Shleifer, A. (2003). Judicial checks and balances. *National Bureau of Economic Research Working Paper Series, No. 9775*. https://doi.org/10.3386/w9775

Lee, C. K., & Strang, D. (2006). The international diffusion of public-sector downsizing: Network emulation and theory-driven learning. *International Organization*, 60(04), 883–909. https://doi.org/doi:10.1017/S0020818306060292

Lee, H.-s. (2019, July 11). Korean firms hit by soaring labor costs. *Korea Times*.

Lee, H., Biglaiser, G., & Staats, J. L. (2014a). The effects of political risk on different entry modes of foreign direct investment. *International Interactions*, 40(5), 683–710. https://doi.org/10.1080/03050629.2014.899225

Lee, H., Biglaiser, G., & Staats, J. L. (2014b). Legal system pathways to foreign direct investment in the developing world. *Foreign Policy Analysis*, 10(4), 393–411. https://doi.org/10.1111/fpa.12026

Lee, J.-W., Park, I., & Shin, K. (2008). Proliferating regional trade arrangements: Why and whither? *World Economy*, 31(12), 1525–1557. https://doi.org/10.1111/j.1467-9701.2008.01143.x

Lee, Y., & Gordon, R. H. (2005). Tax structure and economic growth. *Journal of Public Economics*, 89(5–6), 1027–1043. https://doi.org/http://dx.doi.org/10.1016/j.jpubeco.2004.07.002

Leung, J. C. B., & Nann, R. C. (1995). *Authority and benevolence: Social welfare in China.* Chinese University Press.

Li, Q. (2006). Democracy, autocracy, and tax incentives to foreign direct investors: A cross-national analysis. *Journal of Politics*, 68(01), 62–74. https://doi.org/doi:10.1111/j.1468-2508.2006.00370.x

Li, Q. (2009). Democracy, autocracy, and expropriation of foreign direct investment. *Comparative Political Studies*. https://doi.org/10.1177/0010414009331723

Li, Q. (2016). Fiscal decentralization and tax incentives in the developing world. *Review of International Political Economy*, 23(2), 232–260. https://doi.org/10.1080/09692290.2015.1086401

Li, Q., & Resnick, A. (2003). Reversal of fortunes: Democratic institutions and foreign direct investment inflows to developing countries. *International Organization*, 57(01), 175–211. https://doi.org/doi:10.1017/S0020818303571077

Li, X., & Freeman, R. B. (2015). How does China's new labour contract law affect floating workers? *British Journal of Industrial Relations*, 53(4), 711–735. https://doi.org/10.1111/bjir.12056

Lim, J. (2008). Central banking in the Philippines: From inflation targeting to financing development. *International Review of Applied Economics*, 22(2), 271–285. https://doi.org/10.1080/02692170701880791

Lim, S., & Burgoon, B. (2018). Globalization and support for unemployment spending in Asia: Do Asian citizens want to embed liberalism? *Socio-Economic Review*, 18(2), 519–553. https://doi.org/10.1093/ser/mwy032

Lim, S., Mosley, L., & Prakash, A. (2015). Revenue substitution? How foreign aid inflows moderate the effect of bilateral trade pressures on labor rights. *World Development*, 67, 295–309. https://doi.org/https://doi.org/10.1016/j.worlddev.2014.10.025

Linder, S. H., & Peters, B. G. (1989). Instruments of government: Perceptions and contexts. *Journal of Public Policy*, 9(1), 35–58. www.jstor.org/stable/4007218

Linzer, D. A., & Staton, J. K. (2015). A global measure of judicial independence, 1948–2012. *Journal of Law and Courts*, 3(2), 223–256. https://doi.org/10.1086/682150

Liu, X., Burridge, P., & Sinclair, P. J. N. (2002). Relationships between economic growth, foreign direct investment and trade: Evidence from China. *Applied Economics*, 34(11), 1433–1440. https://doi.org/10.1080/00036840110100835

Lodovici, S. M. (2000). The dynamics of labour market reform in European countries. In G. Esping-Andersen (Ed.), *Why deregulate labor markets?* Oxford University Press.

Lohmann, S. (1998). Federalism and central bank independence: The politics of German monetary policy, 1957–92. *World Politics*, 50(3), 401–446. http://www.jstor.org/stable/25054047

Lombardi, C. B. (2009). Egypt's Supreme Constitutional Court: Managing constitutional conflict in an authoritarian aspirationally "Islamic" State. In A. Harding & P. Leyland (Eds.), *Constitutional courts: A comparative study* (pp. 217–241). Wildy, Simmonds & Hill.

López-Cariboni, S., & Cao, X. (2015). Import competition and policy diffusion. *Politics & Society*, 43(4), 471–502. https://doi.org/10.1177/003232921560 2888

López-Córdova, J. E., & Meissner, C. M. (2011). The impact of international trade on democracy: A long-run perspective. *World Politics*, 60(04), 539–575. https://doi.org/10.1353/wp.0.0016

Louis, M., El-Mahdy, A., & Handoussa, H. (2004). Foreign direct investment in Egypt. In S. Estrin & K. E. Meyer (Eds.), *Investment Strategies in Emerging Markets* (pp. 51–87). Edward Elgar.

Lütz, S. (2004). Convergence within national diversity: The regulatory state in finance. *Journal of Public Policy*, 24(2), 169–197. https://doi.org/10.1017/S0143814X04000091

Madrid, R. L. (2003). Labouring against neoliberalism: Unions and patterns of reform in Latin America. *Journal of Latin American Studies*, 35(01), 53–88. https://doi.org/doi:10.1017/S0022216X0200665X

Magalhães, P. C. (1999). The politics of judicial reform in Eastern Europe. *Comparative Politics*, 32(1), 43–62. https://doi.org/10.2307/422432

Malesky, E. J., & Mosley, L. (2018). Chains of love? Global production and the firm-level diffusion of labor standards. *American Journal of Political Science*, 62(3), 712–728. https://doi.org/10.1111/ajps.12370

Manger, M. S. (2009). *Investing in protection: The politics of preferential trade agreements between north and south*. Cambridge University Press.

Manger, M. S. (2012). Vertical trade specialization and the formation of north-south PTAs. *World Politics*, 64(4), 622–658. https://doi.org/10.1017/S0043887112000172

Manger, M. S., Pickup, M. A., & Snijders, T. A. B. (2012). A hierarchy of preferences: A longitudinal network analysis approach to PTA formation. *Journal of Conflict Resolution*, 56(5), 853–878. http://www.jstor.org/stable/23414713

Manger, M. S., & Shadlen, K. C. (2014). Political trade dependence and north-south trade agreements. *International Studies Quarterly*, 58(1), 79–91. https://doi.org/10.1111/isqu.12048

Mann, M. (1984). The autonomous power of the state: Its origins, mechanisms and results. *European Journal of Sociology / Archives Européennes de Sociologie / Europäisches Archiv für Soziologie*, 25(2), 185–213. www.jstor.org/stable/23999270

Mann, M. (1997). Has globalization ended the rise and rise of the nation-state? *Review of International Political Economy*, 4(3), 472–496. https://doi.org/10.1080/096922997347715

Mansfield, E. D. (1998). The proliferation of preferential trading arrangements. *Journal of Conflict Resolution*, 42(5), 523–543. http://www.jstor.org/stable/174558

Mansfield, E. D., & Milner, H. V. (2012). *Votes, vetoes, and the political economy of international trade agreements*. Princeton University Press.

Mansfield, E. D., Milner, H. V., & Rosendorff, B. P. (2002). Why democracies cooperate more: Electoral control and international trade agreements. *International Organization, 56*(3), 477–513.

Mansfield, E. D., & Reinhardt, E. (2003). Multilateral determinants of regionalism: The effects of GATT/WTO on the formation of preferential trading arrangements. *International Organization, 57*(4), 829–862.

Mansfield, E. D., & Reinhardt, E. (2008). International institutions and the volatility of international trade. *International Organization, 62*(4), 621–652. https://doi.org/10.1017/S0020818308080223

Maoz, Z., & Henderson, E. A. (2013). The world religion dataset, 1945–2010: Logic, estimates, and trends. *International Interactions, 39*(3), 265–291. https://doi.org/10.1080/03050629.2013.782306

Margalit, Y. (2011). Costly jobs: Trade-related layoffs, government compensation, and voting in U.S. elections. *American Political Science Review, 105*(01), 166–188. https://doi.org/10.1017/s000305541000050x

Margaritis, D., Scrimgeour, F., Cameron, M., & Tressler, J. (2005). Productivity and economic growth in Australia, New Zealand and Ireland. *Agenda: A Journal of Policy Analysis and Reform, 12*(4), 291–308. http://www.jstor.org/stable/43199355

Marshall, M. G., & Jaggers, K. (2012). *Polity IV project: Political regime characteristics and transitions, 1800–2012: Dataset users' manual*. University of Maryland. http://www.systemicpeace.org/polity/polity4.htm

Martin, L. L. (1992). Interests, power, and multilateralism. *International Organization, 46*(4), 765–792. http://www.jstor.org/stable/2706874

Massoud, M. F. (2014). International arbitration and judicial politics in authoritarian states. *Law & Social Inquiry, 39*(1), 1–30. https://doi.org/https://doi.org/10.1111/lsi.12050

McKenzie, R., & Lee, D. (1991). *Quicksilver capital: How the rapid movement of wealth has changed the world*. Free Press.

Mearsheimer, J. J. (2001). *The tragedy of great power politics*. W.W. Norton.

Milewicz, K., Hollway, J., Peacock, C., & Snidal, D. (2018). Beyond trade: The expanding scope of the nontrade agenda in trade agreements. *Journal of Conflict Resolution, 62*(4), 743–773. https://doi.org/10.1177/0022002716662687

Milner, H. V., & Judkins, B. (2004). Partisanship, trade policy, and globalization: Is there a left-right divide on trade policy? *International Studies Quarterly, 48*(1), 95–119. www.jstor.org/stable/3693565

Milner, H. V., & Kubota, K. (2005). Why the move to free trade? Democracy and trade policy in the developing countries. *International Organization, 59*(01), 107–143. https://doi.org/doi:10.1017/S002081830505006X

Milner, H. V., & Mukherjee, B. (2009). Democratization and economic globalization. *Annual Review of Political Science, 12*(1), 163–181. https://doi.org/10.1146/annurev.polisci.12.110507.114722

Moran, T. H. (2002). *Beyond sweatshops*. Brookings Institution Press.

Morrison, K. M. (2011). Nontax revenue, social cleavages, and authoritarian stability in Mexico and Kenya: "Internationalization, institutions, and political change" Revisited. *Comparative Political Studies, 44*(6), 719–746. https://doi.org/10.1177/0010414011401213

Mosley, L. (2003). *Global capital and national governments*. Cambridge University Press.

Mosley, L. (2005). Globalisation and the state: Still room to move? *New Political Economy, 10*(3), 355–362. https://doi.org/10.1080/13563460500204241

Mosley, L. (2008). Workers' rights in open economies: Global production and domestic institutions in the developing world. *Comparative Political Studies, 41*(4–5), 674–714. https://doi.org/10.1177/0010414007313119

Mosley, L. (2011). *Labor rights and multinational production*. Cambridge University Press.

Mosley, L., & Uno, S. (2007). Racing to the bottom or climbing to the top? Economic globalization and collective labor rights. *Comparative Political Studies, 40*(8), 923–948.

Moustafa, T. (2003). Law versus the state: The judicialization of politics in Egypt. *Law & Social Inquiry, 28*(4), 883–930. http://www.jstor.org/stable/1215790

Moustafa, T. (2007). *The struggle for constitutional power: Law, politics, and economic development in Egypt*. Cambridge University Press.

Mukherjee, B., Smith, D. L., & Li, Q. (2009). Labor (im)mobility and the politics of trade protection in majoritarian democracies. *Journal of Politics, 71*(1), 291–308. https://doi.org/10.1017/s0022381608090191

Mundell, R. A. (1961). A theory of optimum currency areas. *American Economic Review, 51*(4), 657–665. http://www.jstor.org/stable/1812792

Mundlak, Y. (1978). On the pooling of time series and cross section data. *Econometrica, 46*(1), 69–85. https://doi.org/10.2307/1913646

Murdie, A. M., & Davis, D. R. (2012). Shaming and blaming: Using events data to assess the impact of human rights INGOs. *International Studies Quarterly, 56*(1), 1–16. https://doi.org/10.1111/j.1468-2478.2011.00694.x

Naoi, M. (2020). Survey experiments in international political economy: What we (don't) know about the backlash against globalization. *Annual Review of Political Science, 23*(1), 333–356. https://doi.org/10.1146/annurev-polisci-050317-063806

Naoi, M., & Urata, S. (2013). Free trade agreements and domestic politics: The case of the Trans-Pacific Partnership Agreement. *Asian Economic Policy Review, 8*(2), 326–349. https://doi.org/10.1111/aepr.12035

Naughton, B. (2007). *The Chinese economy: Transitions and growth.* MIT Press.

Neumayer, E., & Plümper, T. (2012). Conditional spatial policy dependence: Theory and model specification. *Comparative Political Studies, 45*(7), 819–849. https://doi.org/10.1177/0010414011429066

Neumayer, E., & Spess, L. (2005). Do bilateral investment treaties increase foreign direct investment to developing countries? *World Development, 33*(10), 1567–1585. https://doi.org/10.1016/j.worlddev.2005.07.001

Nickell, S. (1981). Biases in dynamic models with fixed effects. *Econometrica, 49*(6), 1417–1426. https://doi.org/10.2307/1911408

Nickell, S. (1997). Unemployment and labor market rigidities: Europe versus North America. *Journal of Economic Perspectives, 11*(3), 55–74.

Nooruddin, I., & Rudra, N. (2014). Are developing countries really defying the embedded liberalism compact? *World Politics, 66*(04), 603–640. https://doi.org/doi:10.1017/S0043887114000203

North, D. C., & Weingast, B. (1989). Constitutions and commitment: The evolution of institutions governing public choice in seventeenth-century England. *Journal of Economic History, 49,* 803–832.

Notermans, T. (1993). The abdication from national policy autonomy: Why the macroeconomic policy regime has become so unfavorable to labor. *Politics & Society, 21*(2), 133–167. https://doi.org/10.1177/0032329293021002002

Noy, I., & Vu, T. B. (2007). Capital account liberalization and foreign direct investment. *North American Journal of Economics and Finance, 18*(2), 175–194. https://doi.org/https://doi.org/10.1016/j.najef.2007.04.001

Oatley, T. (2011). The reductionist gamble: Open economy politics in the global economy. *International Organization, 65*(02), 311–341. https://doi.org/doi:10.1017/S002081831100004X

Obstfeld, M. (1994). Risk-taking, global diversification, and growth. *American Economic Review, 84*(5), 1310–1329. http://www.jstor.org/stable/2117774

Obstfeld, M., Shambaugh, J. C., & Taylor, A. M. (2005). The trilemma in history: Tradeoffs among exchange rates, monetary policies, and capital mobility. *Review of Economics and Statistics, 87*(3), 423–438. https://doi.org/10.1162/0034653054638300

Ohmae, K. (1995). Putting global logic first. *Harvard Business Review, 73*(1), 119–125.

Ohmae, K. (1996). *The end of the nation-state.* HarperCollins.

Olney, W. W. (2013). A race to the bottom? Employment protection and foreign direct investment. *Journal of International Economics, 91*(2), 191–203.

Osterloh, S., & Debus, M. (2012). Partisan politics in corporate taxation. *European Journal of Political Economy, 28*(2), 192–207. https://doi.org/https://doi.org/10.1016/j.ejpoleco.2011.11.002

Otjes, S., & Green-Pedersen, C. (2019). When do political parties prioritize labour? Issue attention between party competition and interest group power.

Party Politics, 27(4), 1354068819875605. https://doi.org/10.1177/1354068
819875605

Owen, E. (2015). The political power of organized labor and the politics of foreign direct investment in developed democracies. *Comparative Political Studies, 48*(13), 1746–1780. https://doi.org/10.1177/0010414015592641

Oxford University Centre for Business Taxation. (2017). *CBT tax database* https://www.sbs.ox.ac.uk/faculty-research/tax/publications/data

Paderanga, C., Jr. (2013). *Macroeconomic policy regimes in the Philippines.*

Pastor, J., M., & Maxfield, S. (1999). Central bank independence and private investment in the developing world. *Economics & Politics, 11*(3), 299–309. https://doi.org/https://doi.org/10.1111/1468-0343.00063

Pereira, A. W. (2003). Explaining judicial reform outcomes in new democracies: The importance of authoritarian legalism in Argentina, Brazil, and Chile. *Human Rights Review, 4*(3), 3–16. https://doi.org/10.1007/s12142-003-1009-6

Perroni, C., & Whalley, J. (2000). The new regionalism: Trade liberalization or insurance? *Canadian Journal of Economics / Revue canadienne d'économique, 33*(1), 1–24. https://doi.org/10.1111/0008-4085.00001

Peters, G., & Savoie, D. J. (2000). Globalization, institutions, and governance. In *Governance in the twenty-first century: Revitalizing the public service* (pp. 29–57). McGill-Queen's University Press.

Pierre, J. (2015). Varieties of capitalism and varieties of globalization: Comparing patterns of market deregulation. *Journal of European Public Policy, 22*(7), 908–926. https://doi.org/10.1080/13501763.2014.984749

Pierson, P. (2004). *Politics in time: History, institutions, and social analysis.* Princeton University Press.

Pinto, P. (2013). *Partisan investment in the global economy: Why the left loves foreign direct investment and FDI loves the left.* Cambridge University Press.

Pinto, P. M., & Pinto, S. M. (2008). The politics of investment partisanship: And the sectoral allocation of foreign direct investment. *Economics & Politics, 20*(2), 216–254. https://doi.org/doi:10.1111/j.1468-0343.2008.00330.x

Pinto, P. M., Weymouth, S., & Gourevitch, P. (2010). The politics of stock market development. *Review of International Political Economy, 17*(2), 378–409. https://doi.org/10.1080/09692290903310424

Plümper, T., Troeger, V. E., & Winner, H. (2009). Why is there no race to the bottom in capital taxation? *International Studies Quarterly, 53*(3), 761–786. https://doi.org/doi:10.1111/j.1468-2478.2009.00555.x

Polanyi, K. (2001 [1944]). *The great transformation: The political and economic origins of our Time.* Beacon Press.

Polillo, S., & Guillén, M. F. (2005). Globalization pressures and the state: The worldwide spread of central bank independence. *American Journal of Sociology, 110*(6), 1764–1802. https://doi.org/10.1086/428685

Pond, A. (2017). Worker influence on capital account policy: Inflow liberalization and outflow restrictions. *International Interactions*, 1–24. https://doi.org/10.1080/03050629.2017.1344125

Popova, M. (2010). Political competition as an obstacle to judicial independence: Evidence from Russia and Ukraine. *Comparative Political Studies*, 43(10), 1202–1229. https://doi.org/10.1177/0010414010369075

Przeworski, A., & Sprague, J. (1986). *Paper stones: A history of electoral socialism.* University of Chicago Press.

Quinn, D. P. (2003). Capital account liberalization and financial globalization, 1890–1999: A synoptic view. *International Journal of Finance & Economics*, 8(3), 189–204. https://doi.org/https://doi.org/10.1002/ijfe.209

Quinn, D. P., & Inclan, C. (1997). The origins of financial openness: A study of current and capital account liberalization. *American Journal of Political Science*, 41(3), 771–813. http://www.jstor.org/stable/2111675

Quinn, D. P., & Shapiro, R. Y. (1991). Business political power: The case of taxation. *American Political Science Review*, 85(3), 851–874. https://doi.org/10.2307/1963853

Quinn, D. P., & Toyoda, A. M. (2008). Does capital account liberalization lead to growth? *Review of Financial Studies*, 21(3), 1403–1449. https://doi.org/10.1093/rfs/hhn034

Raess, D., Dür, A., & Sari, D. (2018). Protecting labor rights in preferential trade agreements: The role of trade unions, left governments, and skilled labor. *Review of International Organizations*, 13(2), 143–162. https://doi.org/10.1007/s11558-018-9301-z

Ramseyer, J. M. (1994). The puzzling (in)dependence of courts: A comparative approach. *Journal of Legal Studies*, 23(2), 721–747. http://www.jstor.org/stable/724464

Ranjan, P., & Anand, P. (2020). Indian courts and bilateral investment treaty arbitration. *Indian Law Review*, 4(2), 199–220. https://doi.org/10.1080/24730580.2020.1732693

Ranjan, P., & Raju, D. (2014). Bilateral investment treaties and the Indian judiciary. *George Washington International Law Review*, 46(4), 809–848.

Rasmussen, E. (2009). Introduction. In E. Rasmussen (Ed.), *Employment relationships workers, unions and employers in New Zealand* (pp. 1–8). Auckland University Press.

Razin, A., & Sadka, E. (2018). The welfare state besides globalization forces. *National Bureau of Economic Research Working Paper Series, No. 24919.* https://doi.org/10.3386/w24919

Redoano, M. (2014). Tax competition among European countries. Does the EU matter? *European Journal of Political Economy*, 34, 353–371. https://doi.org/https://doi.org/10.1016/j.ejpoleco.2014.02.006

Reinsberg, B., Kern, A., & Rau-Göhring, M. (2020). The political economy of IMF conditionality and central bank independence. *European Jour-*

nal of Political Economy, 101987. https://doi.org/https://doi.org/10.1016/j.ejpoleco.2020.101987

Rickard, S. J. (2012). Welfare versus subsidies: Governmental spending decisions in an era of globalization. Journal of Politics, 74(4), 1171–1183. https://doi.org/10.1017/s0022381612000680

Rigobon, R., & Rodrik, D. (2005). Rule of law, democracy, openness, and income. Economics of Transition, 13(3), 533–564. https://doi.org/doi:10.1111/j.1468-0351.2005.00226.x

Rius, A. (2013). The Uruguayan tax reform of 2006: Why didn't it fail?

Robertson, G. B., & Teitelbaum, E. (2011). Foreign direct investment, regime type, and labor protest in developing countries. American Journal of Political Science, 55(3), 665–677. https://doi.org/10.1111/j.1540-5907.2011.00510.x

Rodrik, D. (1996). Labor standards in international trade: Do they matter and what do we do about them? In R. Lawrence, D. Rodrik, & J. Whalley (Eds.), Emerging agenda for global trade: High stakes for developing countries. Overseas Development Council Essay No. 20.

Rodrik, D. (1997). Has globalization gone too far? Institute for International Economics.

Rodrik, D. (1998). Why do open economies have bigger governments? Journal of Political Economy, 106, 997–1032.

Rodrik, D. (2011). The globalization paradox: Democracy and the future of the world economy. W. W. Norton.

Rodrik, D. (2018). Populism and the economics of globalization. Journal of International Business Policy, 1(1), 12–33. https://doi.org/10.1057/s42214-018-0001-4

Rodrik, D., & Subramanian, A. (2009). Why did financial globalization disappoint? IMF Staff Papers, 56(1): 112–138.

Rodrik, D., & World Bank. (2006). Goodbye Washington consensus, hello Washington confusion? A review of the World Bank's "Economic growth in the 1990s: Learning from a decade of reform." Journal of Economic Literature, 44(4), 973–987. http://www.jstor.org/stable/30032391

Rogoff, K. (1985). The optimal degree of commitment to an intermediate monetary target. Quarterly Journal of Economics, 100(4), 1169–1189. https://doi.org/10.2307/1885679

Root, H. L., & May, K. (2008). Judicial systems and economic development. In T. Ginsburg & T. Moustafa (Eds.), Rule by law: The politics of courts in authoritarian regimes (pp. 304–325). Cambridge University Press.

Ross, M. L. (1999). The political economy of the resource curse. World Politics, 51(2), 297–322. https://doi.org/10.1017/S0043887100008200

Rudra, N., & Tobin, J. (2017). When does globalization help the poor? Annual Review of Political Science, 20(1), 287–307. https://doi.org/10.1146/annurev-polisci-051215-022754

Ruggie, J. G. (1982). International regimes, transactions, and change: Embedded liberalism in the postwar economic order. International Organization, 36(02), 379–415. https://doi.org/doi:10.1017/S0020818300018993

Russett, B. M., & Oneal, J. R. (2001). *Triangulating peace: Democracy, interdependence, and international organizations.* Norton.

Salacuse, J. W., & Sullivan, N. P. (2005). Do BITs really work? An evaluation of bilateral investment treaties and their grand bargain. *Harvard International Law Journal, 46,* 67–75.

Saravanan, A., & Subramanian, S. R. (2017). Role of domestic courts in the investor-state dispute settlement process: The case of South Asian BITs. *International Arbitration Law Review, 20*(2), 42–54.

Sassen, S. (1995). *Losing control? Sovereignty in an age of globalization.* Columbia University Press.

Saygili, M., Peters, R., & Knebel, C. (2018). African continental free trade area: Challenges and opportunities of tariff reductions, UNCTAD Research Paper No. 15.

Schneider, F., & Frey, B. S. (1985). Economic and political determinants of foreign direct investment. *World Development, 13*(2), 161–175. https://doi.org/https://doi.org/10.1016/0305-750X(85)90002-6

Schreuer, C. (2011). Interaction of international tribunals and domestic courts in investment law. In A. W. Rovine (Ed.), *Contemporary issues in international arbitration and mediation: The Fordham papers (2010)* (pp. 71–94). Brill, Nijhoff. https://doi.org/https://doi.org/10.1163/ej.9789004206007.i-516.25

Schreuer, C. (2016). The development of international law by ICSID tribunals. *ICSID Review—Foreign Investment Law Journal, 31*(3), 728–739. https://doi.org/10.1093/icsidreview/siw017

Seki, K., & Williams, L. K. (2014). Updating the party government data set. *Electoral Studies, 34,* 270–279. https://doi.org/https://doi.org/10.1016/j.electstud.2013.10.001

Sekkat, K., & Veganzones-Varoudakis, M.-A. (2007). Openness, investment climate, and FDI in developing countries. *Review of Development Economics, 11*(4), 607–620. https://doi.org/https://doi.org/10.1111/j.1467-9361.2007.00426.x

Shin, M. J. (2017). Partisanship, tax policy, and corporate profit-shifting in a globalized world economy. *Comparative Political Studies, 50*(14), 1998–2026. https://doi.org/10.1177/0010414016688007

Simmons, B. A., Dobbin, F., & Garrett, G. (2006). Introduction: The international diffusion of liberalism. *International Organization, 60*(04), 781–810. https://doi.org/doi:10.1017/S0020818306060267

Simmons, B. A., & Elkins, Z. (2004). The globalization of liberalization: Policy diffusion in the international political economy. *American Political Science Review, 98*(01). https://doi.org/10.1017/s0003055404001078

Slaughter, A.-M. (2004). *A new world order.* Princeton University Press.

Slemrod, J. (2004). Are corporate tax rates, or countries, converging? *Journal of Public Economics, 88*(6), 1169–1186. https://doi.org/https://doi.org/10.1016/S0047-2727(03)00061-6

Smith, C. A., & Farrales, M. J. (2010). Court reform in transitional states: Chile and the Philippines. *Journal of International Relations and Development, 13*(2), 163–193.

Smith, D. A., Solinger, D. J., & Topik, S. C. (1999). Introduction. In D. A. Smith, D. J. Solinger, & S. C. Topik (Eds.), *States and sovereignty in the global economy* (pp. 1–19). Routledge.

Smithey, S. I., & Ishiyama, J. (2000). Judicious choices: Designing courts in post-communist politics. *Communist and Post-Communist Studies, 33*(2), 163–182. https://doi.org/https://doi.org/10.1016/S0967-067X(00)00002-7

Solingen, E. (2012). Of dominoes and firewalls: The domestic, regional, and global politics of international diffusion. *International Studies Quarterly, 56*(4), 631–644. www.jstor.org/stable/41804821

Solomon, P. H., Jr. (2008). Judicial power in authoritarian states: The Russian experience. In T. Ginsburg & T. Moustafa (Eds.), *Rule by law: The politics of courts in authoritarian regimes* (pp. 261–282). Cambridge University Press.

Solomon, P. H., Jr. (2015). Law and courts in authoritarian states. In J. D. Wright (Ed.), *International Encyclopedia of the Social & Behavioral Sciences* (vol. 13, pp. 427–434). Elsevier.

Staats, J. L., & Biglaiser, G. (2012). Foreign direct investment in Latin America: The importance of judicial strength and rule of law. *International Studies Quarterly, 56*(1), 193–202. https://doi.org/doi:10.1111/j.1468-2478.2011.00690.x

Stallings, B. (2010). Globalization and labor in four developing regions: An institutional approach. *Studies in Comparative International Development, 45*(2), 127–150. https://doi.org/10.1007/s12116-010-9066-8

Stein, A. A. (2016). The great trilemma: Are globalization, democracy, and sovereignty compatible? *International Theory, 8*(2), 297–340. https://doi.org/10.1017/S1752971916000063

Stiglitz, J. (2003). *Globalization and its discontents*. W. W. Norton.

Stinnett, D. M., Tir, J., Diehl, P. F., Schafer, P., & Gochman, C. (2002). The correlates of war (COW) project direct contiguity data, version 3.0. *Conflict Management and Peace Science, 19*(2), 59–67. https://doi.org/10.1177/073889420201900203

Strange, S. (1997). The future of global capitalism; Or, will divergence persist forever? In C. Crouch & W. Streeck (Eds.), *Political economy of modern capitalism: Mapping convergence and diversity* (pp. 182–191). Sage.

Stroh, A., & Heyl, C. (2015). Institutional diffusion, strategic insurance, and the creation of West African constitutional courts. *Comparative Politics, 47*(2), 169–187. http://www.jstor.org/stable/43664138

Strunz, S., Gawel, E., Lehmann, P., & Söderholm, P. (2017). Policy convergence as a multifaceted concept: The case of renewable energy policies in the European Union. *Journal of Public Policy, 38*(3), 361–387. https://doi.org/10.1017/S0143814X17000034

Swank, D. (2002). *Global capital, political institutions, and policy change in developed welfare states*. Cambridge University Press.

Swank, D. (2006). Tax policy in an era of internationalization: Explaining the spread of neoliberalism. *International Organization, 60*(04), 847–882. https://doi.org/doi:10.1017/S0020818306060280

Swank, D. (2016). The new political economy of taxation in the developing world. *Review of International Political Economy, 23*(2), 185–207. https://doi.org/10.1080/09692290.2016.1155472

Swank, D., & Steinmo, S. (2002). The new political economy of taxation in advanced capitalist democracies. *American Journal of Political Science, 46*(3), 642–655. https://doi.org/10.2307/3088405

Tanzi, V. (1995). *Taxation in an integrating world*. Brookings Institution.

Tayssir, O., & Feryel, O. (2018). Does central banking promote financial development? *Borsa Istanbul Review, 18*(1), 52–75. https://doi.org/https://doi.org/10.1016/j.bir.2017.09.001

Thelen, K., & Steinmo, S. (1992). Historical institutionalism in comparative politics. In S. Steinmo, K. Thelen, & F. Longstreth (Eds.), *Structuring politics: Historical institutionalism in comparative analysis* (pp. 1–31). Cambridge University Press.

Thomsen, S. (1999). *Southeast Asia: The role of foreign direct investment policies in development*. OECD Working Papers on International Investment.

Thomson, J. E. (1995). State sovereignty in international relations: Bridging the gap between theory and empirical research. *International Studies Quarterly, 39*(2), 213–233. https://doi.org/10.2307/2600847

Tierney, M. J., Nielson, D. L., Hawkins, D. G., Roberts, J. T., Findley, M. G., Powers, R. M., . . . Hicks, R. L. (2011). More dollars than sense: Refining our knowledge of development finance using AidData. *World Development, 39*(11), 1891–1906. https://doi.org/https://doi.org/10.1016/j.worlddev.2011.07.029

Tsebelis, G. (2002). *Veto players: How political institutions work*. Princeton University Press.

Ulfelder, J. (2005). Contentious collective action and the breakdown of authoritarian regimes. *International Political Science Review, 26*(3), 311–334. https://doi.org/10.1177/0192512105053786

UNCTAD. (1999a). *Investment policy review: Egypt*. https://unctad.org/system/files/official-document/iteiipmisc.11_en.pdf

UNCTAD. (1999b). *World investment report*. https://unctad.org/system/files/official-document/wir1999_en.pdf

UNCTAD. (2012). *UN Comtrade* database. https://comtrade.un.org/

UNCTAD. (2014). *World investment report*. https://unctad.org/system/files/official-document/wir2014_en.pdf

UNCTAD. (2016). *World investment report.* https://unctad.org/system/files/official-document/wir2016_en.pdf

UNCTAD. (2019a). *Bilateral FDI statistics.* http://unctad.org/en/Pages/DIAE/FDI%20Statistics/FDI-Statistics-Bilateral.aspx

UNCTAD. (2019b). *International investment agreements navigator.* https://investmentpolicy.unctad.org/international-investment-agreements

United States International Trade Commission. (2016). *Economic impact of trade agreements implemented under trade authorities procedures, 2016 report.*

van der Cruijsen, C., & Demertzis, M. (2007). The impact of central bank transparency on inflation expectations. *European Journal of Political Economy, 23*(1), 51–66. https://doi.org/https://doi.org/10.1016/j.ejpoleco.2006.09.009

Vandevelde, K. J. (1998). Investment liberalization and economic development: The role of bilateral investment treaties. *Columbia Journal of Transnational Law, 36*(3), 501–528.

Vinuesa, R. E. (2002). Bilateral investment treaties and the settlement of investment disputes under ICSID: The Latin American experience. *Law and Business Review of the Americas, 8*(4), 501–534.

Vogel, D. (1995). *Trading up: Consumer and environmental regulation in a global economy.* Harvard University Press.

Vogel, D. (2000). Environmental regulation and economic integration. *Journal of International Economic Law, 3*(2), 265–279.

VonDoepp, P., & Ellett, R. (2011). Reworking strategic models of executive-judicial relations: Insights from new African democracies. *Comparative Politics, 43*(2), 147–165. http://www.jstor.org/stable/23040830

Waltz, K. N. (1979). *Theory of international politics.* McGraw Hill.

Wang, H., Appelbaum, R. P., Degiuli, F., & Lichtenstein, N. (2009). China's new labour contract law: Is China moving towards increased power for workers? *Third World Quarterly, 30*(3), 485–501. https://doi.org/10.1080/0143659 0902742271

Wang, Y. (2014). *Tying the autocrat's hands: The rise of the rule of law in China.* Cambridge University Press.

Wang, Z. (2017a). Democracy, policy interdependence, and labor rights. *Political Research Quarterly, 70*(3), 549–563. https://doi.org/10.1177/1065912917 704517

Wang, Z. (2017b). Institutionalized autocracies, policy interdependence, and labor rights. *Journal of Human Rights, 16*(4), 473–493. https://doi.org/10.1 080/14754835.2016.1200965

Wang, Z. (2018). Economic competition, policy interdependence, and labour rights. *New Political Economy, 23*(6), 656–673. https://doi.org/10.1080/13 563467.2018.1384452

Wang, Z., & Youn, H. (2018). Locating the external source of enforceability: Alliances, bilateral investment treaties, and foreign direct investment. *Social Science Quarterly*, 99(1), 80–96. https://doi.org/doi:10.1111/ssqu.12412

Ward, D., Kim, J. H., Graham, M., & Tavits, M. (2015). How economic integration affects party issue emphases. *Comparative Political Studies*, 48(10), 1227–1259. https://doi.org/10.1177/0010414015576745

Ward, H., Ezrow, L., & Dorussen, H. A. N. (2011). Globalization, party positions, and the median voter. *World Politics*, 63(3), 509–547. www.jstor.org/stable/23018779

Ware, A. (1996). *Political parties and party systems*. Oxford University Press.

Way, C. (2000). Central banks, partisan politics, and macroeconomic outcomes. *Comparative Political Studies*, 33(2), 196–224. https://doi.org/10.1177/0010414000033002002

Weinberg, J. (2016). European Union member states in cross-national analyses: The dangers of neglecting supranational policymaking. *International Studies Quarterly*, 60(1), 98–106. https://doi.org/10.1093/isq/sqv009

Weiss, L. (1998). *The myth of the powerless state*. Cornell University Press.

Weiss, L. (2005). Global governance, national strategies: How industrialized states make room to move under the WTO. *Review of International Political Economy*, 12(5), 723–749. www.jstor.org/stable/25124049

Werner, W. G., & De Wilde, J. H. (2001). The endurance of sovereignty. *European Journal of International Relations*, 7(3), 283–313. https://doi.org/10.1177/1354066101007003001

Whalley, J. (1996). Why do countries seek regional trade agreements? *National Bureau of Economic Research Working Paper Series*, No. 5552. https://doi.org/10.3386/w5552

Wheeler, D. (2001). *Racing to the bottom? Foreign investment and air quality in developing countries*. World Bank, Development Research Group.

White, J., & Park, J.-m. (2018). GM to shut one South Korea plant, decide on fate of others within weeks. *Reuters*. https://www.reuters.com/article/us-gm-southkorea/gm-to-shut-one-south-korea-plant-decide-on-fate-of-others-within-weeks-idUSKBN1FX042

Wibbels, E., & Arce, M. (2003). Globalization, taxation, and burden-shifting in Latin America. *International Organization*, 57(1), 111–136. http://www.jstor.org.proxy.tamuc.edu/stable/3594827

Widner, J., & Scher, D. (2008). Building judicial independence in semi-democracies: Uganda and Zimbabwe. In T. Ginsburg & T. Moustafa (Eds.), *Rule by law: The politics of courts in authoritarian regimes* (pp. 235–260). Cambridge University Press.

Williams, J. T., & Collins, B. K. (1997). The political economy of corporate taxation. *American Journal of Political Science*, 41(1), 208–244. https://doi.org/10.2307/2111714

World Bank. (2003). *Legal and judicial reform: Strategic directions.*

World Bank. (2015). *Worldwide governance indicators.* http://info.worldbank.org/governance/wgi/index.aspx#doc

World Bank. (2016). *World development indicators.* http://data.worldbank.org/data-catalog/world-development-indicators

World Bank. (2021). *World development indicators.* http://data.worldbank.org/data-catalog/world-development-indicators

World Trade Organization. (2011). *World trade report 2011: The WTO and preferential trade agreements: From co-existence to coherence.* Retrieved from https://www.wto.org/english/res_e/publications_e/wtr11_e.htm

World Trade Organization. (2018). *Regional trade agreements: Facts and figures.* https://www.wto.org/english/tratop_e/region_e/regfac_e.htm

World Trade Organization. 2022. *Regional trade agreements: Database.*

Wright, J. (2008). Do authoritarian institutions constrain? How legislatures affect economic growth and investment. *American Journal of Political Science,* 52(2), 322–343. https://doi.org/10.1111/j.1540-5907.2008.00315.x

WTO. (1999). *Trade and environment: Special studies.*

WTO. (2014). *World trade report.* https://www.wto.org/english/res_e/publications_e/wtr14_e.htm

Wu, G. (2017). Globalization against democracy. In *Globalization against democracy: A political economy of capitalism after its global triumph* (pp. i–ii). Cambridge University Press.

Yergin, D., & Stanislaw, J. (1997). *The commanding heights.* Simon and Schuster.

Zhang, K. (2001). Does foreign direct investment promote economic growth? Evidence from East Asia and Latin America. *Contemporary Economic Policy,* 19(2), 175–185. https://doi.org/https://doi.org/10.1111/j.1465-7287.2001.tb00059.x

Zodrow, G. R. (2007). Should capital income be subject to consumption-based taxation? In H. J. Aaron, L. E. Burman, & C. E. Steuerle (Eds.), *Taxing capital income* (pp. 49–81). Urban Institute.

Zurn, M., & Deitelhoff, N. (2015). Internationalization and the state: Sovereignty as the external side of modern statehood. In S. Leibfried, E. Huber, M. Lange, J. D. Levy, F. Nullmeier, & J. D. Stephens (Eds.), *The Oxford handbook of transformations of the state.*

Index

Note: Use of *italics* indicates figures.

abandonment of capital control, 29
ability: to attract capital, 122; to
  promote trade, 67; to repress labor
  69, 84; to repress workers, 62,
  69
abolish: the practical protection 69;
  the nation-state, 141
abolition of subsidies, 138
accountability, 140
across issue areas, 6, 7, 9, 25, 27, 28,
  30, 31, 59, 61, 93, 144, 148, 150
across-issue area substitution, 10, 27,
  28
adaptation, 17, 59; leads to
  convergence, 59
adaptivity, 2, 4–10, 13–31, 34, 36,
  38, 40, 42, 44, 46, 48, 52, 54, 56,
  58, 62, 64, 66, 68, 70, 72, 74, 76,
  78, 80, 82, 84, 86, 88, 90, 92, 94,
  96, 98, 102, 106, 108, 110, 114,
  116, 118, 120, 122, 124, 128, 130,
  134, 136, 138, 140, 142, 144, 146,
  148, 150
adjustment, 10, 19, 68, 89, 134;
  induces convergence, 20
administration of justice, 38
advanced industrial democracies, 15

advanced industrial goods, 21
Africa, 36, 56, 67, 90
African states, 21, 67
after-tax return, 95
arbitration: tribunals take precedence
  over, 42; awards, 43
audiences, 66, 110
authoritarian government, 37, 55
authoritarian leaders, 36–38
authoritarian regime, 39
authoritarian rule, 94
autocratic governmentst, 130
autocratic rule, 154
autonomous central bank, 29, 138
autonomous judiciary, 39
autonomous monetary policy, 122
avoidance, 26, 27

Baccini, Leonardo, 8, 16, 63, 67, 70,
  73, 74, 77, 78, 84, 91, 154
bargaining: outcomes, 65; position, 8,
  65, 68, 74, 93
barriers: to manipulate trade, 20; to
  harnessing globalization, 22
Basinger, Scott, 89, 90, 92, 102
Bearce, David, 9, 150
behavior, 7, 23, 43, 53, 68

www.ingramcontent.com/pod-product-compliance
Lightning Source LLC
Chambersburg PA
CBHW030329270326
41926CB00010B/1556